RANSOMING THE TIME

Ransoming the Time

By
JACQUES MARITAIN

TRANSLATED BY
HARRY LORIN BINSSE

"Look therefore carefully how ye walk,
not as unwise, but as wise, ransoming the
time, because the days are evil."
(St. Paul, Ephesians, v:16)

GORDIAN PRESS
NEW YORK
1972

Originally Published 1941
Reprinted 1972

Library of Congress Catalog Card Number - 70-165665
ISBN 87752-153-0

To
Raïssa

FOREWORD

THE TOPICS treated in this book seem extremely diverse. Yet the subject-matter is but one: man in his cultural life and in the complex patterns of his earthly destiny. And the essential theme also is one: human conflicts and antinomies can be overcome and reconciled only if first they are perceived in their full dimensions, and if they are viewed in the ontological perspectives of Christian wisdom.

This is not a book of *separated* philosophy, separated from faith, and separated from concrete life. I believe, on the contrary, that philosophy attains its aims, particularly in practical matters, only when vitally united with every source of light and experience in the human mind. Thus it becomes able, in its own intellectual domain, to *ransom the time,* and to redeem every human search after truth, however it wanders, in manifold, even opposite ways.

I hope that the essays I have gathered here may give evidence that Thomist philosophy, which is grounded on tested principles, yet does not slumber comfortably, offers us an equipment enabling us to extend more and more the boundaries of this philosophy itself, and to advance farther into the problems of our time.

I am indebted to the translator of the book, Mr. Harry L. Binsse, who gave all care to and remarkably succeeded in the English interpretation of a very complex French text; to Professor and Mrs. Gordon Andison and to Professor Michael Wallace Fowlie, who kindly gave their invaluable help in connection with some of the chapters; and to Doctor Ruth Nanda Anshen, who was good enough to revise the entire work. To all I wish to express my heartfelt thanks.

J. M.

CONTENTS

RANSOMING THE TIME

CHAPTER I

HUMAN EQUALITY

IN THIS first chapter, we shall consider the idea of equality. When applied to man, this idea, from the very outset, puts the philosopher to the test, for it is surrounded by geometrical imagery that relates to those entities without ontological substance so characteristic of mathematical abstraction. Consequently, its application to human reality demands that the mind work constantly against the grain of this very imagery. In such a case proper discernment is particularly difficult. Yet too many great errors and too many great truths are linked to the concept—false or true—that we form of equality to permit us to evade the issue.

When we speak of living beings of the same species, as we find them in nature—lions, goats, horses—the form of expression we use regarding them relates to the *unity* of their specific nature. And this is the most appropriate form of expression, philosophically speaking. It is probable, however, that if lions thought, lived in society, and had to obey masters of the same species as themselves, those among them to whom obedience was a burden or who suffered injustices would insist upon saying that all lions are *equal* in nature. The expression "equality in nature" appears to be intended to console us for the wounds we suffer from social inequalities, or to satisfy our resentment against these. I shall lay aside consideration of such emotional connotations and take the expression "equality in nature" as purely and simply synonymous with unity of nature. Before turning to the main subject in hand, I should like to observe that the problems of equality concern at once man's psychophysical nature and his social condition. Therefore they cannot be treated by a philosopher without alluding at once to fields of knowledge as disparate as biology, psychology, sociology, and politics.

It seems to me that, faced with the problem of the equality and inequality of men, one can formulate three principal positions regarding it. For the fundamental fact that all men have the same specific nature can be viewed in relation to a system of thought that is either nominalist or idealist or realist. In fact, the great classical themes designated by these academic terms deal with concrete attitudes of the intelligence that are of basic practical importance. I should like to consider these practical attitudes rather than philosophic schools, in which both empiricism and idealism are often either subtly mitigated, or unconsciously impregnated by other master principles. My Empiricists are not Bacon, Locke, Bentham or John Stuart Mill, but rather cheap Nietzschean, Machiavellianist, rightist-Hegelian or rightist-positivist leaders of modern politics; my Idealists are not Plato, Descartes, Berkeley or Kant, but rather cheap Rousseauist, enlightenmentist, Tolstoyan, leftist-Hegelian or leftist-positivist leaders of modern politics. What I should like to outline from this point of view is a kind of working drawing, deliberately reduced to its essential logical integers.

I shall, therefore, first discuss the pure nominalist or empiricist notion of human equality; in other words, the philosophy of enslavement. Secondly I shall discuss the pure idealist notion of human equality, that is, the philosophy of egalitarianism. Finally I shall discuss the realist notion of human equality; here we shall consider the true philosophy of equality which does not suppress inequalities, but bases them indeed on equality, as something more fundamental, and turns them, by virtue of justice, into an equality concerned with the use and fruition of the common good.

First then, the pure nominalist or empiricist notion of human equality.

ANTI-CHRISTIAN PHILOSOPHY OF ENSLAVEMENT

THAT MEN of every colour and every condition should be uniformly designated by the same word *man* is a basic fact accepted by every one. But of what value is this identity in name? For a pure empiricist, for one of those thinking beings who, as Plato put it, cling to the trunks of trees and hug boulders, able to conceive only the things they touch and see, this identity is only a word.

Many a man who has never read philosophy or who has never been sorely troubled by the quarrel about universals, behaves in effect, in this matter, as a pure empiricist. Even if he recognizes that human nature is common to all featherless bipeds, there is nothing more for him in that fact than a simple verbal affirmation charged with no content of significant reality and revealing to his scrutiny no prospect of being or of life worthy of contemplation and honour. Not only is the unity or equality in nature between men—which is not visibly perceived (because it is something perceivable only by the intellect)—less basic in his view than the inequalities, which are themselves manifest and tangible, often in very painful fashion; but the equality of the specific nature of man is for him as though it were not, and the whole burden of reality rests upon the verifiable inequalities between individuals.

These inequalities do exist; they cry out; they cover the whole expanse of human reality. Natural or social, their existence is not exclusively a fact which obtrudes itself upon our observation. Speaking generally, and making reservations for the miseries or indignities with which they may be and often are burdened because our species is an ungrateful and an unhappy sort, these inequalities correspond to the realities of our human condition. With regard to natural inequalities, Saint Thomas Aquinas even says that the intellectual capacity of one soul differs from that of another soul, not only because the actual use of the intelligence is dependent upon the organic and sensitive faculties which are themselves of unequal perfection in various human beings, but also because (the soul being destined to make up with the body a single substance) a certain individual soul destined for a certain body better constituted than others is in itself and intrinsically endowed with a greater intellective power than such a soul destined for some other body.[1]

The empiricist makes no mistake in thinking that there are, and inevitably must be, individual inequalities between men. His error rather consists in seeing and stating *this only* and in practice deeming as nothing the reality and the ontological dignity of that *nature* or essence which all men have in common, and which is perceived by the intellect with the help of the senses, and by transcending the senses.

But it is impossible to live as a pure nominalist and empiricist. Therefore, a sort of recurrence of the instincts and needs of the intelligence will take place, but on a level lower than that of fully formed intelligibility and of essences properly so-called, and this will incite pseudo-scientific cleavages to which people will attribute by compensation all the more value and reality since they have misunderstood the value and reality of the specific essence itself. Here we are faced with a paradoxical process of nominalist rationalization, the logical error of which consists in attributing, without realizing it, the character and value of specific categories to arbitrary groups set up in the fluid mass of individual peculiarities. False hierarchies of pseudo-specific gradations which establish between men inequalities in the same order as those which apply to a lion and

[1] *Sum. theol.* I, 85, 7.

an ass, an eagle and an ant, thus arise as an ideological system whereby men justify the implacable hardening of already given inequalities, or the creation of new ones. This process, pleasing to instinct and passion, first appears in the sphere of the practical intellect; later it reaches out into the speculative sphere when a pseudo-science, taking for its object of study the pseudo-essences in question, seeks to justify the privileges or domineering ambitions of those categories judged to be superior.

Now if it is true that between such and such historically constituted groups of human individuals there exist inequalities, arising from a multitude of accidental circumstances and from a common heritage at once biological and ethico-social, it is none the less true that these inequalities relate to aggregations (collective wholes) and to average values, not to species and essential values. Such groups are only relatively stable; a particular lower group can evolve, can perfect itself, can in its turn achieve superior status. Inferior in some things, that is, participating to a lesser degree in certain resources of the common human capital, it can be superior in other things and more greatly participate in other resources of that capital.

The boundaries between such groups are themselves variable and fluid, and can be broadened or contracted as the mind wishes. And finally these admitted inequalities in no sense apply to every member of the group with the same necessity as do specific inequalities to each member of the species. An ant is essentially incapable of doing what an eagle does and of arriving at the same perfection. But a given child, born in an African tribe, can, if it receives a suitable education, become more intelligent, learned, and virtuous than another given child born in a European nation; a given slave can be better and wiser than his master; a given blind deaf-mute can acquire a culture and an intellectual breadth superior to those of some man endowed at birth with all the senses. The difference which separates the mineral from the vegetable forces itself, by virtue of itself, upon the mind. But when it comes to comparing the characteristics of groups carved out of the common body of mankind, I am as much justified in comparing a resident of Manhattan with a resident of the Bronx as I am in comparing a New Yorker with a Bostonian, an Angevin with a Provençal, a German with a Frenchman, a Nordic with a Mediterranean, a Semite with an Aryan, a Dravidian with an Eskimo. The lion and the ass have no common natural pattern which they more or less fully realize. But primitive and civilized man both participate, to a different degree and with different proportions, in the common virtues possible to mankind; and if the one exemplifies more particularly the daylight riches of the human intelligence, the other exemplifies more particularly the twilight riches of the human imagination and the human instinct. Animals will always be superior to vegetables, but the industrial bourgeoisie can replace the feudal nobility in the leadership of society, and a coloured population can become, if historic circumstances lend themselves thereto, superior to a white population in its qualities of civilization.

Finally, if there are in the providential governance of mankind unequal historic vocations for the various nations and for the great ethnic groups, if there are divine preferences, if the blessings of the forefathers have brought upon their human progenies gifts of unequal brilliance and unequal abundance, all these inequalities are inequalities in fact, not in law, and depend in the last analysis only upon divine freedom. They do not shatter the unity of the human family; they give witness in it to that diversity which springs from the proper condition of what is created, and which calls for completion through mutual help and forbearance; and they make their mark on history naturally, spontaneously, through the very exercise and utilization of the gifts allotted to each. To see therein the manifestation of essential necessities and of determining laws, which it is the proper province of the science and power of man to exploit in order to assure him domination over the universe of men and of things, is the vain fancy of an idle pride. Here, as in everything which touches the well-springs of life, man has no business to subject primordial Acts to his own special providence and to his processes of rationalization. He must accept them from the providence of nature and of its Creator as primary data, dependent, by the very fact that they are primary, upon a domain forbidden to man's control.

The brutal empiricism and the nominalist pseudo-rationalization I have been considering are incapable of taking into account all these truths, the importance of which is vital for humanity. Since the unity of mankind is for the representatives of this kind of thinking merely a word, in practice they harden the natural or social inequalities to which men are heir into differences of species between those groups, existing in fact or arbitrarily imagined, into which they sort mankind. This pseudo-logic, moreover, is not at all disinterested. Just as the life of our instincts constantly underlies and affects that of our intelligence, so the burning inclination toward great sins constantly excites within us the inclination toward great errors. In this case it is collective pride which comes into play, the instinct for domination and cruelty, the passion of hardened hearts, and the tendency to exalt one's own strength by bringing others into submission.

The pseudo-scientific categories into which men are thus divided are either social pseudo-essences or biological pseudo-essences. The first—social pseudo-essences—often correspond (this was generally the case in antiquity) to the various layers of population which, in fact, successive conquests have superimposed on a country. In the days when the caste system was in full flower, what prevented a Brahmin from killing, with a clear conscience, any untouchable whose passing shadow had contaminated him? Or these social pseudo-essences may correspond to the privileges of birth normal in a society of the aristocratic or feudal type, or to the privileges of wealth normal in a society of the mercantile or bourgeois type (and in so doing, they pervert both the idea and the practice of such privileges). They do correspond to the privileges (and serve as a basis for their idea and practice) of a purely cynical "élite" normal in a society of the totalitarian type ruled by a political Party.

The second type of pseudo-scientific category—the biological pseudo-essences—may arise in men's imaginations by virtue of an unconscious process, the origin of which lies in the obscure workings of the will for power, or in the natural ferocity of the defensive instinct of an ethnic group. They may arise in men's imaginations by virtue of a conscious process imitating and justifying the unconscious process. In such a case one finds a systematic perversion of science placed at the service of political imperialism and a monstrous flowering of errors arbitrarily fabricated from the store of biological and anthropological truths and hypotheses. Thus it is that one of the racist theses proclaimed at Nuremberg declares that "there is a greater difference between the lowest forms still called human and our superior races than between the lowest man and monkeys of the highest order."

In either case—whether we are dealing with pseudo-species in the social or the biological order—the royal race, be it social or biological, in effect concentrates in itself, according to the false logic we are considering, all the privileges and dignity of human nature.

The lower categories—and the text I have just quoted states this clearly—are only partially or inchoately human. They are midway between beast and man, so teaches this overbearing philosophy. They are essentially made to serve the royal race; and as this is their final end, so in this also lies their happiness.

If they obey their masters, if they work for them, if, through the toil and trial of the lower categories, their masters succeed in gathering the fruits and the joys of supreme human knowledge or supreme human power, and in conquering the life of the free and the strong, their masters in turn will make them happy. Punishing them for their own good, maintaining them for their own good in a state of slavery, refusing them for their own good the rights and liberty of which they are not worthy, making available to them the necessities of life and the half-animal, half-human joys which alone they are capable of appreciating, and without which they would yield poor returns or might chance to foment some hideous "servile revolt," their masters can bestow no higher benefit upon them than to teach them to find their pleasure and the best reward for their faithfulness in the happiness of those they serve. Scorn here takes the place of pity; the latter, being suitable only to the souls of slaves, is a disease in the souls of the strong. They are heroically prepared for the sacrifice of the weak, whenever the superior interests of the royal race, that is to say of humanity, require it.

More or less on the surface or more or less hidden in the recesses of the unconscious, professed by those who teach it in various degrees and under varied forms, sometimes contrasting with each other, this philosophy of enslavement is the pure form toward which tends every kind of moral or social empiricism which disregards men's equality as a species in nature and sees in it only a word. Whether one looks at it from the point of view of the natural order and the natural truths confirmed by Christianity, or from the point of view of the supernatural life and the supernatural truths which it brought into being, clearly such a philosophy of enslavement wounds Christianity to the heart.

The errors we have been considering are those of the anti-Christian trend toward slavery.

PSEUDO-CHRISTIAN EGALITARIANISM

I COME now to the second attitude to which I referred at the beginning of this chapter—the egalitarian philosophy.

Opposing divagations give rise to each other like the ebb and flow of the tide. Idealism and empiricism are thus bound up in each other. With the empiricist and nominalist denial of the equality in nature between men is contrasted the idealist deification of this equality. For all those who, without knowing it, think as pure idealists, the unity of human nature is the unity of a subsisting Idea, of a Man-in-himself, existing outside time, and of whom all individuals involved in concrete life are merely shadows without substance; in their eyes this realized abstraction is reality itself. Under this purely logical and not ontological conception of the community-in-essence between reasoning creatures, the *homo Platonicus* (I use this expression without in the least wishing to involve Plato himself in the discussion—Plato, who, moreover, being an idealist and knowing well that he was one, was aware of the dangers of idealism and sought strenuously to overcome them)—the *homo Platonicus* absorbs or reabsorbs in himself all the reality of men, the dignity, the greatness and recognized rights of human nature. And as, under this notion, all men are equally himself, the equality in species among them alone becomes the reality, alone has the right to exist, alone is recognized by the mind. The inequalities to which experience testifies are not exactly denied, any more than is the empirical world by Platonic philosophy; rather are they refused consideration, pushed aside by the mind beyond any sphere of existence worthy of the name. Moreover, concerning empirical existence, Rousseau declared, "there is nothing beautiful but that which is not."

The denial I have in mind relates at once, though in different fashion, to natural and social inequalities. Let it be observed in passing that the equalities called natural belong in fact to the ethical order as well as to the psychological and biological orders, and that they in part depend upon the social environment in which the individual comes to maturity. They spring either from the complex pattern set up simultaneously by psycho-physical hereditary tendencies and by environmental conditions—physical, intellectual, moral—or from the personal history of the individual and the exercise of his free will, from what he has acquired or coincided with, good or bad, from his own work and from his own achievements. The idealist who is devoted to the *homo Platonicus* sets up against these natural inequalities a speculative denial. He minimizes them as much as he is able, or thinks that they are above all the result of the artificial stratifications of social life. In fine, they doubtless exist—how can one deny it?—but as a pure accident and a pure, empirical fact, without value for the mind and from which the mind can learn nothing.

As for social inequalities, it is worth noting that some of these are not without connection with the gifts and achievements of individuals (natural inequalities), but, to the extent that they are typically social, they spring from the diversity of the internal structures of society itself, as they have been set up by history, and from the diversity of the conditions of life, which for individuals are the result of the fact that they find themselves bound up in one tissue or another of the social organism. Against such inequalities, the idealist who legislates for the Man-in-himself sets up a practical denial: they should not exist; the Man-in-himself cannot be unequal to himself; his essential dignity is outraged each time one individual is unequal to another and, in short, each time one individual differs from another.

The idealist error, as far as the subject with which we are dealing is concerned, does not lie in thinking that there is an essential equality in nature between men. It lies in the conviction that all human substance reflows within the abstract species alone, and that the reality and value of those individual inequalities which are inscribed in the world of what is particular and historic are as nothing. But these individual inequalities, despite the burden of sorrow or injustice which the sins of men or the vices of institutions may superimpose on them, are in themselves as necessary for the development and flowering of human life as the diversity of parts for the perfection of a flower or a poem.

Nor can idealism itself be integrally lived either. The data of the senses are there, pressing against the door; from time to time they must break in—either to be pushed out thereafter, or else absorbed into the pure idea. From this arises a strange dialectic in which contraries give birth to each other and are in turn absorbed by each other, the data of experience playing a rather barbarous rôle; for, never truly *accepted* by the mind, as they should be by virtue of the dignity of the intelligibles with which they are pregnant, they can carry their proper weight only by violence and in a crude form.

From the point of view of its own inner necessities, the cult of Man-in-himself demands an absolute egalitarianism. Among men, as we have observed, equality alone becomes truly real and worthy to exist, and men partake of the nobility of human nature only in the very measure that they make themselves equal and unified in it. The equality of men, moreover, implies no vital depth, no variety in degree; it is a pure logical form, and implies no internal dynamism. It is produced ready-made by nature, or rather it is the very stamp of the supra-sensible unity and timeless nobility of Man-in-himself imprinted on each of us. In the order of social and political life, the State, in proclaiming it, is only bringing man back to his true essence.

Finally, since by its principle it rules out the consent of the mind to every diversity which breaks the ideal unity of abstract Man, it cannot become in any field an *equality of proportion,* such as that which, according to Thomas Aquinas, is required by distributive justice. It is by every necessity and in every field a pure and simple equality, whose symbol is arithmetic equality. It is the equality of pure unity repeated, of the purely interchangeable and the purely homogeneous. An idea which would make men into angels, transporting into the heaven of separated essences and concentrating in the unity of the hypostasized Species all the qualitative perfection and all the nobility of human nature, thus paradoxically ends, in the empirical world, by bringing about an utter uniformity of men under the law of Number and Quantity, and by transferring to the mass the dignity of the person.

A human mass, as undifferentiated as possible, rejecting as though it were an offense or sacrilege any qualitative inequality annihilating everyone's personal will in its own common will, and having a vocation to become its own Providence here below—is the projection of the privileges of Man-in-himself into the universe of the concrete. The instinctive tendencies and the flame of sin which underlie this error of the spirit are a hatred of all superiority, collective envy and resentment, a thirst to impose a punishment on others for the set-backs and humiliations one has suffered and the sense of guilt which burdens one. It would, moreover, be an error to think that these tendencies belong exclusively to the so-called "popular masses"; they do exist among them, but they are rampant all the more among individuals in a given social group as that group is more differentiated and advanced. In any case they are the very food of absolute egalitarianism.

The first consequence of the principle thus defined is the rejection—not only theoretical but practical—of natural inequalities. All natural privileges and all the privileges of the mind, natural gifts or acquired virtues, must be rigourously levelled. Obviously those qualities which cannot be communicated and have no common measure are objects of a special condemnation. There is room neither for the poet nor for the contemplator in an egalitarian world. Culture as such must be flattened out. In the mental patterns which correspond to all this, there develops an uneasy touchiness regarding any possibility of a hierarchy of value among men, whatever it may be. One of my good friends, a professor in an American university, shocked some of his students by choosing a certain number of great men to characterize the various periods of English civilization which he presented for study in his course. Why great men? It is the mass of men that really matters.[2]

Yet the gifts of nature and natural inequalities exist despite everything. This empirical existence, when egalitarianism passes to another level of thought, obtrudes itself surreptitiously upon the mind. By an unforeseen dialectical twist, it thus comes to pass that upon the level of social and political life, since the mind explicitly rejects the typically social inequalities, it is the natural inequalities which take their place. This kind of naturalism in social matters deserves attention, and partly explains the weakening of structures properly political and the barbarization of civil life in the totalitarian manifestations of egalitarianism. (For, by an effect of the very dialectic of error, that very totalitarianism which belongs in itself to the philosophy of enslavement, is also the last achievement as well as the destruction of egalitarianism.) If, despite all, there are inequalities in society, they must result uniquely from the natural gifts which distinguish one individual from another. Russian communism excludes every social condition other than that of the proletarian in the service of the State; but the Stakhanovist workman receives a salary having no common measure with that of an ordinary workman. National Socialism makes uni-

---

[2]*Cf.* John U. Nef, "The American Universities and the Future of Western Civilization," *Review of Politics,* July, 1939; *The United States and Civilization.* Chicago, University of Chicago Press, 1941. Chapter ix.

form and militarizes all German social life; but the "élite" in charge is categoried and trained according to the principles of eugenics and racism.

Even here a return to the requirements of absolute egalitarianism will inevitably be produced at last. The social order as such being purely egalitarian, the natural gifts, which alone may serve as a basis for the inequalities which in fact exist, cannot be acknowledged as a privilege of the personality they qualify. They lose their personal character, they detach themselves from the individual person in whom they have their roots. It is only to the extent that the individual reflects the mass and focuses in himself the reflections of the mass that natural gifts may be acknowledged. The sovereign domination of the mass thus reaches down into the recesses of the person himself and, for the exclusive benefit of the whole, seizes upon the creative sources hidden at the heart of the person. Everything in man is at the service of the anonymous monster. At this point the mass itself needs to personify itself in a demigod who is at once its master and its saviour.

All the implications I have been pointing out, and which relate to the concrete dialectic of egalitarianism, are just as incompatible with Christian thought as the implications of the philosophy of enslavement. But in the heaven of abstract formulas, and in its idealistic principle, egalitarianism appears to be a false replica of Christian truths. And having an ambiguous nature on the level of the emotions as well as on the level of the intellect, it finds nourishment not only in the vengeful instincts of which I have spoken, but also in generous instincts and truly human aspirations which, although in the end inefficacious, are none the less attempts at or vestiges of a Christian disposition—either aspirations normal to the sentiments aroused by the Gospels or, more often in fact, secularized Christian sentiments. It is the passion for justice which makes the great doctrinaires of equality. With the same words if not with the same voice as Christianity's, they assert against the apologists of slavery the natural equality of men and the equal rights founded thereon. If in the end absolute egalitarianism leads to the worst forms of slavery, it is because of an unhappy fate contrary to its original intention. At its outset it had, or believed it had, only one object—to affirm and defend the dignity of mankind. Its deepest appeal lies in that desire for communion which dwells in the hearts of all men and in that irresistible attraction for all of us which is exercised by anything that tells us—even in perverting its meaning—of the overthrow of the powerful and the exaltation of the humble, of freeing those who are suffering and naked, of summoning all men to the same brotherly feast.

In that restless emotionalism tinged with resentment, and also in those virtues of solidarity and that sense of the universal interdependence of mankind often found joined together in the same believers in the egalitarian thesis, who can distinguish between that which springs from a false love, detesting and ravaging nature, a bitter passion counterfeiting Christian charity, and that which springs from a natural love, from a *caritas humani generis,* which is often abstract and platonic, but which is still in its way a beginning and a remote image of that charity? M. Pierre-Maurice Masson has written an entire book upon the Christianity of Jean-Jacques Rousseau, and this conception is materially precise. Formally it is more nearly true to say that the notions of Jean-Jacques arise from a corruption and from what may be called a "naturalizing" of the Christian gospel.[3] The egalitarian error is at once less hateful and more treacherous than the error of the philosophy of enslavement; less hateful, because it preserves an element of that which is naturally Christian in the human soul; more treacherous, because it corrupts that very element. It is a pseudo-Christian error.

[3]*Cf.* J. Maritain, *Three Reformers,* pp. 200–237.

CHRISTIAN EQUALITY

WE ARRIVE now at the third attitude to which I referred at the beginning of this chapter: the realist idea, the true idea of equality.

From a point of view that is neither nominalist nor idealist but realist, the unity or equality in nature among men is not a mere word nor a logical exigency of an abstract species fictitiously realized. It is ontological and concrete, just as much as the likenesses and affinities which in the external world serve as bases for that positive unity which the species has within our mind. For the universality of our ideas is grounded *in re,* in things, and it would be necessary to have angelic vision to measure the depth of the real relations and the real solidarity connoted by that maxim of the schools.

The equality in nature among men consists of their concrete communion in the mystery of the human species; it does not lie in an idea, it is hidden in the heart of the individual and of the concrete, in the roots of the substance of each man. Obscure because residing on the level of substance and its root energies, primordial because it is bound up with the very sources of being, human equality reveals itself, like the nearness of our neighbour, to every one who practices it; indeed it is identical with that proximity of all to each, and of each to all. If you treat a man as a man, that is to say if you respect and love the secret he carries within him and the good of which he is capable, to that extent do you make effective in yourself his closeness in nature to and his equality or unity in nature with yourself. It is the natural love of the human being for his own kind which reveals and makes real the unity of species among men. As long as love does not call it forth, that unity slumbers in a metaphysical retreat where we can perceive it only as an abstraction.

In the common experience of misery, in the common sorrow

of great catastrophes, in humiliation and distress, under the blows of the executioner or the bombs of total war, in concentration camps, in the hovels of starving people in great cities, in any common *necessity,* the doors of solitude open and man recognizes man. Man also recognizes man when the sweetness of a great joy or of a great love for an instant clears his eyes. Whenever he does a service to his fellow men or is helped by them, whenever he shares the same elementary actions and the same elementary emotions, whenever he truly considers his neighbour, the simplest action discovers for him, both in others and in himself, the common resources and the common goodness—primitive, rudimentary, wounded, unconscious and repressed—of human nature. At once the realness of equality and community in nature is revealed to him as a very precious thing, an unknown marvel, a fundamental basis of existence, more important than all the differences and inequalities superimposed upon it. When he will have returned to his routine pleasures, he will have forgotten this discovery.

The authentic instinct of equality in nature, which naturally underlies and strengthens the fragile conception that our heedless intelligence can gain of this same equality when we retain that realist perspective which I have endeavoured to describe, is no secondary tendency like pride or envy, no matter how deep-seated it is within us; it is a primary instinct, the instinct of communication founded on a common membership in the same specific whole. The realist conception of equality in nature is an inheritance of the judeo-christian tradition; it is a natural prerequisite for Christian thought and life. Just as there is in every being a natural love for God above all else, without which charity would not serve to perfect nature but to destroy it,[4] so also, however it may be weakened by sin, there must be in man a natural love for his own kind without which the love of the gospel for men of every race and every condition would

[4]Cf. *Sum. theol.* I, 60, 5.

be contrary to nature rather than its exaltation. How should we all be called upon thus to love one another in God if we were not all equal in our condition and specific dignity as rational creatures?

Christianity confirms and emphasizes the concrete sense of equality in nature by affirming its historical and genealogical character, and by teaching that here we are concerned with a blood relationship, properly so-called, all men being descended from the same original parents, and being brothers in Adam before they are brothers in Christ. Heirs of the same sin and the same weaknesses, but heirs also of the same original greatness, all created in the image of God and all called to the same supernatural dignity as adopted sons of God, and to coheirship with Christ the Saviour, all redeemed by the same lifegiving Blood, and thus destined to become equals of the angels in heaven,[5] what Christian can look upon man with the demented gaze of racist pride? The *unity of mankind* is at the basis of Christianity. Pius XII asserts it from the eminence of the chair of Peter, when he condemns, as the first of the pernicious errors so widespread today, "The forgetting of that law of human solidarity and charity, required and imposed as much *by the community of origin and by the equality of rational nature among all men,* to whatever people they may belong, as by the sacrifice of redemption offered up by Jesus Christ. . . ." After having recalled to mind the insight which Saint Paul gives us on this matter, the Pope adds, "Marvellous insight which makes us contemplate the human race in the unity of its origin in God; in the unity of its nature similarly composed in all men of a material body and a spiritual and immortal soul; in the unity of its immediate end and of its mission in the world; in the unity of its dwelling place—the earth, the goods of which all men, by natural right, can utilize to sustain and develop life; in the unity of its supernatural end—God

[5] Luke xx:36.

Himself, toward whom all should strive; in the unity of the means to attain this end; . . . in the unity of its relation to the Son of God; . . . in the unity of its redemption worked for all men by Christ."[6]

It is because the Christian conception of life is based upon so concrete, broad, and fruitful a certainty of the equality and community in nature between men that it, at the same time, insists so forcefully on the orderings and hierarchies which spring and should spring from the very heart of this essential community, and on the particular inequalities which they necessarily involve. For in the world of man as in the world of creation, there can be no concourse or communication, no life or movement without differentiation, no differentiation without inequalities.[7]

Christianity fearlessly asserts the necessity of these inequalities; it respects them, furthers them, favours them, for it knows that as long as they remain normal—that is as long as the human will, by a kind of perversion, does not undertake to make them serve as means of exclusion rather than of communication and make them crush the essential equality and the primordial community which they presuppose—the inequalities, which lend variety to human life and intensify the richness of life's encounters, in no way injure the dignities which befit the unity of mankind and the rights which are grounded on this unity. On the contrary, these inequalities make such a unity all the more manifest. Every man is a man in his very essence, but no man is man in essence,[8] that is, exhausts in himself all the riches of the various perfections of which human-kind is capable. In this sense all the diversity of perfections and virtues distributed through the generations of men in space and time is but a varied participation in the common and inexhaustible potentialities of man.

The term *unity of mankind* is the Christian name, and the

---

[6]Encyclical *Summi pontificatus,* October 20, 1939. Italics mine.
[7]Cf. *Sum. theol.* I, 47, 2.   [8]*Cf.* Cajetan, in *Sum. theol.* I, 6, 3.

truest name, of the equality in nature between men. It helps us to purify the idea of that equality from all erroneous associations and implications, whether they arise from a geometric imagination or from a passion for levelling. An arithmetic equality between two numbers excludes all inequality between them, but equality in nature between men, or the unity of human nature, for its full flowering demands individual inequalities. To affirm the equality in nature between men is for idealist egalitarianism to wish that all inequality among them should disappear. To affirm the equality in nature between men, or the unity of human nature, is for Christian realism to wish that those fruitful inequalities, whereby the multitude of individuals participates in the common treasure of humanity, should develop themselves. Egalitarian idealism interprets the word equality on a plane surface; realism interprets it with the dimension of depth as well. Not only should one conceive of equality as something fundamental from which arises an infinite number of differences, but equality itself is a profound thing—organic, intensive, and qualitative. Let us not say that one man is as good as another; that is a nihilistic formula which acquires real meaning only from deep religious pessimism (*vanitas vanitatum, omnis homo mendax*). Let us say that in a man are, *virtualiter*, all men. The Son of Man who "knows what there is within man" perceives in each man all men.

Thus we must assert both that equality in essence which unites men in rational nature and those natural individual inequalities which arise from this very unity or equality. But from this very fact we also recognize that it is equality which is primordial, and inequalities which are secondary. Because, speaking absolutely, the community of essence is of greater importance than individual differences; the root is more important than the branches.

The Church recently gave brilliant testimony to this primacy of equality in nature over derivative inequalities when on October 28, 1939, on the feast of Christ the King and while Europe was going into a period of convulsions which would make us lose hope for her if we had not hope in God, the Pope consecrated over the tomb of Saint Peter twelve bishops belonging to the most diverse peoples and groups of peoples, several of whom were men of colour. "Those who enter the Church, whatever may be their origin and their language," said he on this occasion, "must know that they have an equal right as sons in the house of the Lord, wherein reign the law and peace of Christ." But if this equality in the Church is established upon baptism and the grace of divine adoption, who can fail to see that it necessarily presupposes a similar fundamental equality in the order of nature? The exercise of episcopal government brings into play natural gifts and virtues as well as infused gifts. And here we have white men, according to the regions where they happen to live, who can be governed on the road to their eternal destiny by bishops of the yellow or black race, just as yellow or black men can be governed by bishops of the white race.

With regard to social life it is important at the outset to note that there too, and for the same reasons indicated above, there are and must be equality and inequalities; and that inequalities—which are normal, consubstantial with social life, flourishing everywhere—are and must be secondary. Equality is primary, inasmuch as it relates (as equality pure and simple) to the fundamental rights and common dignity of human beings, and (as equality of proportion) to justice.

Indeed, among all peoples that which is thus secondary, the inequalities, most often conceals that which is primary, not only because in general inequalities exist everywhere and are the more apparent, but doubtless also because in the social order men have always made much of inequalities, in themselves fragile and of human origin, by means of marks and insignia, manifestations of power and trappings of fear, thus trying to solidify and stabilize them. It remains true that, whatever may be the forms of a given society and the inequalities they involve, it is not only a denial of the Evangelical virtues, but in the natural order itself a baseness, an offence against creation, to treat as an *inferior man* a man belonging to some inferior part of the social structure, to make him conceive his inferior social condition as an inferiority of essence. To do this is to place in a relationship of effective prevarication both him who scorns and him who is scorned. If a man is of an inferior social condition, he is there not by virtue of one of those pseudo-essential necessities clarified in the first part of this chapter. Far from relegating him once and for all to his condition, it is only right to honour in him the powers and potentialities of human nature, thanks to which he might have found himself in a higher position if he had been born in some other cradle, or if the fortunes of life had offered him other opportunities, or if he had taken better advantage of those in fact offered him.

Ever since the New Law brought on earth liberated and energized the natural movement of history—in the very depths of the conflict occasioned by its opposing forces, which themselves became energized—this natural movement has not tended to iron out social inequalities; it has tended rather to bring them back to their proper proportions and to their secondary character with respect to common human dignity. To speak more generally, and concerning the demands of inequality as well as of equality, it can be said that, in the toilsome development of mankind and of reason, in proportion as the normal aspirations of the human personality succeed, under whatever given conditions, in more or less perfectly achieving reality, to the same extent the natural law—taken not as an abstract code but in its historical growth, which is itself natural—tends progressively to make explicit the potential requirements contained within its principles, and the positive law tends in its own sphere to open itself more to the influences of nature.

Certain social inequalities result from natural inequalities or are required by them. It is just that that part which by innate or acquired superiority renders more services to the whole should receive more in return. It is also just or equitable that individuals should receive in proportion not to their needs or desires, which tend to become infinite, but to the necessities of their life and development, the means for putting to use their natural gifts. In this sense the more a man has, the more he should receive. The same care that men bestow upon their rare plants or their most beautiful stallions they do not bestow upon the superior persons who are an honour to their own species. This is in itself an offence against nature; even though men's awkwardness is such that it is better for genius not to receive their care.

Other social inequalities, however, are themselves of social origin. It is important to concentrate our attention on these typically social inequalities, of which Pascal liked to point out both the importance and the whimsicality and which egalitarianism least understands. It is from the needs proper to the internal differentiation of the social body, indeed, not from the natural merits of the individuals who happen to be embodied in one or another of its parts, that arise the inequalities in duties and advantages attached to these parts. An imbecile king remains the king. The *orders* of the Old Régime may have given way to the *classes* (in the strict sense of the word)[9] of our present régime, and these in their turn may give way to "bodies" having varied statuses. Always will some inequalities of intrinsically social origin bear witness to the inconquerable originality and vitality which belong to social life as such. It is

[9] *Cf.* Goetz Briefs, *The Proletariat.* New York, McGraw-Hill, 1937.

clear, on the other hand, that such inequalities turn into a perversion of political life and into barbarism if bewildered men wish to erect them into a state of social servitude for the human groups assumed to be inferior.

Social equality itself, in so far as it merits the name, has also a value which is properly and truly social. Although it is based upon unity and equality in nature, it is not to be confused with it; it is rather an expression or development thereof in the social order. This is first of all that equality, recognized and sanctioned by society, in those rights—so hard to specify but none the less real—which we call the fundamental rights of the human person: the right to exist, to keep one's body whole, to found a family (itself assured the enjoyment of its liberties); the right of association, the right to the private ownership of material goods, the right to seek those good things through which a rational creature may perfect himself, the right to travel toward eternal life along the road one's conscience acknowledges as designated by God. It is also that equality in the respect which human dignity requires that social customs show to all men, by treating them all as men, not as things. Then again, it is "political equality, equality of all before the law, whether it represses or protects, the making available to all citizens of public employment."[10] The institution of these last three equalities by the temporal power is derived, as the late Cardinal Verdier wrote, from the "evangelical streams released by Christ throughout the world." It is, finally, that equal condition as coheirs of the effort of all, in accordance with which all should in so far as possible participate "free of charge" in the elementary goods needed for human life.

This social equality is thus, in its own way and like equality in nature, not a surface thing, but lies deep; and it includes essential differences, not only in degrees and modes, but in its

[10]Cardinal Verdier, *Christian Answers to Social Problems,* p. 62.

basis in the law. I have said that this equality, with its differing forms and degrees, has, as the term "social equality" sufficiently indicates, a proper and real social value. Let it be added that it possesses this in a different way from the social inequalities, in this sense that, taken all in all, the inequalities proceed from society more than from nature, whereas social equality proceeds from nature more than from society. It is by virtue either of the exigencies or of the wishes of human nature that, taking into account the different degrees I have pointed out in the domain of natural law, common law, or positive law, social equality assumes in society the proper and real social value about which I have spoken. The fundamental rights of the human person are in themselves anterior to civil society, and the equality of these rights has social value only in so far as society recognizes and sanctions them in its own order. The other kinds of equality, although they derive from nature as their principle, as does society itself, rise up progressively in the midst of society, like a social flowering forth or fructifying of the equality of nature. In any case social equality is not a condition of existence set by "nature" for "all men," like their arms and legs or the colour of their eyes, which social life, unexpectedly coming into being, needs thereafter only to protect, as Jean-Jacques Rousseau would have it. Social equality is a condition of existence which, whether in its various degrees it be postulated or desired more or less imperiously by nature, achieves reality in society. "All men" are not born in this effective condition of existence. The members of a sufficiently developed civil community obtain it from the community through natural law or through positive law, either by virtue of being men (if it is a question of the fundamental rights of the person) or, if it is a question of other kinds of equality, by virtue of being citizens.

In itself, and when its nature is not vitiated by absolute egalitarianism, the multiform social equality which we have been discussing favours the development of natural inequalities, because in opening to each a greater number of possibilities, it favours at the same time differences in growth and in development. And on the other hand it requires that these natural inequalities be compensated for by a process of organic redistribution, by virtue of which the weak and the less favoured share in the benefits which the social whole owes to others.

Similarly, in so far as the true character and the true rôle of social equality are effectively recognized, this social equality, serving as a seemingly natural ground for social inequalities of structure and function, gives them more intrinsic stability than the artifices of constraint can give; yet on the other hand it requires that these social inequalities be compensated for in two ways: first, by the fact that the conditions to which they correspond be not closed but open (open for the circulation of elements which come from other levels); and second, by the fact that in each one of these conditions individuals may enjoy a state of life that is truly human and may really be able to strive (I do not say easily, because without obstacles to override there is no progress for us) for the fullness of human development.

If what I have said concerning the indestructible originality of the social life and its proper differentiations is just, it is an illusion to wish that all may have at the start strictly identical opportunities to mount to the highest degrees in social life. (From the very fact that every one is bound up in a differing social fabric, the initial opportunities of one differ from those of another; and then again it is naïve indeed to believe that the reward of a good life should consist in a change of social level.) But it is proper that the highest social conditions should not of themselves be closed to any one, and even more important, it is proper that in whatever *social* structure men are involved, they should have the same opportunities to achieve—each one according to his effort and his condition—

their *human* fullness, those fruits of wisdom and human virtue whose savour is not identical, but similarly good in each, whether he spends his life in working the earth, in philosophizing or in governing the State. Thus, such notions as that of equality of opportunity or equality of conditions, which egalitarianism would make chimerical, become true and proper if they are understood in the sense not of an equality pure and simple, but of a *proportional* equality.

This *equality of proportion* plays a capital rôle in the temporal community. What Proudhon and the great egalitarianists did not understand was that in the domain of relations between the social whole and its parts, such a proportional equality is justice itself. Having respect for the differences, and hence the concrete inequalities, associated with the carrying on of personal life in the midst of society—equality, by the very fact that it does not relate to an abstract Man-in-himself, but to concrete persons, in a certain fashion seeks to move over into the sphere of these very inequalities. It then becomes the equality of proportion that characterizes distributive justice, which latter deals with each in accordance with his merits. And thus, pervading and reconciling all inequalities, justice to a certain extent restores equality, thereby making civic friendship possible. For, as Thomas Aquinas put it, "friendship is a certain union or society of friends, which cannot exist among persons remote from one another, but has as its prerequisite that they have access to equality. Hence it pertains to friendship equally to use the equality which has been previously established; but it pertains to justice to lead unequals to equality. When this equality has achieved reality, the task of justice is performed. Thus equality is a final end as regards justice, but a principle as regards friendship."[11] Finally, if equality lies at the root and inequality rests in the branches, it is a new kind of equality which, by virtue of justice, friendship, and human compassion

[11]St. Thomas Aquinas, in VIII. *Ethic,* lect. 7.

and by virtue of the communication they provoke, is realized in the fruit.

It is well to insist upon this last statement, and elaborate its implications. Because social life, while postulated by nature, is the work of reason and virtue and implies, however opposed it may be, a movement of progressive conquest of man over nature and over himself, social equality is not something ready-made; it implies in itself a certain dynamism. Like liberty, it is itself an end to struggle for, and with difficulty, and at the price of a constant tension of the energies of the spirit. If, by postulates of nature, it is, in its most general forms, basic and primary, social equality is yet only a seed which must develop and which works in the direction of fruition. It requires not only the exercise of distributive justice in the temporal community; it requires as wide a measure as possible of free participation by all in the necessary good things, material and spiritual, and that redistribution to persons of the common good of which we spoke above. It requires the progress of social justice; the organic development of institutions of law; the participation, in more and more extensive degrees, of persons as such in political life; the transition to conditions which would really offer to each an equal opportunity (equal in the proportional sense) to bring his gifts to fruit, and which would permit the formation of an aristocracy born of personal work, that pays back the good effects of its labour for common use; the sharing more and more by all in the benefits of culture and the mind, and in that inner liberty which is given by mastery over self and knowledge of the truth.

The civilization which we have before our eyes has sought these things, but because it sought them in the wrong way it has often found their very opposites. Doubtless the illiterate craftsmen of medieval France participated more in the commonwealth of the mind than do the middle classes of today, to whom such rare technical marvels as the movies and the radio, used in disastrous fashion, as far as the masses are concerned, provide the delights of a scattered mind and the uniformity of emptiness. I am well aware of all this. Nor do I think that being illiterate is a good thing in itself. We must then renew ourselves, and we must undertake to seek the good in the good way. Such a leaven of equality as has been disseminated by pseudo-Christian egalitarianism has filled the world with unhealthy fermentations; but there is another leaven of equality[12] which is a leaven of justice and is a proper stimulant of human history, and which tends to raise the human mass toward a way of life more truly human, wherein inequalities are not suppressed, but compensated, and subordinated to that high equality of the common use of the good things which nourish and exalt our rational nature. In sum, the error has been to seek equality in a regression toward the basis set up by "nature," and in a levelling down to this base. It should be sought in a progressive movement toward the end which is composed of the good things of rational life becoming in so far as possible and in various degrees accessible to all, and this, thanks to the very inequalities themselves, by justice and fraternal friendship turned away from seeking domination and toward helpfulness and cooperation.

The equality I have been discussing should be called *Christian equality,* not only because it issues from the judeo-christian tradition and conforms with the Christian conception of life, but also because, if it were not for the influence of the Christian leaven injected into secular history, and if it were not for the added stimulus, which in its own sphere temporal civilization receives from Christian energies, this equality could not

[12]"That fundamental equality is active and radiant. . . . It creates a kind of egalitarian *dynamism,* a leaven of equality which perpetually raises the human mass to a way of life where the distances that separate ever diminish, where true brotherhood is without end more perfectly realized. . . ." Cardinal Verdier, *Christian Answers to Social Problems,* p. 43.

succeed in coming to pass. As there is a flowering of the natural law which can be attained only with the help of the virtues of the New Law, there is also a human flowering, a real humanism of civil life which can be attained only with the help of these virtues.

The rôle played by the irrational instincts and tendencies is major in the political life of men. To make possible the existence of a political life in which the dynamism of equality works in the right direction, the habits and customs which spring from the Christian virtues in the human mass must therein tame the irrational with reason and develop right instincts. For the development among men of a real sense of equality without egalitarianism and of that civic love, which is not a gift of nature but an heroic conquest of reason and liberty, in this temporal order which is the very home of conflicts, of weaknesses and of the sins of the world, the sap of the gospel, the sense of supernatural equality of those called to a divine life, the sense of brotherly charity must permeate this temporal order to give it life and lift it up. "Wherever prevails a religion other than ours," wrote Joseph de Maistre, "slavery is the rule, and wherever that religion is weakened, the nation becomes, in exact proportion, less jealous of the general liberty. . . . Government alone cannot govern; it requires either slavery, which diminishes the number of the wills operative within the State, or divine energy, which, by a kind of spiritual *grafting* process, destroys the natural violence of those wills and enables them to act together without harming each other."[13]

Finally, to return to the central theme of this study, the realism of our intelligence is so weak, and the natural love for our own kind so little vigilant, either because of the weakness of our nature or because of the injuries it has suffered, that without the reinforcing comfort of faith and gospel love, it is almost impossible that we should not fall, with regard to the

[13]Joseph de Maistre, *Le Pape,* t. III, c. 2.

equality and the inequality of men, into one of the two errors—empiricist or idealist—which were pointed out at the start. Indeed, a realist conception of equality in nature, if it is to be established among men in a sufficiently general way and with enough force to act effectively upon civilization, can be no less than a Christian conception of that equality.

CHAPTER II

THE POLITICAL IDEAS OF PASCAL

PASCAL'S EMPIRICISM

SUCH a sublime spirit as Pascal cannot even fall into error without scattering sparks of truth in all directions. That is why an examination of his political ideas is so stimulating for any one interested in the philosophy of culture. Much more profound than Machiavelli or Hobbes, it is by the flame of a metaphysical and religious conception of man, at once high and passionate, that Pascal illuminates his political ideas. But these ideas bear witness to that dramatic moment when the classical civilization of Europe, radiant with strength and glory, is hardening inwardly, is already becoming mechanical and forsaking its higher principles. We must therefore, at the outset, make definite reservations concerning the political ideas of Pascal: they are, as it were, the culminating point where appear with equal brilliance the strength and the weakness of his genius. Can mankind live on earth without believing in justice? No, it cannot, says Pascal. Can justice exist among men, even very imperfectly? No, it cannot, says Pascal. Thus, we find ourselves confronted with an irremediable conflict.

When he undertakes to "humble" reason, Pascal is dealing, make no mistake about it, within himself with a geometrical reason more Cartesian than he thinks, and already rationalist—that is to say, taking human reason as the measure of things instead of taking things as the measure of the reason. Indeed he harshly represses it, but he seeks in it the measure for what is or would be rational. It is from this reason which is out of harmony with things themselves that this passionate lover of the real gets the illusory notion of a justice among men which, of itself, should have the same universal application as the propositions of Euclid. He believes that if the human race knew justice, "It would not have laid down that maxim, the most general of all accepted among men, that each follow the customs of his own country."[1] "The brilliance of true equity," he says, "would have subdued all nations, and legislators would not have taken as models, in place of this unchanging justice, the fantasies and caprices of Persians and Germans. One would see it established in all the states of the world and through all the ages. . . ."[2] etc. Here is an abstract and wholly unreal conception of justice. Wait a little more than a century and you will hear Condorcet promulgate this dogma, which at first glance seems self-evident, and which yet means nothing: "A good law should be good for every one"—for man of the age of cave-dwellers as well as for man of the age of the steam-engine, for nomadic tribes as well as for agricultural peoples—"a good law should be good for every one, as a true proposition is true for every one."

Through his genius, Pascal had a foreboding of the disastrous effects of rationalism on politics and against these effects he reacted violently. But how? To avoid this evil, he thought it necessary to beat down reason, and to demand of it solely the avowal of its helplessness. A sort of empiricism which, in him, came from the passionate excess of his attachment to the concrete, a violent and desperate effort to lay bare reality, led him to measure everything against brute fact (this concealing from him the form of law) and to stumble over all the contingencies of experience, without desiring to go beyond them. He sees

[1]Blaise Pascal, *Penseés,* t. II *Œuvres* (*Grands Ecrivains de France,* Hachette, 1921, t. XIII), n. 294 (page 215).
[2]*Ibid.*

that "Larceny, incest, the murder of children and of old people
—all these have been counted virtuous acts."[3] Therefore (and
this is where he makes his mistake) "nothing according to
reason alone is just in itself. . . . Custom makes equity, for this
reason alone: it is accepted."[4]

Finally, Jansenistic theology convinced Pascal that the sin
of Adam changed man's nature and utterly corrupted everything in us. How can we seek thereafter a foundation for justice and reason in the earthly community and in the course of
human events? "There are doubtless natural laws," he writes,
"but that fine corrupted reason of ours itself has corrupted
everything."[5] All our hierarchies, all the ties of our social life,
are, in themselves, mere folly. "Yet true Christians yield to
folly," he adds; "not that they respect it, but that they respect
the will of God who, in order to punish men, has subjugated
them to this folly."[6]

Thus a strange encounter: the Jansenistic theory of a corrupted nature, an imperious zeal for experience, a reaction
against a reason which is impetuous and already rationalist—
conspires to divert him from any consideration of the divine
norms hidden in the depths of nature, converges toward the
anti-metaphysical prejudice which is the great weakness of
Pascal. As a result, there can be, here on earth, only ties of
force and of opinion, subject to the caprice of men and to the
accidents of the historical process. "He who obeys laws because
they are just, obeys a justice of his imagination, not the essence
of the law; law is altogether self-contained; it is law and nothing more."[7] "Not being able to bring it about that right should
be might, men have brought it about that might is right."[8]

Here, then, we have Pascal and Rousseau agreeing on this
major premise: there is no justice in that human community

[3]*Ibid.* (page 217).
[4]*Ibid.* (page 218).
[5]*Ibid.* (page 217).
[6]*Ibid.,* t. II, n. 338.
[7]*Ibid.,* t. II, n. 294 (page 219).
[8]*Ibid.,* t. II, n. 298.

which little by little has been built up through the ages.

They nevertheless reach opposite conclusions, because they differ on the minor premise. For Rousseau's reasoning continues thus: justice must exist, even were we to perish in consequence; therefore everything must be made over in accordance with the plans of the ideal Legislator, and that is possible because man is good by nature. Pascal, on the contrary, thinks that "this is a sure way of losing everything."[9] He says that there must be peace, peace which he holds to be the "sovereign good"[10] in the temporal order. For the sake of the peace of the State, then, we must retain everything and examine nothing, we must proclaim as just whatever is established because it is established. "And thus all our established laws will necessarily be considered just without being examined, because they are established."[11] For Pascal, that acceptance of injustice in the higher interest of the common good would therefore be the only wisdom possible on this earth, since it corresponds to our state of universal depravity.

With Pascal, as with many political theorists of his day, and as later with a Bernard de Mandeville, such pessimistic resignation to an unbridgeable gap between the requirements of justice and those of the welfare of the community seems to be a sign of an astonishing lowering of that quality of the mind which is truly metaphysical and realistic in the inner perception of things. Is it any wonder then that, as an unforeseen result, this kind of Christian cynicism of Pascal's should have found its unhappy realization in the *enlightened despotism* of the next century? Pascal himself wrote, "The wisest of legislators once said that for the good of men we must often deceive them. . . ."[12] The opinions of the people are healthy as such, he thinks, because the people respect ancient customs and established laws, but these opinions are not healthy *in their*

---

[9]*Ibid.*, t. II, n. 294 (page 220).
[10]*Ibid.*, t. II, n. 299.
[11]*Ibid.*, t. II, n. 312.
[12]*Ibid.*, t. II, n. 294 (page 221).

mind, since the people imagine that laws and customs are true
and just, and since they obey them only by reason of this supposed justice. "The people," says Pascal, "take the antiquity
of these laws as an evidence of their truth (not of their authority alone, without truth). . . ."[13] They obey them only because they believe them just."[14]

TRUE AND FALSE JUSTICE

WELL, THEN, here are people's opinions which are healthy, even
in their mind. Saint Thomas Aquinas thought as the people
think. He held that laws are only truly law because they are
just, and that they are binding in conscience only if they are
just. A real justice, not a feigned one, is the foundation for authority in law as it is for peace in the community. If we shatter
this basic order, which links things human to the divine stabilities of the universe, even the strongest empirical defenses of the
social order will remain vain. How much shrewder politically
and more truly realist did Saint Catherine of Sienna show herself to be when she cried to the leaders of the people—*"The
great force of conservation is holy justice."* Philosophically that
is a proposition self-evident, if not to all men, at least "to the
wise," as Saint Thomas would put it. For, the community having been established for the fulfillment of the ends of human
nature, and the latter bearing the impress of God, it is a pure
and simple contradiction in terms to claim to insure the welfare of the community through injustice. To prefer injustice
to disorder, as Goethe put it, is to prefer disorder to disorder,
disorder in the root to disorder in the flower.

But the holy justice of which Catherine of Sienna spoke is
altogether different from the rationalistic justice of the Uto-
pians. Here is another essential point, which calls for the discernment of intelligence. True justice, the justice of the sages
and of the saints, descends from divine reason and permeates

[13]*Ibid.,* t. II, n. 325.   [14]*Ibid.,* t. II, n. 326.

all reality as a living impulse, leading everything to its end. False justice, the justice of the geometricians of non-being, arises from a human reason which refuses at the outset to base itself upon and to be regulated by what is; it veneers the real with the exactions of an asserted *ideal* which, not springing from things—whose essential ordering it would express—and thus not issuing from divine ideas, is an *idol,* dead and death-dealing.

That false justice has deceived many generous minds; it is exactly what spoiled that passion for Justice which in the great French socialist thinker, Proudhon, was so fine, so holy a feeling, Proudhon's fundamental error having been that of reducing justice as a whole, and especially political justice, to the elementary type of justice we call *commutative,* which regulates the exchange of material things. Justice thus conceived applies to men as to *quantities* between whom (as in the case of fair exchange) it calls for pure and simple equality. True justice, as it comes into play in political life, applies to men as to *natures,* to whose particular ends it apportions suitable means, and as to *persons,* who represent for the social whole values more or less important (the scale of which, furthermore, is variable, according to the kinds of society); and in accordance with this value of the persons, considered as parts of the whole, it apportions the advantages which revert from the community to each of its parts.

This true justice, like all things human, progresses concretely from the imperfect to the perfect. It not only distinguishes between the just and the unjust, it inclines from the less to the more just; there is in it a desire, an aspiration toward the most perfectly just. Not only equality in political rights and equality of all before the law, but *equal opportunity* for each in the diversity of social conditions to make his way toward the fulfillment of his earthly life, and equal access for all to the elementary goods of existence and culture (in any given state of civilization) thus correspond to a superior degree of justice;

and this because there is the same fundamental value attached in each of us to the human person, by virtue of the unity of mankind.

But on the other hand, a whole world of unequal functional values is added to this common fundamental value, for the various persons who participate in social life. An endless diversity in conditions of existence, in historical heritages, in circumstances of time and of place, in types of society and stages of development, particularizes the material with which the true justice I am discussing concerns itself. That is why, while we find fixed in all times and in all places within Euclidean space identical laws governing all triangles, justice itself requires that human laws vary according to country and to period, and that custom have the force of law.

For the natural law necessarily requires that what it itself leaves indeterminate be completed by the contingent determinations of human reason and experience; it is therefore, as Saint Thomas says, by virtue of the natural law, and, in the last analysis, by virtue of the eternal law which is in God, that human law is binding. But to say that the law should by its very essence be just is to say it should conform to the conditions laid down by nature for our subsistence and for the fulfillment of our destiny. It is thus that the teachings of Saint Thomas preserve an equilibrium between the requirements of justice and those of the common welfare, that truly human equilibrium which has its roots in the heart of God, and the denial of which makes the earth uninhabitable.

As for variations in the natural law itself, they astonish only those who conceive that law as being I know not what written legal code, stamped upon human minds. On the contrary, that law is *natural* and not written. That is, with regard to the human subject, it develops in time, in accordance with the natural process of the growth of reason. And if it is *natural* in the sense of being valid for man as such, and hence for all human beings whoever they may be, it relates to human nature abstractly taken in itself and is true only with regard to the objective contents of natural law—the intelligible requirements and finalities necessarily implied in human nature and considered in themselves.[15] Not only can it happen that certain of these requirements may elude many ill-disposed human minds which wrongly apply first principles: such facts as depend on material causality prove nothing against justice. That incest and larceny should have been considered lawful by the ancient Germans indicates that subjective deficiencies can vitiate men's judgment in a thousand different ways. All that does not forbid to human substance its constituent structure and its own finalities. Nay more, we must grant that in the course of the various ages of history it is *natural* that the objective requirements of the unwritten law should themselves appear to human beings in a way at first shadowy and dim as twilight, then little by little more perfect, according to the stages in the development of conscience and the ages of civilization.[16] This apperception is destined by nature to improve always. And, finally, there is a perfection, a flowering of the natural law which presupposes in us the light and the efficacy of grace.

Pascal thinks that a selfish instinct for plunder is the origin of private property, and, as he puts it, of the "usurpation of the whole world";[17] for in itself, he again says, equality of

[15]The "law of peoples" (*jus gentium*) differs from the "natural law" in that the objective determinations on which it bears, though *necessarily* depending on first principles (as do those of natural law), do so *on the assumption* of certain circumstances of fact. As for the "positive law," the determinations on which it bears depend on first principles in *contingent* fashion, and consequently require for their establishment the particular decisions of practical reason and human will.

[16]*Cf.* Raïssa Maritain, "Histoire d'Abraham ou la Sainteté dans l'état de nature," *Nova et Vetera*, Fribourg, Switzerland, 1935.

[17]"*Mine, thine.* This dog belongs to me, said these poor children; this is my place in the sun: And there you have the beginning and the pattern for the usurpation of the whole world." Pascal, *Pensées*, t. II, n. 295.

property is just.[18] In this notion he is not guided by natural law and true justice, but by illusory geometrical justice. Usurpation and brigandage—which he cannot help seeing, and which indeed prevail—hide from him the natural and more profound ordinance which calls for personal possession of property by reason of the basic exigencies of human labour-management and for the protection of the liberties of the individual. Then a second error appears forthwith to compensate for the first: "But not being able to bring it to pass," he says, "that man should be forced to obey justice, it was brought to pass that it should be just to obey force,"[19] and he deems it madness to become indignant over this justification of violence and plunder. Chateaubriand saw in that thought the germ of Rousseau's *Discourse on Inequality*.[20] Replacing a natural truth by an unstable equilibrium between two opposite errors which spring from a geometrically-minded reason, Pascal maintains a doctrinal position essentially ambivalent.

So also justice, to his mind, would not merely require that governors decide upon war only in accordance with the rules of law (written or unwritten) and as "vicars" of that multitude whose blood and destiny they are mortgaging; it would also require that decision of war be made by a "disinterested third party,"[21] in every way a stranger to the needs of the common good of the people in question, to its interests as well as to its spiritual heritage and its vocation. But on the other hand

[18]*Ibid.*, t. II, n. 299.   [19]*Ibid.*

[20]"The first man who, having fenced in a bit of ground, had the idea of saying: *this belongs to me,* and found people foolish enough to believe him, was the true founder of civil society. How many crimes, wars, murders, how much misery and horror might he not have spared the human race, who, tearing up the fence-posts or filling in the ditch might have cried out to his fellows: beware of listening to this impostor; you are lost if you forget that the fruits belong to all men and that the land belongs to no one." Jean-Jacques Rousseau, *Discours sur l'Inégalité des Conditions humaines.*

[21]Pascal, *Pensées*, t. II, n. 296.

it is clear that in his opinion to undertake to set up in real life the arbitration of this disinterested third party would be a fine way to spoil everything: justice is not for us, perverted race that we are. Here again, a pair of extreme ideas which counter-balance each other is substituted for one simple truth; and at the same time Pascal and those who think like him forbid us any hope for the progress of a justice less ambitious, but true, which could tend to federate states—beginning with those in the same climate of civilization—in such a way as to substitute for recourse to war the decisions of a superior agency, not in-different to but interested in the welfare of that community of peoples.

Pascal, then, conceives of justice as do the most rigidly visionary rationalists; and in order to come to a conclusion opposed to theirs and to their false justice, he in effect sacrifices justice—the true as well as the false—which is nothing more in his eyes than an indispensable illusion. Here, in the think-ing of a genius, is a harbinger of the confusion which can be-come only more and more aggravated throughout modern times, and which, during an epoch now perhaps nearing its end, will set those cynical plunderers who speak in the name of order against those idealistic plunderers who speak in the name of justice—that is, raging watchdogs against whimpering wolves.

ILLUSIONS AND TRUTHS

IF THE political ideas of Pascal invite these criticisms, it is, in the last analysis, because they refuse to extricate metaphysically the supreme principles of social life. Realist by intention and by impulse, and from many special points of view healthy and vigorous, because of that essential deficiency his ideas do not deserve to be considered as truly realist. They lead of them-selves to the worst illusions, which are the illusions of the sceptics, the sophisticated; the illusions, precisely, of the "realists." The disciples of Machiavelli are the chastisement of Machiavelli. The chastisement of the great empiricists, of whom Pascal is certainly the greatest, lies in all the miscalculations and the crimes gathered together today by the realists of nihilism, who succeed only in sacrificing to absurd myths, in wasting and degrading all the energies, the goods, the virtues, and the substance of men.

Pascal's illusion springs from his very pessimism. Blinded by the sinister whimsicalities, depredations and iniquities which struck his relentless vision, he did not see what immense assets of hidden justice, of real justice, of patient justice, of common justice, of justice of root and of sap, bound to the age-long toil of that "people" which "obeys laws only because it believes them just"[22] and of the leaders who have existed and laboured in communion with the people—what assets of justice remained invested in a civilization which his prophetic sensibility warned him was already being threatened with hidden perils. Solicitous above all to conserve—to conserve the "peace" of that human order of which he saw the fruits, but not the roots—he thought that in order to preserve it, it was sufficient, while letting men believe in its "truth" without believing in it himself, to have the "authority" without truth of laws and of customs, and to have power wielded by a few unjust men of intelligence sacrificing their souls to the happy pursuit of public affairs. A day would inevitably come when, not to conserve but to overthrow, other unjust men of intelligence (intelligence at least of trickery and hatred) would sacrifice not only their own souls, but the soul of the people itself, of the human multitude perverted and hopeless, and their bodies too, as well as their souls, not to the happy pursuit of affairs of state, but to the fixed idea of the universal domination of a class (proletarian), of a "race" (aryan-germanic) or of some new pagan empire or other. On that day man would be able to measure

[22]See p. 37.

(we are beginning to do so today) the benefits of such an illusion.

This basic error, however, does not prevent Pascal's political philosophy from asserting most convincingly certain great truths. Pascal knew that regarding the human species it is a statistical law that in this species the bad comes to pass more frequently than the good. From this we must conclude that it is not enough to affirm that the social order with its structure and its laws is based upon justice and can subsist only by a sustained and constantly renewed effort of justice. We must add that in actual fact, in concrete historical matter, essential justice is realized among us only at the cost of accidental misfortunes and failures without number. What is important above all else, is that political structures and institutions be organized in accordance with the order of nature and justice. If, in specific cases, it happens that we make use of these political structures clumsily or even inequitably, we shall undoubtedly pay for it, but that is a matter of accidental misfortune, and it has all the appearances of an inevitable evil. Thus understood, all that Pascal says about usurpation and folly, about caprice and chance, about the immense amount of curious contingency and whimsicality in men's affairs and in their justice, is given its proper meaning.

But I should like to draw attention to another characteristic of Pascal's political ideas—one more positive and more precise. When the Thomists ask "whether concupiscence is infinite," and when they answer that the concupiscences set up by nature are finite, but that those which depend upon man's reason and man's judgment are infinite,[23] they explain that nature, subordinating to itself with supreme mastery the ends that are peculiar to the instinct, imposes upon these ends a fixed limit, and aims constantly, through all vicissitudes, at the preserva-

[23]Cf. *Sum. theol.* I–II, 30, 3 and 4, and the commentary by Cajetan.

tion of that basic order required by life. They add, however, that this motherly and rectifying power of nature to make everything commensurate with its ends, a power basically always benevolent, vanishes on the threshold of reason. Reason has this peculiar property: it can introduce the infinite everywhere, establish as absolute ends those things which in themselves are only means, and the ends which the reason sets itself escape control in us by any other ends, to the extent that the reason itself has not acknowledged the latter. Reason face to face with being is solitary; it is not, like nature, bound to a fixed limit; there lies hidden in its structure no submerged regulator capable of re-establishing, *in spite of reason,* order within reason. A boundless liberty is the reason's terrifying privilege.

To refuse everything predetermined and ready-made with which nature (which is itself descended from divine reason) supplies us and to abandon the safety of the human family to the play of its fallible reason alone is to make men run an unknown risk. It is to unchain by that very act what Saint Thomas calls "non-natural concupiscences," infinite in scope and of unlimited peril.

The fact remains, however, that the task of politics is in itself a task of reason and of justice (postulated by nature); and if to move forward in step with reason involves frequent slipping and bruising of one's knees, that is better than rotting at a standstill. But—and this is the point I wish to stress—just as the establishment of the social community arises from reason's fulfilling the wishes of nature, so political wisdom should prolong as far as possible into the undertakings of reason what is steadily given by nature. The best régime for man is in this sense a mixed régime (*regimen commixtum*), wherein mingle and harmonize the directives issuing from nature and those which arise from reason. "That which is founded upon sound reason is indeed ill-founded," says Pascal. In other words: that which takes for a basis the universal exercise of sound reason is very ill-based. It is folly to entrust to pure reason alone, as it supposedly exists in each given individual—that is to say, to an instrument which in the majority of cases is faltering—the common task in which the safety of the mass is at stake.

After all, no régime has ever put that folly into practice, but in theory the social metaphysics which derived from Kant and Rousseau (despite Rousseau's irrationalism), postulated it. Hence the troubles and misfortunes of the régimes of individualistic ideology (such as those I have called anarchic democracies [24]) which were constantly forced to act in a way that belied their ideology. Moreover, the inner dialectic of the ideology in question was to lead (at least among peoples not educated for political liberty) to no less a folly, which consists in relegating the common welfare of the multitude to the reason of one man alone—absolute master of all and god of the masses.

For anyone who see things as they are, it is not at all upon the idea of leaving everything to pure reason alone, as it supposedly exists in each of us, that rests the principle of popular consultation, expressed in democratic régimes by the right to vote extended to each citizen. This principle is based upon the idea that since man is by nature a political animal, it is proper that every human person, with his passions and his instincts as well as his reason, and hazarding the bad as well as the good that may come from the latter, should be summoned to political life, at least in the elementary form of the free designation of leaders, as well as of making constitutional decisions affecting the foundations of the common life, and of giving fundamental directives in those basic matters where the instinct of human nature, the hereditary historical sense, the spontaneous reaction of the temperament of a people and the "irrational" feeling for

[24] Cf. *Scholasticism and Politics,* New York, Macmillan, 1940, Chapter IV.

its vocation are more reliable than reason. It is particularly instructive, in this connection, to contemplate the widespread failure of intellectuals, the treason of so many "clercs," in the crisis of the present-day world. Reason—when uprooted from moral virtues, and even from those simple instincts and passions which preserve man's equilibrium in the universe and which are stronger in the common people than in sophisticated persons—such uprooted reason flounders before every appearance of good and is ready to justify everything. The common people, on the contrary, keep in the midst of tragedy a firmer sense of elementary human values, and a better appraisement of the basic interests at stake.

As to everyday decisions and regulations concerning the common task, it will always be true that in any régime it is fitting that such decisions depend on the final practical judgment of a few men, who, representing the whole, relieve the reason of the mass of men from the necessity of supreme and difficult deliberations. This is, however, always on condition that everyone be entitled to be heard in some way—that is, be allowed to take part through his representatives in the deliberation or the counsel which precedes and prepares the final decision (representative system) and on condition that the instruments of that supreme decision (elected officers in a democratic régime) be responsible to the people.

Then again, to be used properly the right of personal suffrage should belong to everyone, not as to an atom or to a pure reason isolated in its divinity, but as to a member of an organic community. Finally, it demands and presupposes—in order that reason may run less risk of going astray (and it does go astray as much with the learned as with the simple, with intellectuals as with manual labourers, with those who are too much informed as with those who are too little)—it presupposes precisely that stability of natural or acquired instincts which membership in an organic community (as well as in a family tradition or a political school) maintains or develops, and without which, in the practical order, reason shifts about at the mercy of the first specious argument.

THE STABILIZING TENDENCIES OF CUSTOM AND OF THE VIRTUES

IT IS HERE that Pascal's teaching is particularly valuable. Everything which in the field of social practice will introduce something of the stability of natural tendencies—not, to be sure, by a despotic drilling of the human being, annihilating character and conscience, but quite on the contrary, by the spontaneous play of institutions and customs—and everything which will thus make it possible to avoid recourse to the deliberations of reason will have, by that very fact and to that extent, its justification. "How right we have been," writes Pascal, "to distinguish men by external things rather than by their interior qualities! Which one of us will take precedence? Which of us will yield to the other? The less clever of us? But I am as clever as he is, and we shall have to fight it out. He has four lackeys, and I have only one: that is perfectly evident, all one has to do is to count; it is up to me to yield, and I am a fool if I dispute it. By this means here we are at peace; and that is the greatest of all goods."[25]

Pascal thus saw the most positive advantage of hereditary rank in the fact that it reduces the intelligence to a simple observation of fact, without leaving room for the play of reason and the boundlessness it brings with it. What he says on this subject is of value not only with regard to hereditary rank[26] in a monarchical régime, but with regard to all institutions whose

[25]Pascal, *Pensées*, t. II, n. 319.

[26]"The greatest evil is civil wars. Such are inevitable if one attempts to recompense merits, for every man will say that he has merit. The evil to be feared from a fool, who attains rank by right of birth, is neither as great nor as inevitable." *Ibid.* t. II, n. 313. *Cf.* n. 320a.

natural play gives rise to "clear" and "incontestable"[27] observations of fact.

We understand then in what sense Pascal was right to attach so great an importance to custom. For custom is a strange thing, which has its starting point in the play of reason, but which crystallizes along the road and has as its destination a *second nature*. It reintroduces then into rational life itself the fixed ways belonging to nature, it is the normal corrective for the contingencies and innumerable difficulties with which the play of reason—and the antagonism of individual reasons, with their differing points of view and their colliding passions—threatens to burden us.

All arts except the art of politics (which is not only an art, but also, and first of all, prudence) ask nothing better than to begin anew each time they find a superior form. Thus industry is constantly changing. But Saint Thomas observes that the art of politics, precisely because it is also prudence and is dependent on the ethical order, should accept changes only when the superiority of the new form from the point of view of the common good is such that it compensates for that injury which the *change in the laws* inflicts upon the social body, by depriving law of the support of custom.[28] Here is a matter of no little importance. It is less by imposed changes of a mechanical kind than by internal development, and by adaptation to conditions ceaselessly changing, that new things properly come into being in the social order.

The integral realism of Saint Thomas Aquinas, whose motto might well be that of Leo XIII, *vetera novis augere,* is, it is true, very different from Pascal's empirical, pessimistically bitter conservatism. But Pascal's concept of custom, taken over and enlarged in an Aristotelian sense, leads to conclusions which go beyond this conservatism. More profoundly indeed than

[27]*Ibid.,* t. II, n. 320a.
[28]Cf. *Sum. theol.* I–II, 197, 2, C. and ad. I; 97, 3.

custom, although in strict relation to it, the creators in the human being of quasi-natural tendencies far superior to the mechanisms of habit—tendencies truly human and progressive— are those vital improvements in the spiritual powers of the soul called *habitus,* and firm dispositions. And the most important among these are the virtues. The virtues are not customs, even though they are acquired by practice. They are *habitus,* internal qualities perfecting the soul in its possession of itself. And that kind of reason, whose practical insufficiencies, even misdeeds, Pascal quite rightly denounces, is an isolated reason, set up in a sort of inhuman condition of theoretical abstraction regard- ing human matters themselves. According to Saint Thomas, the practical reason is set up in a permanent and general state of good working order only if it is bound in the human soul to its natural and quasi-natural regulators, which are the right tendencies of our essence and the virtues.

By reflecting along these lines on the principles of Pascal, we understand—to come back to the central problem of political philosophy offered by the last two centuries—under what con- crete conditions it is proper to summon all human persons who are members of a state to participate, in differing degrees, in its political life. Not only does an organic democracy presuppose legal institutions which protect liberty and prevent the exercise of suffrage from being distorted, but it also implies, and this above all else, the education of the masses. I do not mean mere instruction which enriches the intellect, I mean ethical educa- tion which develops the virtues and good tendencies, the spon- taneous uprightness of the will, of the instincts, of the feelings, and of the moral reflexes. And indeed such an education is inconceivable without religious life and without the grafting of divine gifts on our souls.

If we have good reason to feel that the struggle waged by our forefathers against political slavery grew out of Christian seeds planted in temporal history (sometimes seeds unfortunately weakened and debased), with still greater reason are we justified in affirming that in fact the authentic ideal thus pursued can be guaranteed only against deadly deviations and against its own self-destruction by effectual Christianity. For the existential realization of its very principle, an organic democracy has need of that relatively high level of general morality, and of that adequate stability (though compatible with the weakness and deficiencies of man), of average upright-ness in the instincts which Christianity alone is able to insure in a manner at once general, durable, and efficacious, by means of the virtues to which it gives life as well as the "fine cus-toms," social habits, and common rules which are linked up with them. Such a democracy will not "tolerate" the Christian religion, it will invoke, substantially postulate, its internal and vital inspiration. On the other hand, such a democracy will pre-suppose a constant watchfulness against pharisaism and the too natural tendency to impose religious domination by external and political means. And it will presuppose the complete elimination from the Christian conscience of that Jansenist leaven, with the exaggerated pessimism it involves, which so well suits the "old man" and which hardens our pagan heart in its terrible and stubborn engrossment in severing social and political life from justice and the gospel.

CHAPTER III

THE METAPHYSICS OF BERGSON

PRELIMINARY OBSERVATIONS

THE VERY title of this chapter raises a question and requires some sort of justification. Bergson was a born metaphysician; how otherwise could he have been a great philosopher and a great renovator of the mind? But would Bergson himself have been willing to say that he undertook a metaphysical life-work or that he propounded a metaphysical system for his contemporaries? I do not think so. In this there is both an indication of Bergson's admirable modesty—not, indeed, unaware of its own quality—and an effect of that unbounded, scrupulous *conscience* and extraordinarily lucid *consciousness* (I use both words—a psychological *consciousness,* awareness, of himself and a meticulous scientific *conscience*) by reason of which he held himself strictly within the results which he believed he was justified in expecting from his method, which is an experiential or *empirical* method, utilizing indeed the most intelligent and the most refined of empiricisms, but still at root empirical.

Here we are at the very outset, before we have even made a real beginning, at the heart of the matter. The whole is in every part, especially for a philosophy of a vital-organic and, as it were, biological variety (this, be it noted in passing, makes Bergson and Aristotle neighbors): we cannot take up one problem without all the others being also present. Let us hope, despite this, that we may develop the present discussion without going into everything at the same time and not without parcelling out our ideas in some suitably ordered sequence.

In the days when I, in company with the little group associated with Charles Péguy and Georges Sorel, enthusiastically followed Bergson's lectures at the Collège de France, what we looked for was the revelation of a new metaphysics, and it was that which the lecturer himself seemed to promise us.

This was not the case, in reality. Bergson did not give us that metaphysics; he never intended to do so. And for many among us that was a very vivid disappointment; it seemed to us that a promise on which we relied had not been kept.

When we look back on all this today, distance casts a new light on things. When Bergson revived the worth and dignity of metaphysics in the minds of his listeners, minds engaged to their sorrow by agnosticism or materialism, when he said, with an unforgettable emphasis, to those minds brought up in the most depressing pseudo-scientific relativism, "it is in the *absolute* that we live and move and have our being,"[1] it was enough that he should thus awaken in them a desire for metaphysics, the metaphysical *eros:* that was accomplishment enough. And nothing is perhaps more moving than that species of detachment with which he freely let that desire, once aroused, travel its own road, in the minds of everyone, and lead some to a metaphysics which was not his metaphysics, which was even directly opposed to his metaphysics, until there should be, on deeper terms, relating not so much to philosophic conceptualization as to the spiritual directives of philosophy, new meetings of the mind.

If Bergsonian philosophy never completely avowed the metaphysics it involved, and which it could have brought forth into the light of day, if it remained much more rigidly linked to the

[1]These words were pronounced by Bergson in his lectures at the Collège de France.

science of phenomena, and more dependent on the latter than its lively reaction against the pseudo-metaphysics of scientism would have led one to suppose, it was because that very reaction had been managed from its outset by a radical empiricism. It is with the very weapons of anti-metaphysical science—with experience, but an *experience* incomparably more true and more searching—that Bergson sought to overcome the false cult of scientific experience, the mechanistic and determinist experimentalism which a philosophy of vulgar simplification claimed to be necessary for modern science. In this way he hoped for the possibility of a philosophic method (to use his own words) "rigorously drawn from experience (internal and external)," and which "does not allow the assertion of a conclusion that in any way whatever goes beyond the empirical considerations on which it is based."[2] Here is a singularly bold declaration of integral empiricism.

Determined to remain rigidly faithful to the method thus defined, it would seem that Bergson was progressively drawn to forswear the metaphysical in order more and more to fall back on the experimental. For one thing, what he expected from his philosophy was not the elaboration of a metaphysics which would be placed on a level in the scale of knowledge higher than experimental knowledge (thus, indeed, he objected when his philosophy was compared with metaphysical doctrines so elaborated and so *placed*); what he expected from his philosophy was that it make fertile the experimental sciences and that it even arouse the latter (especially the biological sciences) to certain new directions. For another thing (but I postpone discussion of this to my next chapter) he was to move not so much in the direction of a metaphysics as in the direction of a philosophy of morals and religion, precisely because there only could he find the experiential knowledge which he needed to

[2]Letter to the Reverend Father de Tonquédec (June 12, 1911), *Études,* 20 février 1912, p. 515.

follow, in accordance with the method he had once and for all adopted, the upward movement of his enquiries.

Yet it is clear that there is a metaphysics implied in Bergson-ism. And even if it were only in the nature of *excursuses,* of what one might call marginal trials, Bergson could not but from time to time give his explicit attention to the principles of that metaphysics. It is with that metaphysics, in an attempt to extricate it as a whole and examine its value, that we shall here be concerned.

THE INTUITION OF DURATION

IT IS WELL to indicate first certain elements relating to the gene-sis of the Bergsonian metaphysics. What is truly central and primary in that genesis is the deepening of the sense of *duration.*

Let us recall the passage where Bergson himself supplies us with important and precise indications of the history of his thought. "In my opinion," he wrote to Harald Höffding, "any summary of my views will deform them as a whole and will, by that very fact, expose them to a host of objections, if it does not take as its starting point, and if it does not continually revert to, what I consider the very centre of the doctrine: the intuition of duration. The representation of a multiplicity of 'reciprocal penetration,' altogether different from numerical multiplicity—the representation of a heterogeneous, qualitative, creative duration—was my point of departure, and the point to which I have constantly returned. It requires of the mind a very great effort, the breaking of many frames of reference, something like a new way of thinking (for that which is imme-diate is far from being that which is the easiest to perceive); but once you have attained that representation and possessed it in its *simple* form (which must not be confused with a reconstruc-tion by concepts), you feel obliged to shift your point of view on reality; you see that the greatest difficulties have arisen from the fact that philosophers have always put time and space on the same line: you see that the greater number of those difficulties are eased or dispelled."[3]

Arising above all from a close study of modern science and modern physics, and perhaps brought about—if we are prone to believe certain evidences thereof—by the examination of the arguments of the Eleatics against movement, what, in this, has been the central discovery of Bergson? I am not thinking at the moment of the Bergsonian *theory* of duration, nor of the Bergsonian *theory* of the intuition of duration. I am thinking of that kernel of *genuine intellectual intuition* which was for Bergson a discovery of duration.

In discussing the central intuition from whence proceed the great philosophical doctrines and the intermediary "image" between the absolute simplicity of that intuition and the complexity of its conceptual interpretations, Bergson writes: "What first of all characterizes that image is the power of *negation* it carries in it. Confronted with currently accepted ideas, with theses which seemed self-evident, with assertions which had until then passed muster as scientific, it whispers in the philosopher's ear, *impossible!* Impossible even though data and reasoning would appear to urge you to believe that it is possible and real and sure. Impossible because a certain experience, confused perhaps but decisive, speaks to you by my voice; impossible because it is incompatible with the data that are alleged and the reasons given, and because therefore these data are wrongly observed, those reasonings false. . . . Later on [the philosopher] will be able to vary in what he affirms; he will not vary in what he denies. And if he varies in what he affirms, it will again be by virtue of the power of negation immanent in the intuition or in its image."[4]

---

[3]Letter to Harald Höffding (in Höffding, *La Philosophie de Bergson*, Paris, Alcan, 1916, pp. 160–61).

[4]"L'Intuition Philosophique," *Revue de Métaphysique et de Morale*, 1911, pp. 810–11. (*La Pensée et le Mouvant*, Paris, 1934, pp. 138–39.)

Thus, according to Bergson himself, his basal intuition of duration above all carried with it a negation. And of what sort was that negation—so powerful and invincible? Real time *is not* the spatialized time of our physics; and this is true indeed, for the various times of the physicist are mathematical entities which are built up on complex patterns of spatio-temporal measurements, and which are doubtless based on real time, but are not that time. The latter is in the ontological, not the mathematical, order. And the negation in question goes much further. Not only is real time *not* the spatialized time of physico-mathematics; motion is *not* a scattering of positions succeeding and replacing each other; reality is *not* reducible to reconstruction worked out after the event, reality is *not* a reiteration of identical happenings, reality is *not* that concatenation of immobilities and of ready-made elements, without internal ontological substance or propensity or internal power of expansion, conceived by the mechanist.

Still there is not merely a negation, however strong, however important, however fruitful, in the intuition Bergson has had of duration. There is also a positive content in that intuition. (Herein I still do not accept that intuition in the conceptual form in which Bergson has thought it; but, by an abstractional procedure which I am well aware is not devoid of a certain presumption, I try to rediscover this intuition in so far as it has been an authentic intellectual intuition—in other words, within the very peripheries where, I believe, it evinces truth.) The positive content, then, of the experience under discussion seems to me to relate to the internal progress of the life of the psyche, or the lived movement, wherein, on a level deeper than that of consciousness our psychic states are fused in a potential multiplicity which is one nevertheless, and by which we feel that we are moving forward through time—that we endure while we change in a way which is really unfragmented, and yet which enriches us qualitatively and triumphs over the inertia of matter.

Here indeed is an experience of the concrete reality of *duration,* of *existence continuing itself,* of our deep *psychic life,* in which is enfolded, implicitly present, the irreducible metaphysical value of the act of being. Let us have confidence in the light of metaphysical abstraction, let us not fear the extreme purification which abstractive or eidetic intuition involves, and which does not attenuate but rather concentrates into an absolutely crucial simplicity that which is most important in the real and that which before everything makes the real manifest. This experience of the lived duration of the soul will transfigure itself, will open out directly not only on duration, but on *existence,* or rather upon the actual *esse* in its pure consistence and its intelligible amplitude, will become the metaphysical intuition of this act: *to be.* This further step Bergson did not take. With all this intuition of psychic duration, faultless to the extent that it involved an authentic intellectual intuition, he did not himself grasp all the ontological content with which it was, and despite all would continue to be, pregnant; he did not express to himself that actuality and that generosity of being, and that creative abundance which permeates action and movement (and which indeed derives from the cause of being)—in short, everything ontological which his intuition in fact attained in the experience of psychic duration. On the contrary, he at once conceptualized his intuition in the *notion,* in the idea (to my mind equivocal and misleading) of that which it is proper to call, in an historical and systematic sense, *Bergsonian duration.*

INTUITION AND CONCEPTUALIZATION

HERE WE ARE face to face with a great—and a forbidding—mystery of intellectual life. There is no intuition *per modum cognitionis,* there is no intellectual intuition without concepts and conceptualization. And yet the intuition can be true and fruitful (indeed it is, to the extent that it is truly intuition, infallibly true and fruitful) and the conceptualization in which it finds expression and in which it takes place can be mistaken and illusory.

How can this be? Let us first of all remember that the intelligence sees by and in the concepts which it, in a living way, produces from its own depths. Everything in the way of concepts and ideal constructions that the intelligence—ceaselessly leading its insatiable hunger for reality over the whole extent of exterior and interior experience, the whole extent of truths already acquired, perpetually on the *hunt for essences,* as Aristotle put it—causes to surge up in itself is only to serve that *sense of being* which is indeed the deepest thing in the intelligence, and to achieve an intuitive discernment which is the act itself of the intelligence. In those matchless moments of *intellectual discovery,* wherein we seize for the first time upon a pulsing, intelligible reality in the seemingly infinite abundance of its possibilities for expansion, and wherein we feel rising and confirming itself in our deepest beings that intellectual word which makes such reality manifest, we then know well what the intuitive power of the intelligence is, and that it is exerted by means of concepts.

True enough, but then we shape that intellectual word as the ultimate term of all the immense equipment of conceptual tools, of the universe of ideas and images already dwelling within us, which results from the years and years of the workings of knowledge to which we have yielded ourselves from the first wakening of reflection in our mind. If there is some serious lack, or if there are warpings and distortions in that universe; in other words, if the doctrinal equipment with which we are already supplied admits of errors and deficiencies, the effort of the mind through which the intelligence—by virtue of the active light which is within it—suddenly extricates from experience and from the accumulation of data and from all sensory contacts the freshness, murmuring with life, of some new countenance of the real . . . it touches that countenance, grasps it, looks upon it; the intelligence has brought it forth out of things; with it the intelligence ends its act of intellection, for it is things that that act seeks out; it does not stop at signs or statements . . . well then, the effort of the mind which achieves an authentic (and to that extent infallible) intuition will thus only reach reality by and in signs which, being produced and patterned under the ægis of a preexisting equipment encumbered with errors and deficiencies, will ill express that intuition and will express it in statements more or less erroneous—sometimes seriously, irremediably erroneous. This will be the case as long, at least, as our general scheme of concepts has not been recast, perhaps by virtue of that very intuition and the ruptures it produces.

At the heart of every great philosophic system there is thus a very simple and yet inexhaustible insight—Bergson has singled it out in a celebrated passage—which on some occasion has overwhelmed the mind with its certitude. With every great philosopher and every great thinker there is a central intuition which in itself does not mislead. But that intuition can be conceptualized, and in fact in a great number of cases is conceptualized, in a mistaken, perhaps even pernicious, doctrine. So long as he remains bound to his own ideas, the philosopher himself cannot effectuate discernment in this matter; yet some day a proper discernment must be effectuated. How grand a dramatic spectacle is this! Here we have an intuitive certitude through which the real suddenly yields itself to the mind, through which the real and the mind suddenly enjoy a mutual ecstasy; and here is at the same time and in the same event, since all this cannot take place without a conceptualization drawn from our invested capital, the risk of deceiving oneself more or less seriously and of jeopardizing an entire, well-tested system of statements held as true by the sages. To avoid this risk, will the mind turn away from the real which offers itself, away from being for an instant overtaken by an aspect which had never before been manifest to the mind? That is impossible. The mind knows that its first duty is not to sin against the light. It must subject to the most careful verification its conceptual equipment, but it cannot prevent itself from rushing toward being. No matter what the price. It is required of the mind not to fall into error, but first of all, it is required of the mind that it *see*.

THE BERGSONIAN CONCEPTUALIZATION OF DURATION

BUT LET US cease from this digression and return to the idea, the notion of Bergsonian duration. I have said that in my judgment it is an illusory notion.

Why and how? We were considering, a while back, the primarily *negative* signification of intuition. Well, the Bergsonian notion denies *more* than does intuition; it stretches that negation beyond the proper content of intuition. The Bergsonian notion of duration does not merely say that real time is not the spatialized time of our physics, that change is not a scattering of positions succeeding each other, that movement is *non-divided, undivided,* that is to say *one* in act and of such nature that if it be divided, its own proper quality together with its unity is thereby suppressed (in this sense Aristotle went so far as to say that *6* is different from *3 plus 3*). Even more—and this is what is false—the Bergsonian idea would have movement be *non-divisible, indivisible,* and such that no parts in it can be distinguished from each other, even were they potential as in all *continua*. And it would have time not be *something* of change or of movement, *distinct* from change itself and *distinct* from the subject of change—indeed, the uninterrupted flux of the impermanence of change. Real time is that, it is this flux of impermanence, which is to say that it is that which is the least substantial in the world. And yet the Bergsonian notion of duration would not have it be that.

And what does this notion do in its *positive* aspect? It makes of time something substantial; it seems indissolubly to lump together in one same idea-image the idea of substance and the idea of time and the idea of psychic flow and multiplicity, all this making that "snowball which gets bigger as it moves forward" of which Bergson has so often spoken.

Instead of directing itself toward being and instead of opening out into the metaphysical intuition of being, as the nature of things requires, the Bergsonian experience of duration, in brief, took a wrong direction to conceptualize itself—while at the same time, in so far as it is experience, it continued, without saying so, to pulse with all the ontological content discussed above. Bergsonian experience of duration, then, has conceptually opened out into an unstable and fleeting notion of *time* as *substitute for being,* of *time* as primary stuff of the real and specificating object of metaphysics, of *time* as first object not, of course, of the intelligence, in the sense in which Aristotle said that being is the first object of the intelligence, but of that twisting of the intelligence back onto itself which would have it recover the virtualities of instinct and which is called Bergsonian intuition and which for Bergson replaces the intelligence as a power vitally apprehending the real, despite the fact that he himself momentarily considered calling it itself "intelligence."

A METAPHYSICS OF MODERN PHYSICS

To PRESS the discussion further, we can note that metaphysics—the science which is wisdom, the highest sort of knowledge which human thought can attain—from its beginning constituted itself as transcending time. It was born when the intelligence of the philosophers lifted its head above the flood of succession. But from the very moment when the physico-mathematical method permitted the setting up of a science of phenomena *as such,* with the condition that concepts shall be resolved only within the *measurable* and *sensible* and the rôle of the ontological be reduced to the construction of "explanatory" ideal entities (*entia rationis*), intended to sustain a tissue of mathematical law-structures unifying phenomena, from that moment one can say that thought, coming back to the world of the senses, took up its abode in time. It required three centuries and the Kantian revolution to make men see what had happened.

What then is to become of metaphysics? If it is faithful to itself and to what is, metaphysics will transcend the science of phenomena as it transcends time, and it will at the same time recognize that that science, from the very fact that it consists in an *empiriological* or *empiriomathematical* analysis of the real, is autonomous with regard to the analyses of an ontological order to which philosophy proceeds—precisely because science does not itself contain, hidden away in it, a philosophy.

But if one denies to metaphysics that transcendence and that autonomy with regard to science and yet would wish to set up a metaphysics, one's only recourse is to seek out that metaphysics not at a level above that of the world appropriate to the mathematization of the sensible, but in its own depths. It will be necessary to seek within the physico-mathematical tissue a metaphysical substance, a stuff with which the physico-mathematical cognition of nature is unconsciously pregnant.

But where dwells this physico-mathematical cognition if not in the flux itself? What does it strive to organize through its formulas if not the relational stabilities which it isolates in the very flow of sensible becoming? Bergson's stroke of genius has been to see that if phenomenal science itself enfolds and hides, on its own level and in its formal object, a metaphysical stuff, that stuff can only be time. It is in time that we must immerse ourselves in order to find a knowledge which shall no longer have for its direct goal the necessary and the universal, but the flux itself of the singular and the contingent, pure movement considered as the very substance of things. All this presupposes, as Bergson perfectly well saw, the absolute superseding of the concept and a total inversion of the natural movement of the intelligence. In this same *time,* in which physics dwells without wishing to ponder its reality (for physics is indeed well satisfied with its mathematical substitute) and which physics translates into spatial symbols and the reality of which mechanicism suppresses, in this *time* metaphysics will fasten upon the absolute itself, which is invention and creation.

Much more basically dependent on modern physics than the immanent Cause of Spinoza, which substantialized the mechanistic explications of a still youthful phenomenal science, Bergsonian duration achieves in metaphysics the very soul of pure empiricism or of pure experimentalism, of which modern physics has become aware as it progressed and with which it approaches reality in order to explain it. The last pages of *Creative Evolution* are supremely significant in this connection. "It seems then," writes Bergson, "that parallel to this physics [modern], a second type of knowledge should have set itself up. . . . It is to the inwardness of becoming that it would have transported us by an effort of sympathy. . . . If [this knowledge] were to succeed, it is reality itself which it would clasp in a final embrace."[5] And again, "An experience of this type is not a non-temporal experience. It merely seeks, beyond spatialized time wherein we believe we see continual rearrangements of parts, the concrete duration wherein ceaselessly operates a radical recasting of the whole."[6] And again, "The more one reflects upon it, the more one will find that this conception of metaphysics is that which modern science suggests."[7] "Thus understood," he finally says, "philosophy is not only the return

[5]*L'Évolution Créatrice,* Paris, Alcan, 1909, pp. 370–71; (*Creative Evolution,* New York, Holt, 1911, pp. 342–43).

[6]*Ibid.,* Paris Ed., p. 392; New York Ed., p. 363.

[7]*Ibid.,* Paris Ed., p. 371; New York Ed., p. 343.

of the mind to itself, the coincidence of the human consciousness with the living principle from whence it emanates, an establishment of contact with the creative effort. Philosophy is the deepening of becoming in general, the true evolutionism, and hence the true continuation of science."[8] In short, and properly speaking, metaphysics consists in "seeing in time a progressive growth of the absolute";[9] it is summed up in the affirmation that *time is creator*.

Such, it seems to me, considering what is most basic about it, has been the genesis of the Bergsonian metaphysics, and at the same time these considerations have already indicated a few of its essential characteristics.

BERGSONIAN IRRATIONALISM

IT IS from *this,* from this fundamental discovery (and, in truth, as we have seen, ambivalent discovery) which Bergson thought he had made concerning duration that issues as a secondary (if inevitable) characteristic the *irrationalism* of the Bergsonian philosophy. This irrationalism is secondary, not primary. It is as though involuntary; I should even say that it goes against his grain. And that creates a fundamental difference between Bergson's thought and a thought by first and deliberate intention inimical to the intelligence, like the thinking of Klages.[10] Still the Bergsonian philosophy is an irrationalist philosophy: Irra-

---

[8]*Ibid.,* Paris Ed., p. 399; New York Ed., pp. 369–70.

[9]*Ibid.,* Paris Ed., p. 372; New York Ed., p. 344.

[10]"You are perfectly right," Bergson wrote to Jacques Chevalier, "in saying that all the philosophy I have expounded since my first *Essay* affirms, against Kant, the possibility of a supra-sensible intuition. Taking the word 'intelligence' in the very broad meaning given it by Kant, I could call 'intellectual' the intuition I speak of. But I should prefer to designate it as 'supra-intellectual,' because I believed I must restrict the sense of the word 'intelligence,' and because I reserve this name for the set of discursive faculties of the mind, originally destined to think of matter. *Intuition bears toward spirit."* (April 28, 1920. Letter published in the book *Bergson,* by Jacques Chevalier.)

tionalism is the ransom set by the errors we discussed a few pages back in the conceptualization of the fruitful realities toward which moved, in so far as it was a genuine intellectual intuition, Bergson's original intuition.

For one thing no labour of metaphysical reflection, properly so called, had preceded this intuition and prepared the conceptual equipment which it was to use. There was no metaphysics of being nor of the intelligence, and no previously worked out critique of knowledge (the first chapter of *Matière et Mémoire* clearly shows that at that time Bergson believed he could still do without a choice between the idealist conception and the realist conception of knowledge; later on he was freely to assert that if he must choose between two *isms,* as he put it, it is realism he would choose, and with no hesitation.) From the great metaphysical tradition of humanity, it is only through Plotinus that Bergson received the λόγος σπερμάτικος—a *logos* singularly precious, indeed, and which perhaps was to go further than philosophy. Bergson's original training was entirely scientific, or rather scientistic; it was from Spencer that he emanated. And that very fact renders more moving for us, and even more deserving of gratitude the work he has done for the rediscovery of the spirit. But this also explains certain deficiencies in that work.

Then again (and this is only another aspect of the same consideration, this also was a legacy of the modern philosophic tradition, unrectified by a sane metaphysics of knowledge) the one and only sure recourse to which thought might have access was in Bergson's eyes, and was exclusively to remain, *experience.* Faced with the contradictions and the fluctuations of abstract knowledge, experience alone (as though it itself were not inevitably indicated in abstract knowledge)—experience alone in his eyes had any philosophic value. Hence if experience—an experience more profound than the experience of the laboratory sciences—seems to admit me to the presence of a *creative time*

and a *change which is substance* and a duration which is a kind
of *pure act in becoming,* well then, let logic and the principle
of identity and all the rational requirements of the intelligence
perish as they must. All that is secondary from the point of view
of the truth which I hold. This kind of desperate energy whereby the intelligence tears itself to pieces and prefers to deny
its most vital law and its very existence rather than loosen its
grip, rather than let go the truth which a deficient conceptualization causes the intelligence to hold badly, but to hold onto
for dear life—we find this desperate energy in several of those
philosophers who today call themselves existentialists, in
Heidegger, for example, and in Berdyaev. It was for this that
William James expressed his gratitude to Bergson with charm-
ing frankness, when he thanked Bergson for having helped
him to liberate himself once and for all from logic. Such deliv-
erances are scarcely more profitable than an immersion in the
river of Heraclitus, in which one does not bathe twice, for one
drowns the first times one tries it. For Bergsonism, the con-
tinuous duration of life escapes all logic, and cannot accommo-
date itself to the principle of non-contradiction; from this it
follows, as has been said, that "the method made necessary by
that density proper to the things of the soul can only be entirely
irrational." [11]

That assertion is taken from one of the best statements yet
made of Bergsonism from the point of view of Bergson, and it
has the merit of leaving no doubt in the reader's mind on this
point of capital importance.

One of the results of this actual irrationalism, and one of its
expressions, indeed its specific and systematic expression, is the
Bergsonian theory of the *intelligence,* essentially incapable of

[11]Vladimir Jankélévitch, "Prolégomènes au Bergsonisme," *Revue de
Métaphysique et de Morale,* Oct.-Dec., 1928, p. 42 (later published as
a book).

understanding life, capable only of knowing matter and making geometry, and the Bergsonian theory of *intuition*. Here we have that which in Bergsonism plays the rôle of a metaphysics of knowledge. These are well-known portions of the teaching of Bergson on which it does not seem to me that there is any need to elaborate here.

On the subject of the theory of intuition, a theory which, as Bergson wrote Höffding, occurred to him later than the theory of duration, I shall point out only one thing.[12] An intuition which requires a kind of violent recovery, through an effort contrary to our nature, of the instinctive virtualities spaced out along the course of zoological evolution; an intuition "which prolongs, develops, and carries over into thought whatever remains of instinct in man,"[13] which buries us in concrete perception in order to deepen and broaden it, which is, thanks to the instrumentality of the will, an expansion of the perception of the senses and the consciousness,[14] a painful effort wherein "the faculty of *seeing*, bending and twisting back on itself" should no longer be "but one with the act of *willing*"[15]—such an intuition it seems very difficult effectively to consider as a *supra-intellectual* intuition. I am nevertheless convinced that if the Bergsonian conceptualization here requires criticism, it still expresses in a deficient way views which are profoundly true on the supremely vital act of the intellect, on that which in the intellect is the most genuinely intellectual and is more valid

[12]Cf. *Introduction à la Métaphysique* (*The Introduction to a New Philosophy*, translated by Sidney Littman; John W. Luce & Co., Boston, 1912) later reprinted in *La Pensée et le Mouvant* (Chapter VI); *L'Évolution Créatrice*, notably p. 192 (New York Ed., pp. 176–77) and p. 290 (New York Ed., p. 268); "L'Intuition Philosophique," (*Revue de Métaphysique et de Morale*, Novembre, 1911, notably pp. 89 and 827), later reprinted in *La Pensée et le Mouvant*, Chapter IV.

[13]Letter to Harald Höffding (see p. 56), p. 163.

[14]"La Perception du changement," p. 8 (*La Pensée et le Mouvant*, Chapter V, p. 169).

[15]*L'Évolution Créatrice*, p. 258 (New York Ed., p. 237).

than the reason. However questionable may be the Bergsonian intuition, as Bergson describes it, true intellection, that is to say intellectual intuition, often slips into it on the sly. It is the intelligence which gives value to all this, even though Bergson objects to the intelligence. (And I fully realize that he uses the word intelligence in a sense other than that commonly given it. Yet it is precisely the intelligence in its common meaning that he thus seeks to make suspect.)

THE BERGSONIAN CRITIQUE OF THE IDEA OF NOTHINGNESS

THREE THEORIES, it seems to me, supply us with the metaphysical backgrounds of or the metaphysical keys to Bergsonism. These are the Bergsonian critique of the idea of nothingness, the Bergsonian theory of change, the Bergsonian critique of the possible.

If what I said at the outset concerning Bergson's position with respect to metaphysics is just, it will be understood that these three theories appear in his work as tentatives for projects, or as sketches (as though seen through a window open for a moment and then quickly closed) for what could be the bases of a Bergsonian metaphysic, rather than as essays intended to supply the foundations of a doctrine properly so called. Yet I am convinced that Bergson has set down in these three theories ideas to which he attached the greatest importance and which he has worked out very thoroughly and very carefully. The critique of the idea of nothingness may be found in *Creative Evolution*. The theory of change appears in two lectures given at Oxford in 1911 on the *Perception of Change*. The critique of the possible was made at an Oxford philosophical conference in 1920, and was developed in an article published in a Swedish review, *Nordisk Tidskrift,* in 1930. This article and the 1911 lectures were gathered together in 1934 in Bergson's most recently published volume, *La Pensée et le Mouvant.*

First of all a few words concerning the critique of the idea of nothingness.[16] Bergson therein upholds the thesis that the idea of absolute nothingness, the idea of the nothingness of the whole being, is a *pseudo-idea,* which we never really *think.* Since the understanding as such is able to perceive or record only *presences,* not *absences,* to think the nothingness of a thing is to posit the reality of another thing, of a thing which drives the first from existence, and which replaces it. "The unreality of a thing consists in its being driven out by other things." If negation appears in our formulas, it is only through extra-intellectual motives, affective or social, by reason of which—for example, to anticipate someone else's possible mistake—we fix our attention on the reality replaced or driven out, of which we then say that it *is not,* while leaving indeterminate the reality that replaces or drives out, of which we are effectively thinking but thinking without concern. The fact is that we think only the *plenum,* and that to picture to oneself the nothingness of a thing is in truth to depict another thing which drives the first away and takes its place. It follows that to think absolute nothingness implies a contradiction.

This singular thesis is justified only by an original misunderstanding: it is obvious that one will strive in vain to picture nothingness to oneself; one will not succeed. But the idea of nothingness is not a representation of nothingness, it is a *negative idea:* its content is not a "nothingness" which one would picture as something (on that score indeed one can picture the nothingness of a thing only as its expulsion by another). The content of the idea of nothingness is *being* affected by the sign of the negative; it is *non-being.* The proper activity of the intelligence suffices for the shaping of this idea. And as it is only the idea of being, but of being indicated as denied, the idea of the nothingness of a thing in no way consists in the replacement of that thing by another which would drive it out. From this it follows that the idea of absolute nothingness, which

[16]*Ibid.,* Paris Ed., pp. 298–323; New York Ed., pp. 275–299.

means purely and simply the expulsion of all things—but not by other things which would replace those expelled—in no way implies a contradiction, in no sense is a pseudo-idea.

But *why* did Bergson set up this critique, in our opinion fallacious, of the idea of nothingness?

In his thinking it was a question of struggling against the temptation of Spinozism, a temptation natural to each philosopher. "Scarcely had he begun to philosophize" when the philosopher asks, *"Why is there such as thing as being?"* And this question implies, says Bergson, the supposition that nothingness is before being, that being is "spread over nothingness as on a carpet." If we admit that question, we can answer it only by granting, with Spinoza, a being as cause of itself which is alone capable of "conquering non-existence" and which "plants itself in eternity even as logic plants itself"[17] and which will cause to perish all effective causality, all contingency and all freedom in things, these being but the endless unrolling of this hypostasized logic. But this question is only a pseudo-problem (we have just see how Bergson believes that he has demonstrated this); the problem should not be posed at all, and the Spinozist reply is as illusory as that which provoked it.

Yet Bergson, in his desire to strike at Spinozism, hits a blow at all metaphysics. If his critique is justified, the idea of a Being existing through itself, of the *Ipsum esse subsistens,* the idea of the divine aseity is a mere pseudo-idea and a *hypostasierung* of logic, as is Spinoza's idea of substance, *causa sui.* For it is the idea of the contingency of things, the idea that they could not-be, in other words the idea of the possibility of the nothingness of things, which compels the mind to conceive that Being and its necessity. And even that idea of the possibility of nothingness would be a pseudo-idea.

We have seen that it is nothing of the sort. And the idea of the Being-by-itself is in no sense the substantiation of logic and

[17]*Ibid.*

of logical necessity. It relates rather to a pre-eminently real necessity, to the infinite necessity by virtue of which there exists a Being so rich and superabundant and independent that its very essence is its act of existing, of knowing, and of loving.

But for Bergson the question *Why do things exist?* constitutes a pseudo-problem and rests on a pseudo-idea. As a result the classic distinction between the necessary and the contingent is definitively a pseudo-distinction, and that *which is not necessary* posits itself through itself. Thus we perceive in a rapid flash of enlightenment why a Bergsonian theodicy, a rational demonstration of the existence of God in the Bergsonian system, is not possible. It is by another road that, for Bergson, this existence will be attained. Bergsonian metaphysics, following its own line of approach, arrives at the admission that God, prime source of the creative spurting forth, probably exists as a supremely concentrated duration and life; it cannot demonstrate that such exists. And it cannot determine whether this God, who exists *in fact,* is or is not necessary in Himself, and infinitely necessary *by right.*

THE BERGSONIAN DOCTRINE OF CHANGE

DID NOT the critique of the idea of nothingness have somewhat the character of an argument *ad hominem?* In any case was it not above all intended to sweep the premises clear—following a method dear to Bergson—of one of those pseudo-problems by means of which, a little too easily perhaps, he frees philosophy of many an embarrassment? Let us now consider the Bergsonian doctrine of change. It has a much stronger positive value and makes us enter far more deeply into the intimacies of Bergsonian metaphysics. But it shows us also what sort of positive virtualities were contained in the critique of the idea of nothingness.

Let us look carefully at a few specially significant passages in the "Perception of Change." *"There are changes, but there*

*are not, under change, things which change: change has no
need of any support. There are movements, but there is no inert,
invariable object which moves:*[18] *movement does not imply
something mobile."*

Doubless the utilitarian preoccupations of the sense of sight
have accustomed us to chop movement up into successive positions, so that "movement would seem added onto the mobile
as an accident." "But we shall have less difficulty in perceiving
movement and change as independent realities if we turn to
the sense of hearing. Listen to a melody, permit yourself to be
cradled in its embrace: do you not have a sharp perception of
a movement which is not attached to anything mobile, of
*change without anything that changes? That change is enough;
it is the thing itself."* [Italics mine, here and in the following
quotation.] "Once we have abstracted these spatial images,
there remains *change—pure, self-sufficient, and in no way
divided, in no way attached to a 'thing' which changes."*

"Let us, then, revert to the sense of sight. Meditating upon it
more closely, we perceive that even here movement requires no
vehicle, nor change a substance . . ." "But in no way is the
substantiality of change as visible, as touchable, as in the realm
of the inner life . . ." "Thus whether it is a question of the
inner or the outer, of us or of things, reality is mobility itself.
That is what I meant when I said that there is change, but that
there are no things which change."

"Confronted with the spectacle of this universal mobility,
some of us will be seized with dizziness. Such minds are accustomed to *terra firma* . . . They think that if everything is
in passage, nothing exists, and that if reality is mobility, it no
longer exists at the moment when one thinks it—it escapes the
mind. The material world, they say, is going to dissolve, and
the mind is going to drown in the torrential flux of things. Let

---

[18]The words "inert, invariable" were added by Bergson in the second
edition of his lecture. See in this connection Footnote 19.

them be at rest! Change, if only they will look it in the face, without any interposed veil, will soon seem to them as that which in all the world is most substantial and most enduring."[19]

Otherwise stated, and to turn again and ever to Bergson's own words, *if change is not everything, it is nothing;*[20] it is not only *real,* but *constitutive of the reality,*[21] it is the *very substance of things.*[22]

The Bergsonian metaphysics is then indeed the metaphysics of pure change. In my opinion there has not been enough emphasis placed on the central importance for the whole Bergsonian philosophy of the metaphysical doctrine which I have just summarized. That doctrine supplies us with a key to Bergsonian philosophy. We are here confronted with one of the most determined and one of the boldest attempts ever made to drive out being and replace it with becoming—not indeed after the fashion of Hegel's panlogism; on the contrary, after the fashion of an integral empiricism. Yet two things are clear: in the first place, if it is true that being is the connatural object of the intelligence and that it constitutes, if I may put it so, the climate in which the intelligence thinks what it thinks, this metaphysics of pure change must be considered as not thinkable. For to say that change is the very substance of things is to say that things change inasmuch as they are and in so far as they are. And therefore inasmuch as they are and in so far as they are, they cease to be what they are, they leave their being, they no longer are what they are but are something else. Secondly, in order to try to think this, it is necessary to find some-

---

[19]*La Pensée et le Mouvant,* pp. 185–189. It is to be noted that, according to the views of Thomas Aquinas, substance is not an "inert" object; on the contrary it is the very root of action. Substance is *"invariable" in itself,* that is to say in so far as it is the primal being of a thing. But substance varies, substance moves—through accidents, which are *its* secondary being, and are not at all things superimposed upon another thing.

[20]*Ibid.,* p. 183.   [21]*Ibid.,* p. 190.   [22]*Ibid.,* p. 197.

thing better than the intelligence, or to turn the intelligence against itself, and in any case to deny, as did Heraclitus of old, the principle of non-contradiction.

This doctrine of pure change at the same time affords us useful insight into certain implications of Bergsonian intuition, which here is seen to be clearly "anti-intellectualist," as it does likewise into certain implications of Bergsonian duration. Bergsonian duration is nothing else but time. "Real duration," Bergson writes, "is that which has always been called *time,* but time perceived as indivisible";[23] it is an *indivisible* time and one in which *the past endures.* "The conservation of the past in the present is nothing more than the indivisibility of change."[24] "It suffices that we convince ourselves once for all," we read once more, "that reality is change, that change is indivisible, and that in an indivisible change, the past is one with the present."[25] In short, "it is a question of a present which endures."[26] Those few phrases show us the altogether characteristic meta--physical content of Bergsonian duration.

Furthermore Bergson explains to us that all the difficulties raised by philosophers over the problem of substance and the problem of movement "sprang from our closing our eyes to the indivisibility of change." And he adds, "If change, which is evidently constitutive of all our experience, is the fleeting and elusive thing about which the majority of philosophers have spoken, if one sees in it only a scattering of positions which replace other positions, we are forced into re-establishing continuity between these positions by means of an artificial bond. . . ." It is thus, he thinks, that the figment of a substance distinct from change was born. "Let us try on the contrary," he continues, "to perceive change as it is, in its natural indivisibility. We see that it is the *substance itself of things.*"[27]

---

[23]*Ibid.,* p. 188.
[24]*Ibid.,* p. 196.
[25]*Ibid.,* p. 196.

[26]*Ibid.,* p. 192.
[27]*Ibid.,* pp. 196–197.

These statements seem to me highly significant. I point out parenthetically that here we pass over from the true assertion that change and movement are *undivided* into the erroneous assertion that they are *indivisible,* and that Bergson attacks with equal vigour two altogether different conceptions: the conception of motion as a *scattering of positions which replace positions,* which is a very false concept against which Aristotle and the best philosophers have not failed to make objection, and the conception of motion as that *"fleeting and elusive thing about which the majority of philosophers have spoken."*[28] And they did well so to speak, for that is exactly what motion is. Since, moreover, motion is that, it follows that the being to which our intellect at once tends when it thinks things, the being which by itself exercises existence, and the notion of which, far from being the notion of a bond between positions of change, is *anterior* to the notion of change—it surely follows that *substance* must be really distinct from movement and from change: it is *substance* which changes; change is not *substance.*

But that which I should like above all to emphasize is the bond which unites the thesis of the substantiality of change to that of creative time. We must understand this last expression as being rigorously meant. We are dealing with a time that is properly creative; motion is the absolute, and that absolute grows of itself, it creates and creates itself as it unfolds; "following the new conception through to the end" we come, says Bergson in *Creative Evolution,* "to see *in time a progressive growth of the absolute."*[29]

And finally why should this be stated if it is not that Bergson expressed and conceptualized in the notion of time, not in that of being, an intuition which, aiming at the concrete duration of the psychic life, attained—through that duration and in it—that deeper reality which is *being itself* and substantial *existence* and the very *activity* thanks to which, through

[28]*Ibid.,* p. 196.   [29]*See* note 9, this chapter.

the motion of the first cause, being still superabounds. To tell us what he saw, Bergson should have said *being;* he said *time.*

The result is that we are to "see in time a progressive growth of the absolute."[30] This amounts to saying that change precedes being and that becoming exists by itself, enjoys *aseity* as well as creative power. Contingency and becoming, change and diversity posit themselves. Posit time, and things make themselves. Or rather they make themselves through an expansion of the creative being, that is to say of the pure creative act, which we have lumped together with things, with their being and with their changing, in the same ambiguous notion, which improperly transcribes a true intuition by causing it to speak falsely. The *intentions* of Bergsonism are fundamentally opposed to every form whatever of pantheism; yet one cannot see how a certain pantheism is not in line with the internal logic of those concepts through which in fact the Bergsonian system finds expression.

Yet on the other hand, if change is *indivisible,* and if consequently one cannot distinguish in it parts which succeed one another—of which one has disappeared when another begins to exist—if the past, the past as such, continues to exist and "preserves itself of itself, automatically,"[31] we must say, inasmuch as we also say that the past passes, we must say that *that which no longer is, still is.* In a memory that is true indeed. For the memory preserves in the intentional being of its images that which no longer is. But in things? Again as always we come up against the principle of non-contradiction, and we have to undertake to break through it in order not to be ourselves broken by it.

THE BERGSONIAN CRITIQUE OF THE POSSIBLE

IT IS POSSIBLE to go even more deeply into the metaphysical roots of Bergsonism. One then comes to the denial of the *pos-*

[30]*Ibid.*   [31]*La Pensée et le Mouvant,* p. 193.

sible, in the sense of a real possible, or of potentiality—a denial already involved, in truth, by the critique of the idea of nothingness.

Were things *possible* before they existed? No, Bergson replies. It is an illusion to think so. The possible does not precede the act.

Now he undertakes to prove this thesis by an analysis of the psychological and cognitional function of the idea of a real possibility. But from the very outset he misunderstands that idea. He takes real possibility to be a *virtual or ideal pre-existence,* that is *an image of tomorrow* already provided in things today, and in which there lacks only the act to exist; in short, he takes real possibility to be something actual lacking only existence—a notion of the possible which is indeed scandalous for an Aristotelian or a Thomist!

Once supplied with such a pseudo-idea of the possible or of potentiality, it is simple enough to explain that here is only a pseudo-idea, and that it springs from a *retrospection,* from a projection which we extend into the past at the instant when *that which was not yet* comes to exist. At that specific moment, says Bergson, and at that moment only, at the moment when it is, the new thing is thought as *having been* possible. Thus in fact it begins *to have been* possible only at the moment when it *is.*

In this so subtle an argument let us let the philosopher himself speak. "At the foundation of the doctrines which fail to recognize the radical novelty of each moment of evolution, there are many mistakes, many errors. Above all there is the idea that the possible is *less* than the real and that, for this reason, the possibility of things precedes their existence . . . If we put to one side closed systems, subject to purely mathematical laws, able to be isolated because duration does not bite into them; if we consider the whole of concrete reality, or merely the world of life, and even more the world of consciousness, we find that there is *more,* and not *less,* in the possibility of each of successive positions than there is in their reality. For the possible is only the real with an added act of the mind which casts back into the past the image of the real once it has been produced." A work of art *will have been,* but actually *is* not, possible. "As reality step by step creates itself, unforeseeable and new, its image is reflected behind it in the indefinite past. Thus reality is at all times found to have been possible. But it is at that precise moment that it begins always to have been possible. And this is why I said that its possibility, which does not precede its reality, will have preceded it once reality appears. The possible, then, is a mirage of the present in the past . . . The idea, immanent in the greater part of philosophic systems and natural to the human mind, of possibles which realize themselves by acquiring existence, is, therefore, pure illusion. One might as well claim that flesh-and-blood man springs from the materialization of his image perceived in a mirror. . . . Is it not . . . absurd . . . to suppose that the future designs itself in advance, that possibility existed prior to reality?" "There is an effective stirring of unforeseeable moments." "One has to take one's stand: it is the real which makes itself possible, and not the possible which becomes real."[32] It would be impossible to state in more absolute fashion that everything is in act (*in actu*) at the same time that everything is becoming.

Here the fundamental error, as we pointed out a moment ago, relates to the nature of the *possible,* which is considered as something actual by one remove, and which at once, unless we deny becoming, can only be ideal, and retrospectively indicated by a future perfect. In reality what happens in change at a given moment in no sense existed in the preceding moment as something *already actual* but not yet made manifest; what is to be is in no way *already realized* under any form whatever.

[32]*Ibid.,* pp. 126–33.

Yet what a subject becomes, not being a simple extrinsic qualification, must affect the subject in its being: but cannot affect
it as regards what it already is (that is, in act), because what it
already is, it is; that it does not become. Therefore the new
qualitative endowment affects the subject, and is drawn from
it, as though from a kind of capital fund or an ontological fertility which is in no way reducible to any being in act, and
which actuality from all sides invests and sustains in the being,
but which in itself is absolutely non-actual, not realized, is pure
determinability—in a word, potentiality. This is real possibility,
and wherever there is change and becoming, it necessarily precedes whatever new actuations the subject receives. If, moreover, it is quite true that the possible is recognized after the
event, after it is realized, it is precisely because potentiality—
being nothing that may be uttered, for everything which may
be uttered is in act—is purely *ad actum,* and is knowable only
through act.

It is indeed the mark of that which is created—of that which
can increase, acquire, undergo, of that which depends on another—to bear in its inner inwardness this metaphysical un-
evenness, which is completely levelled off only in the Being
itself subsisting, in Being which can become nothing, because
it is supereminently everything. In everything which is not
God, reality is the realization of a possible.

For Bergson, on the contrary, what things become they of
course were not, but before becoming so, they already were
everything that they could be. From the very fact of their being
actual, they pass over into another actuality. It is sufficient for
things to be, and to be in act,—I mean in their continuity with
the effusive actuality whence emanates that universal *élan,*—in
order for them to become other. Here we are confronted with
a "new method of thinking" which consists in the full and entire substitution of the verb *change* for the verb *be.* Here is an
affirmation of *pure actuality,* not of Parmenidean being, or of

Spinozist substance, but of *movement* itself and of becoming. "We have only," as wrote M. Jankélévitch, "to make a transposition in order to pass from the impassible universe of Spinoza to the qualified universe of Bergson."[33] Let us not say "transposition"; the word does not seem to me quite appropriate; let us rather say "reversal." In its metaphysical significance, Bergsonism gives the appearance of being a Spinozism reversed.

From whence it comes to pass that certain interpreters of Bergsonism, particularly the philosopher I have just quoted, themselves aflame with the same fire as enflamed Spinoza, evoke Bergson in the Spinozist sense. It is essentially important, says M. Jankélévitch, to refuse to allow oneself to be drawn into the shadows of virtuality; all must be in clarity and in act. And he continues: "From the very moment when the shadow of the possible invades the universe, giving rise to the illusory optics of finality, of (possible) disorder and of indifference, the idea occurs to us that perhaps things might have been other than they are," and that idea gives birth in us to the wonder which affects "fanatics" confronted with the spectacle of the world.

I do not at all believe that Bergson would be inclined to yield to the fanaticism of Spinoza and of his present-day disciples. On the contrary he holds his own philosophy to be determinedly anti-Spinozist. And it is not *substance*—on the contrary, it is *change*—which for him is *pure actuality*. But in such cases one can say that extremes meet.

Even though he frontally opposes Spinoza, Bergson has in common with him one major premise of absolutely primordial importance—the denial of potentiality in things. For Bergsonian metaphysics, and here we touch on basic questions which order the destiny of a philosophy, everything is pure act —pure act in perpetual growth, radical recasting and constant motion of the ever new. Here was matter from which could

[33]*Ibid.,* p. 95.

be drawn a whole system of atheist metaphysics. Yet we know that it is not at all in this direction that Bergson chose to go. Far from it! He chose to affirm a personal God, as well as the spiritual nature of the soul and free will. The question is to find out whether in this his metaphysics helped him, or whether in a certain sense in this he himself triumphed over his metaphysics, and whether, between very different and even opposite possibilities of development (here once more the possible holds us in pursuit!), it was not extra-philosophic factors which made him decide.

THE UNFORESEEABLENESS OF BECOMING

THE ROOT motive for Bergson's elaboration of his critique of potentiality is, I believe, his desire to safeguard the unforeseeableness of becoming, not only the absolute unforeseeableness of free acts and the relative unforeseeableness of contingent happenings in the course of nature, but also what he calls the "radical unforeseeableness" of every moment in the universe. This feeling for *unforeseeableness,* as I have just observed, can lead a philosopher into excesses and errors. In itself it is a highly philosophic feeling and one which we should not let lie quiescent within us. I have explained that when it is understood in its exact meaning, the Aristotelian idea of potentiality, far from threatening, in fact justifies this feeling of unforeseeableness. Certain too elementary expositions of theodicy might seem to compromise it. In reality the God of Saint Thomas safeguards as much as the God of Bergson the unforeseeableness of concrete becoming. If He knows all things from all eternity, and the feather which tomorrow will fall from the wing of a certain bird, it is not because the history of the world should be only the unfolding of a *ready-made scenario.* It is, on the contrary, that all the moments of the whole of time are present for the divine Eternity, who sees in its own instant, and hence always, everything creatures do, have done, will do in the very instant that it *happens,* and hence in an eternal freshness of life and newness.

If, as I have indicated at the beginning, Bergson did not desire to erect a whole system of metaphysics, his metaphysics is nevertheless one of the most profound, most penetrating, and most audacious of our time. The critical discussion thereof I have endeavoured to conduct in this chapter is in homage to his greatness. For the errors for which one is justified in reproaching him could only take shape as the ultimate, logical consequences of the projection, in a field of conceptualization unhappily altogether empiricist and nominalist, of intuitions and of truths which touch at the very roots of things.

CHAPTER IV

THE BERGSONIAN PHILOSOPHY OF MORALITY AND RELIGION

A BOOK LONG AWAITED

BERGSON's *Creative Evolution* appeared in 1907; twenty-five years later, in 1932, Bergson published his *Two Sources of Morality and Religion*. This book was not only the result of a long and patient labour of meditation performed with that scientific conscience and that care in the accumulation and verification of data and documents which Bergson's method exacts in so high a degree; it was also a victory over serious illness, and is one of the purest and most moving of available testimonies to the life of the spirit.

We had all for a long time been aware that Bergson was preparing a moral philosophy and that he even intended to enter upon questions of theodicy.[1] What would this morals, this theodicy be? A few disciples had chanced some timid anticipatory essays, inevitably rather thin, and tending in different

[1] As to theodicy, very few indications were to be found in the first books of Bergson. He wrote to Höffding, in 1912: "That problem [of God], I have not really touched in my works; I believe it to be inseparable from moral problems, in the study of which I have been absorbed for some years; and the few lines of *Creative Evolution* you are alluding to have been placed here only as a stepping-stone." He also wrote to another friend that his critique of the idea of nothingness was only an objection directed against Spinoza, and that even in *Creative Evolution* he aimed at portraying the existence of a transcending and creative God. (*Cf.* the review *Études*, February 20, 1912.)

directions, and even more extremist in their conclusions inasmuch as the internal directive principle, the principle of vital equilibrium, was lacking.

Others wondered whether indeed an ethics could ever arise from a philosophy which, despite its irrationalism, seemed as if it were settled in the slightly disdainful coolness of pure speculation, and as if it were rather scornful of practical human affairs (in fact no one was less a pragmatist than Bergson).

During this entire time, Bergson laboured in silence. He was reading, he was building up for himself a vast historical, ethnological and sociological documentation; he was meditating the history of humanity. He was reading the great spiritual writers —those we call mystics. Already in 1906 he spoke to me of Saint Theresa of Avila, and said to me that in his opinion the philosophers would do well to become a little more mystical, and the mystics a little more philosophical. Mystic. Perhaps that word bothers some people; yet after all we must call things by their right names. Thirty years ago in France, the word "mystic" stirred up all sorts of reactions of mistrust and uneasiness; one could not hear it spoken without immediately being on one's guard against an eventual invasion of fanaticism and hysteria. What is the situation in regard to this in the New World? I do not know. With us, in any case, a more careful observation of reality has caused these parasitical connotations to fall by the wayside, and now we understand better and better that the more or less pathological counterfeits of the mystical life are doubtless numerous, but that the true mystics are the wisest of men and the best witnesses for the spirit. Bergson himself has had a great deal to do with this change.

I was saying, then, that for a long time he had been reading the mystics. But I must at once emphasize that he did not read them with that curiosity of the collector, of the hobbyist in rare plants or exotic butterflies, which is sometimes displayed in regard to them by certain historians who are firmly determined to be on guard against them, to look down at them, to prevent the questions they have raised from entering their hearts. He read the mystics as one consults witnesses, eager himself for any traces of the spiritual he might find in this sad world, and perfectly prepared to allow any evidence of it, no matter how cumbrous and unsettling it might be, to exert on him its full weight. The mystics are dangerous beings. We have heard that often enough. Inevitably and from the beginning there is a betrayal of yourself in your manner of reading them. As you read, and by the way you read, they judge you.

Bergson read them humbly, and with love.

THE BASIC THEME OF THE TWO SOURCES

ONE FINE DAY, without any notices in the press, without informing any one, not even the author's closest friends, after twenty-five years of anticipation, the work was published. A classic from the day it appeared, it smashed the narrow framework of the rationalist, idealist and sociologist ethics, or pseudo-ethics; it outlined an ethics which does not shut man in on himself, but reveals and respects in him (and in this the title of the book is remarkably appropriate) the well-springs of moral experience and of moral life. He affirmed in magnificent language, and with a new emphasis, that humanity and life can be loved effectually only in Him who is the Principle of humanity and life; he recognized, if not the absolute truth of Christianity, on which he withheld judgment, at least the unique value and the transcendence of the fact of Christianity.

I shall not set forth in detail the contents of the *Two Sources of Morality and Religion;* that would take up too much space. We know, on the other hand, that Bergson's thought constantly progressed until his death, but he did not publish any statement concerning his more recent views. I shall restrict myself to the *Two Sources* and to a rapid résumé of its essential theses.

I should like at once to point out for one thing that Bergson herein brought us something profoundly new in relation to his previous work, what I would call an unforeseen spiritual substance—unforeseeable he doubtless would himself say—unforeseen because it stemmed from the very roots of his own inner life; and for another that he has ordered and organized that spiritual substance in a logical whole which in itself seems on the contrary to bring us very little that is new and to be merely the expected and foreseen projection of themes already elaborated in *Creative Evolution. Intuition* and *conceptualization*—we know how significant and at times dramatic is the contrast between them in many philosophies, but especially in Bergsonism.

The fundamental theme of the *Two Sources* is the distinction and opposition between that which in moral life proceeds from *pressure* and that which proceeds from *attraction*. Pressure comes from social formations, and from that law of fear to which the individual is subject with regard to those rules of life imposed by the group and intended to assure its preservation, and which seeks only to turn to the routine and ferocious automatism of matter.

Attraction comes from the call of superior souls who commune with the *élan* of the spirit, and who penetrate into that infinitely open world of freedom and love, which transcends psychological and social mechanisms; *attraction* comes from the *call of the hero,* and from the propulsive force of the emotion which at once invading the soul, makes it free, because it awakens the soul to its most secret inner vitality. To the law of *pressure* and the law of *attraction* are linked two quite separate forms of morality: *closed* morality which, to put it briefly, is that of social conformism, and *open* morality, which is that of holiness.

A similar distinction must be made according to Bergson concerning religion: on one side we would have *static religion,* of which the beliefs of primitive peoples offer us a typical example, and which corresponds to the somewhat biological necessities implied by the conservation and historical movement of social groupings on the surface of the earth. By virtue of these necessities, a myth-making function must develop as a defensive reaction of nature against the dissolving power of the intelligence, in particular against the representation by the intelligence of the inevitability of death, and against the representation by the intelligence of a discouraging margin of contingency between initiative taken and desired effect.

This gives Bergson the opportunity to incorporate, while placing them on their proper level and criticizing their excessive pretentions, modern works on ethnology and sociology which relate to primitive mentality, magic, totemism, and mythology.

On the other hand we have *dynamic religion,* which is above all a vocation to the mystical life. In his chapter on dynamic religion, Bergson studies Greek mysticism, Oriental mysticism, the Prophets of Israel, Christian mysticism; and at the conclusion of this study he considers himself justified in saying that Christian mysticism alone has reached real achievement.

And it is the experience of the mystics which leads him to the existence of God. This existence, which his previous philosophic speculation on the *élan vital* and on the primary centre of movement wherefrom it springs made possible of conjecture, now compels unconditioned acceptance. How? By witness of those who have experience of things divine. We must believe the mystics about God, as we do the physicists about matter; both are competent, they both know whereof they speak.

In the last chapter of his book, to which he gave the title "Mechanics and Mysticism," Bergson, as if eager to add his testimony, offers us his ideas on many of the questions, in the cultural, social, and moral orders, which today torment humanity. The connection between this chapter and those that precede it is not very strong. But the author's concern to provide us, in the twilight of his life, with the warnings of a wholly free and wholly disinterested wisdom is only the more significant and moving. I shall not have space here to discuss this chapter.

I shall only point out that, taking the opposite view to a very wide-spread and superficial opinion, Bergson asserts that *mechanics* and *mysticism,* far from being opposites by nature, attract each other and require the completion of the one by the other. "Man will rise above earthly things," Bergson writes, "only if a powerful equipment supplies him with the requisite fulcrum. . . . In other words, the mystical summons up the mechanical. . . ." And, on the other hand, "We must add that the body, now larger, calls for a bigger soul, and that mechanism should mean mysticism. . . . Machinery will find its true vocation again; it will render services in proportion to its power, only if mankind, which it has bowed still lower to the earth, can succeed, through it, in standing erect and looking heavenwards."[2]

TWO POINTS OF VIEW

IN ORDER to try to appraise the latest developments of Bergsonian thought as they appear in the *Two Sources* one can take two vastly differing points of view, look at things from two widely different perspectives: the perspective of conceptualization and of doctrinal construction, of philosophy as a system; and the perspective of intentions and guiding intuitions, of philosophy as a spirit. We shall begin with the first. From that point of view it would be fruitless to hide the fact that Bergson's ideas on morals and religion call for serious reservations in spite of the great truths on which they cast light.

The metaphysical apparatus of Bergsonism is responsible for

[2]*Les Deux Sources de la Morale et de la Religion,* Paris, 7e Ed., Alcan, 1932, pp. 334–35; *The Two Sources of Morality and Religion* (Tr. by R. A. Audra and C. Brereton), New York, Holt, 1935, pp. 298–99.

this. The "ontological gap" and radical empiricism which wound this metaphysics have often and rightly been pointed out, especially in connection with the *Two Sources*. That serene elevation of thought, that scrupulous concern for the integral testimony of experience, that happy and powerful subtlety which we admire in Bergson—all this cannot avail as a complete remedy for such doctrinal deficiencies. Moreover, I must limit myself to the statements contained in the *Two Sources*. I am aware that Bergson did not express in these statements many thoughts he considered at this time to be private opinions (he wished his friends to read "between the lines"); I also know that his constantly alive effort of discovery did not stop at the *Two Sources* and continued progressing, above all in the religious field. But in this philosophical discussion I am allowed to take into account only those points of doctrine which Bergson offered to us in his books.

Considering in itself the system of interpretation proposed by Bergson in the *Two Sources,* one might ask whether his attempt to discover and comprehend the spiritual in its highest forms, to the extent that that attempt is bound up with the system of ideas propounded in *Creative Evolution,* does not, despite everything, amount to a reduction of the spiritual to the biological. I mean a biological itself made so transcendent that it is conceived as the creative source of all worlds, but which ever remains biological, in so far as the word relates to those levels of life, above all characterized by the organic and the psychic, on which life manifests itself in the animation of matter, and on which consequently immanent activity is bound up with conditions of transitive action and of productivity. Of course it is true enough that outside the world of grace and of supernatural life, man's spirituality never transcends what is biological except in a more or less imperfect fashion.

Let us at once try to develop precisely a few aspects, first of the Bergsonian conception of morality; second, of the Bergsonian conception of religion; and third, of the Bergsonian conception of the mystical life.

THE BERGSONIAN THEORY OF MORALITY

IT HAS BEEN justly observed that in matters of moral philosophy there exist two possible attitudes: one, which we may call *idealist,* being purely reflexive, refuses to distinguish between the speculative order and the practical order; it makes moral life the fundamental element, and if I may put it so, the very vitality of all thought; it moreover recognizes no other thought but human thought, which it calls Thought, with a capital T. The other attitude we might call *cosmic;* focussed upon being, it acknowledges that man is *situated* in a universe which spreads beyond him in every direction, and sees in the moral life of man a particular case in universal life, made specific within this universal life by the existence of free will.

The attitude of the ethics of Saint Thomas Aquinas is a cosmic attitude; that of Bergsonian ethics is also cosmic. And we cannot insist enough upon the importance of the renewal which modern thought thus owes to Bergson. He has recognized the dependence of moral philosophy with regard to metaphysics and the philosophy of nature, and has linked to a philosophy of the universe the destinies of the philosophy of human action. He thus delivers us from the last surviving attraction of Kantianism, and rediscovers the great philosophic tradition of humanity.

An ethics of the cosmic type cannot possibly dispense with a system of the world; the universe of freedom presupposes the universe of nature and fulfills a wish of the latter: I must know where I am and who I am, before knowing, and in order to know, what I should do. All that is fundamentally true; on all that Bergson and Saint Thomas are at one. But it is immediately obvious that the problem now shifts ground and relates to the validity of that metaphysics and system of the world proposed for our consideration. Is the world, as Bergson believes, a creative evolution? Or is it, as Saint Thomas believes, a hierarchy of growing perfections? Is man's intellect capable of attaining being, and does it consequently possess a power of regulation over life and action so that, as Saint Thomas Aquinas puts it, reason is the proximate rule of human acts? Or indeed is that which keeps man in contact with reality, with the dynamic *élan* that constitutes the secret of the real, is that, as Bergsonism would have it, a sort of instinct, as it were a vital inspiration, which runs through us from the depths of our souls, an instinct which emotion, above all, is apt to stir into action, to awaken? In each case, clearly enough, the edifice of ethics will be differently constructed. We are grateful to Bergson for having founded his ethics in a metaphysics; but we must note that that metaphysics is the metaphysics of the *élan vital,* and that the metaphysics of the *élan vital* does not take into account many essential truths.

Bergsonian ethics carries on and completes the fundamental theme of Bergsonian metaphysics: life is essentially a creative dynamism, but one which advances only under the burden of a dead weight, the obstacle constantly created by habit, by the "slipping back," which *is* matter. Thus, from our very first moral experience we feel ourselves caught between two dependencies: on the one hand a dependency with regard to the social disciplines which put pressure on us and which appear to us interior, because they have become habit; on the other hand a dependency with regard to the universal *élan* of life, which draws us on when we yield to the hero's call. We are inhabited: pressure and aspiration are both natural energies which are in us without being of us. Here we have, in the case of social pressure, an *obligation* to which Bergson seems to ascribe only a sort of physical meaning; in the case of liberating aspiration, an *emotion,* resembling grace, whether natural or supernatural, itself conceived as an irresistible attraction, a victorious allurement.

In all this, and in the restitution of a certain profound *docility,* as an essential element of moral life, we find precious truths. But what of morality itself? What shall we consider the specific task of morality? It has vanished into thin air. Reduced to its essential work, and especially if it is considered in its basic natural structures, morality is a very humbly human thing, and not brilliant or glorious—rough and resolute, patient, prudent, argumentative, hard-working. For that poor devil, a rational being, it is a question of finding his way as best he can along the paths of happiness, using as he must a certain little light which places him above the whole bodily world, and thanks to which he is in a position to choose freely, to select for himself his own happiness, to say yes or no to whatever guides and hawkers offer to show him the way. It is a matter of taking oneself in hand by means of reason and freedom. And to what end? In order to decide that it is reasonable to obey a Law one has not made. What weariness! It is a thankless task to take oneself in hand, when one is as uninteresting a thing to look upon as is a man. And it is thankless to put freedom into use, especially when it is, in the last analysis, to do what Someone else wills. All this is a work of man, a work of reason and of thwarted freedom. How can we wonder that in a sense it seems to be volatilized by an *irrationalist* philosophy, for which the intelligence is good only to make tools, which teaches that the motives for acting come only after the decision to act has been taken, which does not succeed in conceiving free will except as a very high peak of vital spontaneity? The most captivating thing about Bergsonian ethics is precisely that morality, in the strictest sense of the word, has been eliminated from it. In it, man is caught between being something *social,* infra-rational, and something *mystical,* supra-rational.

Truth to tell, he is torn between the two, and when he becomes conscious of this, he will perhaps regret the absence of morality's exacting effort, but effort toward autonomy. Bergson does not leave us any means of choosing between the service of society and the call of the hero, between piety which imitates and fervour which invents. A kind of Manichæan cleavage is here the price paid for a thoroughly empiricist conception, in which to act can only be to yield to a force. Only reason, which is the principle of a moral universe distinct at once from social obedience and mystical impulse, can recognize, in dependence on the laws proper to that universe, the internal hierarchy which subordinates the social entity to the mystical and at the same time reconciles them with each other. But to posit that subordination and that reconciliation is to get away from Bergsonism.

If I had space here to delve deeply into things, I should have to recall at this point the central importance for ethics of the notion of *end;* since the human being is ordered to a certain end by the nature of things and by his ontological structure, ethics and the human will are dependent upon *another,* whom they should welcome, and are involved in the great cosmic play of being. But it is reason that knows that end—reason, and the will which accepts it freely and which freely chooses the means of attaining it. Thus the universe of morality is a universe of freedom, founded on the universe of nature. A cosmic type of morality we indeed must have, but on condition that reason and freedom are at the heart of the cosmic. Now the idea of end—the idea on which all this depends—is absent from Bergsonian morality as from Bergsonian metaphysics; that gap is the inevitable result of Bergsonian irrationalism.

One might say that for a philosophy of being, which is the philosophy of Saint Thomas, the temper of ethics is *cosmic rational;* for Bergson, it is *cosmic irrational.* Here everything for Bergson springs from a creative *élan* which ceaselessly pushes forward universal life; and moral generosity, the particular work of the hero of the moral life, is only the furthest and highest apex of that *élan* of universal life, which pushes on from degree to degree in the midst of so many set-backs. There is not, finally, any distinct order which constitutes the proper order of morality. But for Saint Thomas, for the philosophy of being, the order of the moral life is the order of the practical reason guiding the freedom of the human being to the true end of that being; and this order constitutes a *specific and autonomous* order in the bosom of universal metaphysical order, and yet founded upon it. And God, who is the Head and the Principle of universal order and universal life and who thus has no opposite and whom nothing resists, is also, Himself, the Principle of being, the Head and the Principle of that specific and autonomous order which is the moral order, and of that specific life which is the moral life, wherein man can offer his own refusal to the divine Will. If reason is the rule of human acts, it is so to the extent to which it is a participation in that eternal law which is creative wisdom itself.

Here then, all things considered, we have, for Bergsonism, an ethics of the creative *élan* or of creative evolution which preserves, I dare say, all of morals except morality itself; we have, for a philosophy of being, an ethics of creative wisdom, which in securing the specificity of morality, nevertheless recognizes its biological roots and social conditioning and makes the social disciplines a part of morality in so far as they are in conformity with reason; and, on the other hand, leaves morality open to the transcendent demands, to the most profound purifications and the highest regulations of the mystical life.

THE BERGSONIAN THEORY OF RELIGION

So is it also with the Bergsonian theory of religion. Bergson has admirably appraised, that is to say he has reduced to very modest proportions, the ambitious speculations of the sociological school on primitive mentality. In particular he calls attention to the fact that the thought of primitive man obeys the same laws as our own, under altogether different conditions and therefore with quite different results. I cannot resist quoting two pages here—pages which serve as a perfect example of the good nature whereon the wisdom of metaphysicians on occasion permits itself to smile:

"Let us take for instance one of the most interesting chapters in M. Lévy-Bruhl's books, the one dealing with the first impressions produced on primitive man by our fire-arms, our writing, our books, in a word by everything we have to give him. We find this impression disconcerting at first. We should indeed be tempted to attribute it to a mentality different from our own. But the more we banish from our minds the science we have gradually, almost unconsciously, acquired, the more natural the 'primitive' explanation appears. Here we have people before whom a traveller opens a book, and who are told that the book gives information. They conclude that the book speaks, and that by putting it to their ear they will hear a sound. But to look for anything else in a man unacquainted with our civilization would be to expect from him an intelligence far greater than that of most of us, greater even than exceptional intelligence, greater even than genius: it would mean wanting him to re-invent the art of writing. For if he could imagine the possibility of depicting words on a sheet of paper he would possess the principle of alphabetic, or more generally of phonetic, writing; he would straightway have reached a point which civilized man has reached only by a long accumulation of the efforts of a great number of exceptional men. Let us not then speak of minds different from our own. Let us simply say that they are ignorant of what we have learnt.

"There are also, we added, cases where ignorance is coupled with an aversion to effort. Those would be the ones grouped by M. Lévy-Bruhl under the title of 'ingratitude of the sick.' Primitive men who have been treated by European doctors are not in any way grateful; nay, more, they expect payment from the doctor, as if it were they who had done him a service. But having no notion of our medical science, no idea that it is a science coupled with an art, seeing moreover that the doctor is far from always curing his patient, and finally considering that he certainly gives his time and his trouble, how can they help thinking that the doctor has some interest, unknown to them, in what he does? And why, instead of striving to shake off their ignorance, should they not adopt quite naturally the interpretation which first occurs to their minds, and from which they can profit? I put this question to the author of *La Mentalité primitive,* and I shall evoke a recollection, a very ancient one, though scarcely older than our old friendship. I was a little boy and I had bad teeth. There was nothing for it but to take me now and again to the dentist, who at once showed no mercy to the offending tooth; he pulled it out relentlessly. Between you and me, it hardly hurt at all, for the teeth in question would have come out of their own accord; but I was no sooner seated in the dentist's chair than I set up a blood-curdling yell, for the principle of the thing. My family at last found out a way to make me keep quiet. The dentist, taking care to make a noise about it, would drop a fifty-centime piece into the glass from which I was to rinse my mouth (asepticism was unknown in those far-off days), the purchasing-power of this sum being at that time ten sticks of barley sugar. I must have been six or seven, and was no stupider than most boys. I was certainly capable of guessing that this was a put-up job between the dentist and my family to bribe me into silence, and that they conspired together for my particular good. But it would have needed a slight effort to think, and I preferred not to make it, perhaps from laziness, perhaps so as not to change my attitude towards a man against whom my tooth was indeed bared. So I simply went on not thinking, and the idea I was bound to form of the dentist then stood out automatically in my mind in letters of fire. Clearly he was a man who loved drawing teeth, and he was even ready to pay for this the sum of half a franc."[3]

[3]*Ibid.,* Paris Ed., pp. 158–60; New York Ed., pp. 139–41. Quoted by permission of Henry Holt and Co.

Thus can "primitive mentality" be found in civilized man. The data to be found in today's newspapers would allow me to illustrate that assertion with examples not quite so innocent as that of young Bergson's tooth.

But let us come back to the theory of religion. In my opinion what spoils the Bergsonian theory of *static religion,* despite his many profound observations, is his refusal to discern in it the natural energy of human reason, as it operates in the midst of those incoherences and contradictions which Bergson so well analyzes, and which relate to a mental universe bathed and inundated by the waters of the imagination; the obscure natural workings of the metaphysical intelligence, the natural pursuit of and feeling for the absolute are thus disregarded. Instead of that, religion in its primitive and strongly socialized forms, the religion Bergson calls static, together with the myth-making function which is linked to it, seems to him like a defensive reaction against the dangers of the intelligence.

The embarrassment caused by these fascinating theories is like that caused by the aphorisms of genius. Consider such an aphorism; you may well express a truth equally profound by saying just the opposite. For instance, selecting as samples a few of the most celebrated aphorisms of classical French literature: *One can face neither the sun nor death without flinching. Man is a thinking blade of grass. Genius is patience long drawn out.* Well, suppose I say: *One can face unflinchingly the sun and death?* Or: *Man is* NOT *a thinking blade of grass?* Or: *Genius is impatience long drawn out?* It seems to me these aphorisms are as good as the first. Bergson thinks that the intelligence discourages and that it inspires fear, and that the myth-making function, translating great biological instincts, is necessary to give man heart to live. On the other hand one may think that the spectacle of life is indeed depressing—"You have multiplied men," says the psalmist, "but you have not multiplied joy,"—and that intelligence, with its primordial metaphysical certainties, inspires one with the courage to live, and that the myth-making function is a kind of refraction in the realm of the imagination of the intellect's practical encouragements. After all, it would be quite possible for both these ways of thinking to be true at the same time.

However that may be, it is ever the same process of severing and opposing (to use a word certainly too strong, one could call it Manichæan) that, for Bergson, separates static religion, religion in its inferior forms, socialized and materialized, from dynamic religion, open to the universality of the spirit. That which might constitute the unity of both, that is to say the ontological value, now hidden, now exposed, of certain perceptions and certain beliefs, disappears in both the one and the other.

For even as regards dynamic religion the logical implications of the Bergsonian distrust of intelligence tend to attenuate that objective content of knowledge, those properly intellectual data whose supra-rational value one cannot affirm without at the same time affirming the rational values they envelop. It is the entire domain of *truth* communicated to man by the formulas and the assertions of faith which finds itself thus disregarded. As a matter of fact, if this is the case, it is so because in the philosophical order itself Bergson began by failing to recognize the value of *metaphysical reason,* properly so called. Against the heritage of this reason he continues to raise criticisms most unjust, and the picture that he draws of the ideas of Plato and Aristotle is distorted by the nominalistic and irrationalistic prejudices of his own metaphysics.

THE BERGSONIAN THEORY OF THE MYSTICAL LIFE

LET US GO on to what Bergson tells us of the mystics in the *Two Sources.* If one considers things less from the point of view of the spirit whose instinct he followed than from the point of

view of the doctrinal conceptualization he proposes, one is
compelled here also to make certain reservations.

When the mystics say that they are united to their Principle
as to the life of their life, they do not think they are welcom-
ing some vital *élan* or some anonymous creative effort. They
already know the name of the One to whom they cling: they
already know—by the faith they have in common with all
those who have received the revealed Word—who is this God,
and what are His designs upon men.

The question of knowing whether the principle to which the
mystics are bound is the transcendent cause of all things[4]
seemed, in the *Two Sources,* secondary to Bergson. The mystics themselves are not uninterested in that question; they answer it with a definite affirmative. They testify (and on this
point it seems to me that Bergson's book at least leaves us in
an equivocal state) that their will and their soul are impelled
not toward the joy of a creative urge definitively free of all end,
but on the contrary toward an infinite end; and that the pro-
digious energy which moves them has meaning and existence
only as it carries them on to that final end wherein they shall
be established in a ceaseless life.

They testify (and it is the whole problem of the validity of
dogma that they thus set and that they resolve—a problem
which Bergson, wishing to remain purely a philosopher, has
not set, but one to which I do not see how one can give appropriate answer if one accepts his basic criticism of the concept and of conceptual formulas) . . . the mystics testify that
their experience of divine things has living faith as its proximate and proportioned principle, and that if that experience is
obscure and is obtained by love, it is nevertheless a supreme
knowledge, since the intelligence is nourished in this not-
knowing by its most noble Object.

Finally, to come to the problem of action and of contempla-

[4]*Ibid.,* Paris Ed., pp. 256, 269, 281; New York Ed., pp. 228, 239, 250.

tion, the mystics testify that if contemplation overflows into action, still it is not precise to write—I criticize the expression more than the thought; I shall come back to that in a moment —it is at least ambiguous to write as did Bergson that the final state for contemplation is to *spoil itself in action* and in an *irresistible urge which casts the soul into the most vast undertakings.*

FROM THE POINT OF VIEW OF THE SPIRIT AND OF DIRECTIVE INTUITIONS

WE HAVE BEEN considering, from the point of view of conceptualization and doctrinal construction or of philosophy as a system, some important matters contained in the *Two Sources,* and on that score we have been obliged to make several criticisms. Everything changes its aspect if we change the point of view to one of philosophy as *spirit,* of directive intentions and intuitions. In such case we may give ourselves the joy of admiration, pure and simple.

There is nothing more moving, nothing which in a sense better bears witness to the transcendence of the spirit, than to see an untiringly courageous thought, in spite of its philosophical equipment and by virtue of fidelity to the light within, follow a pure spiritual trajectory and thus come to the very doors at whose threshold all philosophy stops short (but which Bergson himself was to pass through some years later).*

*Mme. Henri Bergson has made public part of her late husband's will, dated February 8, 1937. Here are a few sentences from this document: "My reflections have led me closer and closer to Catholicism, in which I see the complete fulfillment of Judaism. I would have become a convert had I not seen in preparation for years the formidable wave of antisemitism which is to break upon the world. I wanted to remain among those who tomorrow will be persecuted. But I hope that a Catholic priest will consent, if the Cardinal Archbishop of Paris authorizes it, to come to say prayers at my funeral." A priest did in fact fulfill this wish. Henri Bergson died on January 4, 1941.

I indicated a moment ago the reservations which concern for correct doctrine obliges us to make with regard to the general interpretation that Bergson proposes for the mystical life. As a matter of fact, the delinquencies I have pointed out in that interpretation show above all that philosophy *alone* is not enough in these matters. To the extent that philosophy, in its desire to use merely philosophical means, believes that it should not explicitly consider the reality of grace and the mystery of the Cross—in other words, to the extent that philosophy believes it should refuse to enter into continuity with theology in its treatment of such matters—to that extent philosophy will remain unable to reach in their specific causes the things of mystical life, with whatever good faith the philosopher honours them. And what pure philosopher has ever studied all those things with greater good faith, with a more humble and generous love, than Henri Bergson?

It is high time to indicate the gratitude we owe him for the admirable pages he has devoted to the mystics, pages which reveal a marvellously faithful and loving attention with regard to realities felt as present and efficacious. Bergson here reduces to nothingness the indigent constructions of vulgar phenomenalist psychology; and if one bears in mind the anti-mystical prejudices to which I alluded at the beginning of this chapter, one cannot help thinking that Bergson offers the mystics fine compensation when he dwells upon the *intellectual robustness* of these souls, who attained a life in some fashion superhuman. Let us take a look at his own words. I quote some pages from the *Two Sources:*

"We may therefore conclude that neither in Greece nor in ancient India was there complete mysticism, in the one case because the impetus was not strong enough, in the other case because it was thwarted by material conditions or by too narrow an intellectual frame. It is its appearance at a given moment that enables us to follow in retrospect its preparatory phases, just as the volcano, bursting into activity, explains a long series of earthquakes in the past.

"For the complete mysticism is that of the great Christian mystics. . . .

"When we grasp that such is the culminating point of the inner evolution of the great mystics, we can but wonder how they could ever have been classed with the mentally diseased. True, we live in a condition of unstable equilibrium; normal health of mind, as, indeed, of body, is not easily defined. Yet there is an exceptional, deep-rooted mental healthiness, which is readily recognizable. It is expressed in the bent for action, the faculty of adapting and re-adapting oneself to circumstances, in firmness combined with suppleness, in the prophetic discernment of what is possible and what is not, in the spirit of simplicity which triumphs over complication, in a word, in supreme good sense. Is not this exactly what we find in the above-named mystics? And might they not provide us with the very definition of intellectual vigour?

"If they have been judged otherwise, it is because of the abnormal states which are, with them, the prelude to the ultimate transformation. They talk of their visions, their ecstasies, their raptures. These are phenomena which also occur in sick people and which are part of their malady. An important work has lately appeared on ecstasy regarded as a psycho-asthenic manifestation. But there exist morbid states which are imitations of healthy states; the latter are none the less healthy, and the former morbid. A lunatic may think he is an emperor; he will systematically introduce a Napoleonic touch into his gestures, his words, his acts, and therein lies his madness: does this in any way reflect upon Napoleon?

"In just the same way it is possible to parody mysticism, and the result will be mystic insanity: does it follow that mysticism is insanity? Yet there is no denying that ecstasies, visions, raptures, are abnormal states, and that it is difficult to distinguish between the abnormal and the morbid. And such indeed has been the opinion of the great mystics themselves. They have been the first to warn their disciples against visions which are

quite likely to be pure hallucinations. And they generally regarded their own visions, when they had any, as of secondary
importance, as wayside incidents; they had to go beyond them,
leaving raptures and ecstasies far behind, to reach the goal,
which was identification of the human will with the divine
will. The truth is that these abnormal states resembling morbid
states, and sometimes doubtless very much akin to them, are
easily comprehensible, if we only stop to think what a shock
to the soul is the passing from the static to the dynamic,
from the closed to the open, from everyday life to mystic
life. . . .

"We cannot upset the regular relation of the conscious to the
unconscious without running a risk. So we must not be surprised if nervous disturbances and mysticism sometimes go
together; we find the same disturbances in other forms of
genius, notably in musicians. They have to be regarded as
merely accidental. The former have no more to do with mystical inspiration than the latter with musical.

"Shaken to its depths by the current which is about to sweep
it forward, the soul ceases to revolve around itself and escapes
for a moment from the law which demands that the species
and the individual should condition one another. It stops, as
though to listen to a voice calling. Then it lets itself go, straight
onward. It does not directly perceive the force that moves it,
but it feels an indefinable presence, or divines it through a
symbolic vision. Then comes a boundless joy, an all-absorbing
ecstasy or an enthralling rapture: God is there, and the soul
is in God. Mystery is no more. Problems vanish, darkness is
dispelled; everything is flooded with light. But for how long?
An imperceptible anxiety, hovering above the ecstasy, descends
and clings to it like its shadow. This anxiety alone would suffice, even without the phases which are to come, to distinguish
true and complete mysticism from what was in bygone days
its anticipated imitation or preparation. For it shows that the
soul of the great mystic does not stop at ecstasy, as at the end
of a journey. The ecstasy is indeed rest, if you like, but as
though at a station, where the engine is still under steam, the

onward movement becoming a vibration on one spot, until it
is time to race forward again.

"Let us put it more clearly: however close the union with
God may be, it could be final only if it were total. Gone, doubtless, is the distance between the thought and the object of the
thought, since the problems which measured and indeed constituted the gap have disappeared. Gone the radical separation
between him who loves and him who is beloved: God is there,
and joy is boundless. But though the soul becomes, in thought
and feeling, absorbed in God, something of it remains outside;
that something is the will, whence the soul's action, if it acted,
would quite naturally proceed. Its life, then, is not yet divine.
The soul is aware of this, hence its vague disquietude, hence
the agitation in repose which is the striking feature of what
we call complete mysticism: it means that the impetus has
acquired the momentum to go further, that ecstasy affects indeed the ability to see and to feel, but that there is, besides,
the will, which itself has to find its way back to God. When
this agitation has grown to the extent of displacing everything
else, the ecstasy has died out, the soul finds itself alone again,
and sometimes desolate. Accustomed for a time to a dazzling
light, it is now left blindly groping in the gloom. It does not
realize the profound metamorphosis which is going on obscurely within it. It feels that it has lost much; it does not yet
know that this was in order to gain all.

"Such is the 'darkest night,' of which the great mystics have
spoken, and which is perhaps the most significant thing, in
any case the most instructive, in Christian mysticism. The final
phase, characteristic of great mysticism, is imminent. To analyze
this ultimate preparation is impossible, for the mystics themselves have barely had a glimpse of its mechanism. Let us con-
fine ourselves to suggesting that a machine of wonderfully
tempered steel, built for some extraordinary feat, might be in
a somewhat similar state if it became conscious of itself as it
was being put together. Its parts being one by one subjected
to the severest tests, some of them rejected and replaced by
others, it would have a feeling of something lacking here and

there, and of pain all over. But this entirely superficial distress would only have to be intensified in order to pass into the hope and expectation of a marvellous instrument. The mystic soul yearns to become this instrument. It throws off anything in its substance that is not pure enough, not flexible and strong enough, to be turned to some use by God. . . . *Now* it is God who is acting through the soul, in the soul; the union is total, therefore final. . . .

"A calm exaltation of all its faculties makes it see things on a vast scale only, and, in spite of its own weakness, produce only what can be mightily wrought. Above all, it sees things simply, and this simplicity, which is equally striking in the words it uses and the conduct it follows, guides it through complications which it apparently does not even perceive. An innate knowledge, or rather an acquired ignorance, suggests to it straightway the step to be taken, the decisive act, the unanswerable word. Yet effort remains indispensable, endurance and perseverance likewise. But they come of themselves, they develop of their own accord, in a soul acting and acted upon, whose liberty coincides with the divine activity. They represent a vast expenditure of energy, but this energy is supplied as it is required, for the superabundance of vitality which it demands flows from a spring which is the very source of life. And now the visions are left far behind: the divinity could not manifest itself from without to a soul henceforth replete with its essence. Nothing remains to distinguish such a man outwardly from the men about him. He alone realizes the change which has raised him to the rank of *adjutores Dei,* 'patients' in respect to God, agents in respect to man. In this elevation he feels no pride. On the contrary, great is his humility. How could he be aught but humble, when there has been made manifest to him, in mute colloquy, alone with The Alone, through an emotion in which his whole soul seemed to be absorbed, what we may call the divine humility? . . .

"The love which consumes him is no longer simply the love of man for God, it is the love of God for all men. Through God, in the strength of God, he loves all mankind with a divine love. This is not the fraternity enjoined on us by the philosophers in the name of reason, on the principle that all men share by birth in one rational essence: so noble an ideal cannot but command our respect; we may strive to the best of our ability to put it into practice, if it be not too irksome for the individual and the community; we shall never attach ourselves to it passionately. Or, if we do, it will be because we have breathed in some nook or corner of our civilization the intoxicating fragrance left there by mysticism. Would the philosophers themselves have laid down so confidently the principle, so little in keeping with everyday experience, of an equal participation of all men in a higher essence, if there had not been mystics to embrace all humanity in one simple indivisible love? This is not, then, that fraternity which started as an idea, whence an ideal has been erected. Neither is it the intensification of an innate sympathy of man for man. Indeed we may ask ourselves whether such an instinct ever existed elsewhere than in the imagination of philosophers, where it was devised for reasons of symmetry. With family, country, humanity appearing as wider and wider circles, they thought that man must naturally love humanity as he loves his country and his family, whereas in reality the family group and the social group are the only ones ordained by nature, the only ones corresponding to instincts, and the social instinct would be far more likely to prompt societies to struggle against one another than to unite to make up humanity. The utmost we can say is that family and social feeling may chance to overflow and to operate beyond its natural frontiers, with a kind of luxury value; it will never go very far. The mystic love of humanity is a very different thing. It is not the extension of an instinct, it does not originate in an idea. It is neither of the senses nor of the mind. It is of both, implicitly, and is effectively much more. For such a love lies at the very root of feeling and reason, as of all other things. Coinciding with God's love for His handiwork, a love which has been the source of everything, it would yield up, to anyone who knew how to question it, the secret of creation. It is even more metaphysical than moral in its essence. What it wants to do, with God's help, is to complete the creation of the human species. . . ."[5]

"In reality," again adds Bergson, "the task of the great mystic is to effect a radical transformation of humanity by setting an example."[6] And what was it that Saint Paul said? It is our task to complete that which is lacking (as far as application, not merit, is concerned) of the sufferings of the Saviour—in other words to continue the work of redemption in time as His instruments—to the point, as said Saint John of the Cross, "of quitting one's skin and all the rest for Him." That is why Christians receive baptism: and not in order to thank God for not being like other men, even like that publican. . . .

Short of making an analysis through *inherent proper causes,* which theological instruments alone permit, by informing a philosopher of the realities which are grace, the theological virtues, and the gifts of the Holy Spirit, it is impossible to discuss the mystical experience with more depth and with a more intense, farsighted sympathy than does the author of *Two Sources.* Perhaps theologians themselves might find in the pages quoted above matter fit for instruction. We can see, on the other hand, that if at certain times in other passages which I do not here reproduce the conceptual expression may call for reservations, the spirit which animates all this study of Bergson's can only elicit our admiration. And even as Bergson seemed to subordinate contemplation to activity and to vast undertakings, his thought really had quite a different meaning. During one of our last conversations I questioned him in this matter. He answered that it was not in his mind to assert any primacy of action over contemplation. He meant simply to say that the contemplation of the perfect mystics is a contempla-

[5]*Ibid.,* Paris Ed., pp. 242–51; New York Ed., pp. 216–23. Quoted by permission of Henry Holt and Co.
[6]*Ibid.,* Paris Ed., p. 256; New York Ed., p. 228.

tion of love which, because it essentially implies the giving of self, requires an overflow into action, in accordance with the obligations and the opportunities of the moment; and that this overflowing, when it takes place, gives testimony to the full transformation of the human soul, regarding the will as well as the powers of knowledge.

If Bergsonian theodicy is evidently very deficient in the order of demonstration and rational knowledge, or rather, is inexistent in so far as it is rational, nevertheless that humility by which the philosopher in all this *believes* those who have journeyed into the realm of things divine, and who have returned from it, is not only a great testimony to the internal hierarchy of wisdoms, it also insures him against the risk of errors from which it might have been particularly difficult for his philosophical conceptualization by itself to escape. He henceforth knows with certainty that God exists, and that He is personal, and that He is freely creative. If the dangers of pantheism are in my opinion inherent in the Bergsonian metaphysics, Bergson himself has deliberately made his choice against pantheism. He has asked the mystics to instruct him; they have not led him astray. They have taught him the great secret, which the Gospels revealed, even though in a sense it be accessible to natural reason. What the testimony of the mystics clearly tells us, writes Bergson, is that "divine love is not something of God, it is God himself."[7]

I have just said that in a sense reason alone could have discovered the truth that God is Love—the highest truth to which the reason of itself can attain. True, but the reason did not do so. It required the help of those positive historic contributions which the judæo-christian tradition calls revelation. If the revelation of the divine Name to Moses, *I am who I am,* taught the reason from above what the reason itself could have known but did not know how to discover, by how much stronger

[7]*Ibid.,* Paris Ed., p. 270; New York Ed., p. 240.

reason is this true of the revelation made to Saint John: *God is love*. Let me point this out: if you consider the relation between the creature and God, then to say that God not only should be loved, but that He loves, and I mean with the madness proper to love, that there can be relations of friendship, of loving forgiveness, of a common life, of shared happiness, between the creature and God—all that implies the supernatural order of grace and of charity. Both this supernatural truth, and this experience, help the reason to understand the meaning of that same word, God is love, in so far as it asserts that in God to love is the same as to exist, which is a truth of the natural order. It is the most resplendent sign of divine glory, as our reason can attain it, that love, which presupposes intelligence and which is above all an overflowing, an ultimate superabundance of the life of spiritual living beings, should be in God identical with the very essence and the very existence of God. In that sense Love is His Name above all names: it is His Gospel Name.

The mystics have taught Henri Bergson this name, causing him at one bound to outstrip his whole philosophy. If the philosopher "attaches himself to mystical experience," he writes, "Creation will appear to him as God undertaking to create creators, that He may have, besides Himself, beings worthy of His love."[8] Let us say, rather: to create gods, transformed in God by love and in love, and then we rejoin Saint Paul and Saint John of the Cross.

Given the very special method here followed by Bergson; that is to say, given that, in order to philosophize on divine things, he consulted the experience of mystics, it is not astonishing that certain echoes of a properly supernatural order which spring from the living faith of his instructors should have passed over into his philosophy. One can thus understand that, whatever may be the insufficiencies of his theory of dy-

[8]*Ibid.*, Paris Ed., p. 273; New York Ed., p. 243.

namic religion, what matters most to the Christian is nevertheless there. When, in connection with the coming of Christianity, he says, in his own special phraseology, "The essence of the new religion was to be the spreading of mysticism,"[9] or again, "In this sense religion is to mysticism what vulgarization is to science,"[10] what does he affirm if not the central truth which Saint Thomas sets forth in the following terms: "The new law, at least that which is principal in it, is not a written law, but is infused in the heart, because it is the law of the new covenant. What is above all important in the law of the new covenant, and that in which lies *all its power,* is the grace of the Holy Spirit which is given by living faith. . . . "[11] From whence it follows that without love I am nothing, as Saint Paul says, and that the perfection of charity, the union which transforms the soul in God, is *of precept,* not indeed as a thing immediately to be realized, but as a goal toward which to strive, each in accordance with his condition.

I have pointed out that the system developed in the *Two Sources* with regard to static morality and dynamic morality retains all of morals except morality itself.

This formula, doubtless too severe, must evidently be understood as applying to the strictly rational and human content of ethics, and it relates to Bergsonian conceptualization. In considering on the other hand the spiritual intentions of the doctrine, one must grant that it brings us very precious enlightenment on the subject of the conditions, the environment, the social orchestration of morality, and also concerning its internal dynamism.

For one thing, it puts us on our guard against the enormous amount of deliberate or unconscious imitation, of routine, of social reflexes, and of social conformity which threaten the

[9]*Ibid.,* Paris Ed., p. 255; New York Ed., p. 227.
[10]*Ibid.*   [11]*Sum. theol.,* I–II, 106, 1.

moral life within us. For another it warns us that in fact, in concrete reality, moral life loses all truly transforming value in us if it is not infused with a call and a vocation, with an *élan* and a desire, with an insatiable desire, with a mad desire, and for what, if not for holiness? Because what Bergson terms the call of the hero is very evidently the call of the saint. In thus having the moral fastened to the supramoral, that is to say the divine, in having the law appendant to love and freedom, Bergson saves morality.

AFTER TWENTY-SEVEN YEARS

MY FIRST published work was a severe criticism of Bergsonism. It appeared late in 1913.[12] The last chapter of this book was called "The Two Bergsonisms"; I there distinguished what I called the *Bergsonism of fact,* which I criticized, from what I called the *Bergsonism of intention,* which I believed to be orientated toward Thomistic wisdom.

I take the liberty of quoting here some lines from this chapter. With great temerity I addressed myself, as it were, to Bergson, and I said: "You glimpse the existence of a personal God. It is not the God of the learned; it is a living and active God, it is the God of the whole man. Can you continue to deal with Him as a theorist does with an idea, and not as a man with his Lord? There are secrets which He alone can reveal. You yourself are one of these secrets. You would know your end and the means to attain it if you knew these secrets. But you will only know them if it pleases God to reveal them Himself. Truly, philosophers play a strange game. They know very well that one thing alone counts, and that all their medley of subtle discussions relates to one single question: why are we born on this earth? And they also know that they will never

---

[12]*La Philosophie Bergsonienne, Études Critiques,* Paris, Rivière, 1913. Seconde édition revue et corrigée, et augmentée d'une préface de 86 pages, Paris, Téqui, 1930.

be able to answer it. Nevertheless they continue sedately to amuse themselves. Do they not see that people come to them from all points of the compass, not with a desire to partake of their subtlety but because they hope to receive from them one word of life? If they have such words, why do they not cry them from the housetops, asking their disciples to give, if necessary, their very blood for them? If they have no such words, why do they allow people to believe they will receive from them something which they cannot give? For mercy's sake, if ever God has spoken, if in some place in the world, were it on the gibbet of one crucified, He has sealed His truth, tell us; that is what you must teach. Or are you indeed masters in Israel only to be ignorant of these things?"

How then, after so many years, can I fail to see in the last developments of Bergson's philosophy an answer to the anxious questions I then raised?

This master, who freed in me my metaphysical desire, and whose doctrine I had in turn criticized—through love of the truth, as he well knew—this master was generous enough not to hold these criticisms against me although they touched what is most dear to a philosopher, his ideas. He wrote some years ago that, though having but little acquaintance with Saint Thomas, each time he met with one of his texts along the way, he had found himself in agreement with him; and that he was gladly willing to have his philosophy placed in the same stream as flowed from Saint Thomas. I do not cite this with some ludicrous idea of annexing Bergson to Thomism. But rather because he himself was perfectly willing to think that I had not been wrong in saying that his philosophy contained certain as yet undeveloped virtualities, and because it thus happened that as last we met one another as it were halfway, each having journeyed unwittingly in such a manner as to approach the other: he, toward those who alone represent without betraying it the faith to which I belong, I toward a comprehension, a little less deficient, of the human task of those who seek without yet having found.

Charles Du Bos once spoke of the kind of euphoria to which an intelligence *too felicitous in being right* is in danger of abandoning itself. Twenty-seven years ago I well knew that it was not myself, but the long tradition of wisdom of which Saint Thomas is the great Doctor, that was in the right as against the metaphysical system of Bergson. But I did not yet know that even if one is never too much in the right, this is nevertheless so great a privilege, and so undeserved, that it is always appropriate to apologize for it. It is a courtesy which must be offered to truth.

CHAPTER V

WHO IS MY NEIGHBOUR?

THE PROBLEM I should like to consider in this chapter is a very difficult one, but it is of vital importance. I think that there is a decided advantage for us in courageously facing this problem, and becoming aware of its reality, even if we are unable to do much more. The question is to determine whether the diversity of religious creeds, an evident historical fact, is an insurmountable obstacle to human cooperation.

Surely it is a paradox that despite the state of religious division in which mankind lives, good fellowship, brotherly intercourse and a spirit of union can be established between men in the earthly commonwealth, while each of them is bound to his God and is attached with all his heart to his faith in Him and to the form of worship he renders Him. But man himself is a paradox. And more astonishing still appears the "exceeding great love" of Him who loved us first and whose very predilections work for the welfare of all.

Nothing in history, indeed, goes to show that religious feeling or religious ideas have been particularly successful in pacifying men. Religious differences seem rather to have fed and sharpened their conflicts. And yet, if it is true that human society must bring together in the service of the same terrestrial common good men belonging to different spiritual families, how can the peace of that temporal society be lastingly assured if first in the domain that matters most to the human being— in the spiritual and religious domain itself—relationships of mutual respect and mutual understanding cannot be established? I prefer the word fellowship to "tolerance," for it connotes something positive—positive and elementary—in human relationships. It conjures up the image of travelling companions, who meet here below by chance and journey through life—however fundamental their differences may be—good humouredly, in cordial solidarity and human agreement. Well, then, for the reasons I have just mentioned, the problem of good fellowship between the members of the various religious families seems to me to be a cardinal one for the new age of civilization, the rough outlines of which are beginning to take shape in our present night. I should like to quote in this connection the words pronounced by Pope Pius XII at his coronation: "Our thoughts go out also in this solemn moment to all those who are outside the Church and who, we should like to think, will rejoice to learn that the Pope prays to Almighty God for them also and wishes them every possible good."

A deliberate attempt to bring closer together the believers of the various religious families is something relatively new. On a solemn occasion, Pope Pius XI called upon all men of good will to such an attempt. No doubt this attempt is partly due to the imminent dangers, to the spiritual evils threatening us: open atheism publicly warring against God, or pseudo-theism seeking to turn the living God into some protecting genius for the State or some demon of the race. If that is so, we must admit that it is a stern lesson for believers. Was it needful that God permit the frightful degradation of mankind that we are witnessing today, so many persecutions and so much suffering, to teach those who believe in Him to go down into the real depth of their own hearts, even into those mysterious regions where we more or less faintly hear the hand of the God of love knocking at our bolted doors?

Let me say immediately that this attempt at rapprochement might easily be misunderstood. I shall therefore begin by clearing the ground of any possible sources of misunderstanding. Such a rapprochement obviously cannot be effectuated at the cost of straining fidelity, or of any yielding in dogmatic integrity, or of any lessening of what is due to truth. Nor is there any question whatever either of agreeing upon I know not what common minimum of truth or of subjecting each one's convictions to a common index of doubt. On the contrary, such a coming together is only conceivable if we assume that each gives the maximum of fidelity to the light that is shown to him. Furthermore, it obviously can only be pure, and therefore valid and efficacious, if it is free from any *arrière-pensée* of a temporal nature and from even the shadow of a tendency to subordinate religion to the defense of any earthly interest or acquired advantage.

I am sure that everyone is agreed on these negative conditions I have just enumerated. But one aspect of the paradox I mentioned at the outset is that, as soon as we pass on to positive considerations, each one sees the very justification and the very reason for being of this good fellowship between believers of different religious families mirrored in his own particular outlook and in his own world of thought. And these outlooks are irreducibly heterogeneous, these worlds of thought never exactly meet. Until the day of eternity comes, their dimensions can have no common measure. There is no use closing one's eyes to this fact, which simply bears witness to the internal coherence of the systems of signs, built up in accordance with different principles, on which human minds depend for their cognitive life. Fundamental notions such as that of the absolute oneness of God have not the same meaning for a Jew as for a Christian; nor has the notion of the divine transcendence and incommunicability the same meaning for a Christian as for a Moslem; nor the notions of person, of freedom, grace, revelation, incarnation, of nature and the supernatural, the same meaning for the Orient as for the Occident. And the "non-violence" of the Indian is not the same as Christian "charity." No doubt it is the privilege of the human intelligence to understand other languages than the one it itself uses. It is none the less true that if, instead of being men, we were patterns of Pure Ideas, our nature would be to devour each other in order to absorb into our own world of thought whatever other such worlds might hold of truth.

But it happens that we are men, each containing within himself the ontological mystery of personality and freedom; in each of us the abyss of holiness of the Supreme Being is present with His universal presence, and He asks to dwell there as in His temple, by manner of a gift of Himself to us. Well, each one must speak in accordance with his outlook. I suppose there are readers of this book who do not share my own creed. I shall try to tell them as briefly, but also as frankly and as precisely as possible—and this frankness is itself one of the characteristics of mutual confidence—how the paradox of fellowship I am at present examining can be solved for me, a Catholic, from the point of view of a philosophy which takes into account the data of Christian theology. I do not apologize for this excursion into the field of theology, it is required by the subject I am discussing.

THE CATHOLIC DOCTRINE CONCERNING
THE STATUS OF NON-CATHOLICS BEFORE GOD

IT IS WELL known that, according to the Catholic Faith, God, after having spoken in various and imperfect ways through the prophets, spoke once and for all, in a perfect and final manner, through His own uncreated Word, who took flesh in the womb of a virgin of Israel in order to die for mankind. And that the deposit of this revelation of the Word of God was confided to a living and visible body, made up both of just men and of sinners, but specially assisted by the Spirit of God in its mission of truth and salvation. Thus authority plays a most important part for Catholics. But apart from dogmas and their connected truths and apart from the discipline of salvation, freedom plays a big part also, and the diversity of opinions in human affairs is far greater in the Catholic Church than is generally realized by those not in it. I know that the teaching of the Church can deal with every matter connected with faith; but in being integrally mindful of this teaching, I can still disagree most sharply with other Catholics about political or social matters: democracy, trade unionism, the late war in Spain or the second World War, as well as about philosophical or historical questions. This is because it is only to the purity and integrity of the Word of God that the faithful are bound as such; the teaching authority of the Church intends of itself only to safeguard this living deposit of truth, just as the disciplinary authority of the Church has no other object than to enable the faithful to live by that truth. It is to the First Truth in person, speaking to my heart, that I adhere by means of the statements of dogma that bring the revelation to all. As a Catholic and by my Catholic Faith, I am bound in conscience to no human, theological or philosophical opinion, however well founded it may be, and still less to any judgments on contingent or worldly matters, or to any temporal power. Nor am I bound to any particular form of culture or civilization, and still less of race or blood. I am bound uniquely to what is universality itself and superuniversality: to the Divine, to the words and precepts of Him who said, "I am the Truth, I who speak to you."

That in brief is how the Catholic outlook appears to me. Catholic theology teaches that it is upon our love, as Saint John of the Cross says, that we shall be judged; in other words, that salvation and eternal life depend on charity. It teaches that charity presupposes faith and has its root in faith, in other words, in truth divinely revealed. It teaches that *explicit* faith in Christ, illuminating the human mind regarding the inmost secrets of divine truth and life, is not only the requisite means for souls to attain the highest degree of conformity with God and divine union, and a prerequisite for peoples to achieve a firm position of general morality and perfectly human civilization, but that that faith is also the response of reverence justly due to God's gift, inclining His glory toward us. Explicit faith in revealed truth, therefore, is the first duty of everyone who is not incapable of hearing through his ears and in his heart the word of God. But Catholic theology adds that faith together with grace are offered to all souls, even if they are unable to know the truth explicitly in its integrity. If those souls are in good faith and do not refuse the internal grace offered to them, they have *implicit* faith in Christ and accept implicitly the entire divinely revealed truth, even if they only believe, having no clearer light, that God exists and saves those who seek Him.[1] (And God knows much better than do they themselves whether they believe that.)

If, therefore, Catholics hold that there is no salvation outside the Church, you can see that this maxim can shock only those who understand it wrongly and who are ignorant of what is commonly taught concerning the "soul of the Church." All it means to us is that there is no salvation outside the Truth, which, explicitly or implicitly, is freely offered to all. And does that not seem fully in harmony with the nature of man and his essential dignity? Surely if there were salvation outside the Truth, I should not want such a salvation, for I prefer the Truth to my joy and freedom; or rather I know that only the Truth can give me real joy and set me free.

We believe that there is no salvation outside the Truth, and the fact that all men do not explicitly know the Truth, the fact of religious division, far from being a good in itself, is a mark of the distress of our condition. But we also hold, as I have just explained, that the Truth speaks to every man's heart; and God

[1] *Cf.* Heb. xi:6.

alone knows who those are, in whatever part of the world they may be born and whether or not they live under the régime of His publicly revealed word, who truly and efficaciously hear His interior and secret word. We believe that there is no salvation outside Christ, but we also believe that Christ died for all men and that the possibility of believing in Him—either explicitly or implicitly—is offered to all. We believe that there is no salvation outside the Mystical Body of Christ, but we also believe that those who visibly belong to that Body by confessing the faith and by the sacraments, and are thus designated to continue in time the work of redemption and receive more generous effusions of the vehicles of grace, are not its only members. We hold that every man of good faith and right will, provided he does not sin against the light and does not refuse the grace interiorly offered to him, belongs, as we put it, to the Soul of the Church, or, in other words, is invisibly and by the motion of his heart a member of the visible Church and partakes of her life, which is eternal life. And no man, withal, whether Christian or non-Christian, can know whether he is worthy of love or of hatred.

Catholics are sometimes reproached with speaking to others in a domineering or patronizing manner. Human weakness being what it is, that may well be the case with some. Yet in reality, their position is far from being a comfortable one. They are twice wounded, with the wounds of their faults and with the requirements of their God. Not only does their reason show them that other religions can also transmit to mankind many great truths, although in their eyes incomplete or mixed—and on occasion, if it is a question of certain techniques of natural spirituality or of psycho-physical mastery of self—certain truths which the Gospel did not take pains to teach. But what is more important still, they see that, through the very supernatural truth which they have received—not as a monopoly but as something to give to others—men belonging to other spiritual families, even poor idolaters, can, if they are of good faith and if their hearts are pure, live better than some members of their own religious family. And who would not lose heart, if he were not helped by grace! The tree bends, says Saint Thomas Aquinas, under the fullness of its fruit. The Church rejoices over the testimony she is required to give, and the Christian rejoices in her. She knows that it is a bounden duty to acknowledge the holy reality of privileges received. For the divine freedom gives as it pleases to whomever it pleases. But, as Saint Paul puts it, it is in a fragile vessel that each faithful soul contains grace. That he should have on his pitiable human shoulders some measure of the burden of divine truth in no way justifies the believer in being supercilious or patronizing; rather he feels inclined to excuse himself and to ask forgiveness of every passer-by. *Euntes ibant et flebant;* going, they went and wept. I know well that there are men—and it is perhaps to make up for their little practical faith—who despise others and ceaselessly repeat: we believers, we respectable people, we Christians, we Catholics, at times even we "born" Catholics, as if they were not born sinners like everyone else. They never suspect that, by thus placing their pride in evidence of their religion, they make those who see them want to blaspheme the Almighty.

THE BASIS OF GOOD FELLOWSHIP AMONG MEN

OF DIFFERENT CREEDS, CONSIDERED ON THE SPIRITUAL LEVEL

To RETURN to the question of the fellowship of believers. I think it is clear what the basis of such a fellowship is in the Catholic outlook. This basis is not of the order of the intellect and of ideas, but of the heart and of love. It is friendship, natural friendship, but first and foremost mutual love in God and for God. Love does not go out to essences nor to qualities nor to ideas, but to persons; and it is the mystery of persons and of the divine presence within them which is here in play. This fellowship, then, is not a fellowship of beliefs, but the fellowship of men who believe.

The conviction each of us has, rightly or wrongly, regarding the limitations, deficiencies, errors of others does not prevent friendship between minds. In such a fraternal dialogue, there must be a kind of forgiveness and remission, not with regard to ideas—ideas deserve no forgiveness if they are false—but with regard to the condition of him who travels the road at our side. Every believer knows very well that all men will be judged—both himself and all others. But neither he nor another is God, able to pass judgment. And what each one is before God, neither the one nor the other knows. Here the "Judge not" of the Gospels applies with its full force. We can render judgment concerning ideas, truths or errors; good or bad actions; character, temperament, and what appears to us of a man's interior disposition. But we are utterly forbidden to judge the innermost heart, that inaccessible center where the person day after day weaves his own fate and ties the bonds binding him to God. When it comes to that, there is only one thing to do, and that is to trust in God. And that is precisely what love for our neighbour prompts us to do.

There are some people who do not like that word, "love." It embarrasses them, because it has become hackneyed, and because we hear it as well from lips that have gone to rot, or from hearts that worship themselves. God is not so squeamish. The Apostle John tells us that God is self-subsisting Love.

There is only one proper and fitting way through which peace and union can come to men, and that is through love: first, love springing from nature for beings—for those poor beings who have the same essence as we have ourselves, and the same sufferings, and the same natural dignity. But that love is not enough, for the roots of strife are too strong for it. There must be a love of higher origin, immediately divine, which Christian theology calls supernatural, a love in God and for God, which both strengthens in their proper sphere our various inclinations toward one another in the natural order, and also transcends them to infinity. Charity is very different from that simple human benevolence which philosophers praise, which is noble indeed in itself, yet inefficacious in the end. Charity alone, as Bergson observed in his great book, *The Two Sources of Morality and Religion,* can open the heart to the love of *all men,* because, coming from God who first loves us, charity desires for all men the same divine good, the same eternal life, as it does for ourselves, and it sees in all human beings the summoned of God, streaming, as it were, with the mysteries of His mercy and the prevenient gifts of His goodness.

I should like to dwell a moment on the inner law and the privileges of this friendship of charity, as regards precisely the relations between believers of different religious denominations (as well as between believers and non-believers). I have already made it sufficiently clear that it is wrong to say that such a friendship *transcends dogma* or exists *in spite of* the dogmas of faith. Such a view is inadmissible for all those who believe that the word of God is as absolute as His unity or His transcendence. I know very well that if I lost my faith in the least article of revealed truth, I should lose my soul. A mutual love which would be bought at the price of faith, which would base itself on some form of syncretism or eclecticism, or which, recalling Lessing's parable of the three rings, would say: "I love him who does not have my faith because, after all, I am not sure that my faith is the true faith and that it bears the device of the true ring," in so saying would reduce faith to a mere historic inheritance and seal it with the seal of agnosticism and relativity. Such a love, for anyone who believes he has heard the word of God, would amount to putting man above God.

That love which is charity, on the contrary, goes first to God, and then to all men, because the more men are loved in God and for God, the more they are loved themselves and in themselves. Moreover this love is born in faith and necessarily presupposes faith, at least the implicit faith I mentioned earlier. And it remains within faith, while at the same time reaching out to those who have not the same faith. That is the very characteristic of love; wherever our love goes, it carries with it our faith.

Nor does the friendship of charity merely make us recognize the *existence* of others—although as a matter of fact here is something already difficult enough for men, and something which includes everything essential. Not only does it make us recognize that another exists, and not as an accident of the empirical world, but as a human being who exists before God, and has the right to exist. While remaining within the faith, the friendship of charity helps us to recognize whatever beliefs other than our own include of truth and of dignity, of human and divine values. It makes us respect them, urges us on ever to seek in them everything that is stamped with the mark of man's original greatness and of the prevenient care and generosity of God. It helps us to come to a mutual understanding of one another. It is not supradogmatic; it is suprasubjective. It does not make us go beyond our faith, but beyond ourselves. In other words it helps us to purify our faith of the shell of egotism and subjectivity in which we instinctively tend to enclose it. And it also inevitably carries with it a sort of heart-rending, attached, as is the heart, at once to the truth we love and to the neighbour who is ignorant of that truth. This condition is even associated with what is called the "ecumenical" bringing together of divided Christians; how much more is it associated with the labour of bringing into mutual comprehension believers of every denomination.

I distrust any friendship between believers of all denominations which is not accompanied, as it were, by a kind of compunction or soul's sorrow—which would be easy and comfortable; just as I distrust any universalism which claims to unite in one and the same service of God, and in one and the same transcendental piety—as in some World's Fair Temple—all forms of belief and all forms of worship. The duty of being faithful to the light, and of always following it to the extent that one sees it, is a duty which cannot be evaded. In other words the problem of conversion, for anyone who feels the spur of God, and to the extent that he is pricked by it, cannot be cast aside, any more than can be cast aside the obligation of the apostolate. And by the same token I also distrust a friendship between believers of the same denomination which is, as it were, easy and comfortable, because in that case charity would be reserved to their fellow-worshippers, there would be a universalism which would limit love to brothers in the same faith, a proselytism which would love another man only in order to convert him and only in so far as he is capable of conversion, a Christianity which would be the Christianity of *good* people as against *bad* people, and which would confuse the order of charity with what a great spiritual writer of the seventeenth century called a police-force order.

THE COOPERATION OF MEN OF DIFFERENT CREEDS, CONSIDERED AT THE TEMPORAL LEVEL

IT FOLLOWS from what I have said that from the Catholic point of view (which is mine) a rapprochement between believers of diverse religious denominations can be accomplished, on the religious and spiritual level itself, only by and in friendship and charity, by and in the pure spirituality and freedom of love. It cannot in any way involve any less intangible, more definite, more visible communion, expressed in the order of the speculative and practical intellect by some community of symbol or of sacred ritual. But on the level of the temporal and profane life (and that is indeed quite another level) it is proper that the effort toward union should express itself in common activities, should be *signed* by a more or less close cooperation for concrete and definite purposes, whether it be a question of the common good of the political community to which we all respectively belong, or of the common good of temporal civilization as a whole.

No doubt in that field it is not as believers but rather as members of a given fatherland, as men bound together by customs, traditions, interests and particular outlooks of a fleshly community, or as men having in common a given concrete historical ideal, that believers belonging to different religions are called upon to do a common work. But even in that common temporal task, ethical and spiritual values are involved, which concern the believer as such. And in that common temporal task itself, the mutual good will and fellowship I have been discussing remain factors of primary importance (I say primary; I do not say sufficient) for the pacification of men. In this sphere of temporal and political life, the most suitable phrase is not the phrase *love of charity*, but rather *civic friendship*, which is a virtue of the natural order, that must, however, be leavened by charity. It is a great pity that in an agonized world, men who believe in the supernatural, enchained as they are by so many sociological prejudices, should be so slow to broaden their hearts and to cooperate boldly in order to save from the inheritance of their fellows the elementary values of threatened humanity. From the English *Blue Book* anyone may learn about the atrocities and abominations committed in Nazi concentration camps, which blaspheme the image of God in the human person. But why were these things, that the British Government had known very well for many years, published only when war had already broken out? Anyone may also discover for himself the similar degradation of the human person practiced in Soviet prisons and concentration camps or during the persecution of the Kulaks. If a true feeling for justice and friendship had, at the appropriate time, brought into play the firm intervention of free peoples against such indignities—not by war, but by normal political or economic pressure and for aims purely and truly disinterested—in place of their seeking business accommodations with butchers, maybe the world could have avoided today's dreadful convulsions.

It is impossible to exaggerate the vital importance, so little understood by the sectarian liberalism of the nineteenth century and by the paganism of the present, of the spirit of friendship in human society. Perhaps by force of contrast the extreme sufferings and the terrible conflicts that men are undergoing today will at least have the effect of awakening in a goodly number of them a feeling for friendship and cooperation.

The cruel anomaly with which we are concerned here lies in the fact that historically, as I have pointed out, religion seems to have done as much to divide men and sharpen their conflicts as it has to pacify them. This anomaly is linked with what is deepest in man's nature. If man is not drawn above himself toward eternal values, he becomes less than human; and when he makes use of these eternal values for the sake of his own world of weakness and sin, he uses them to feed and strengthen, and to hallow his passions and malice. To this contradictory situation there is only one key; that key is charity. Religion, like everything great and noble and demanding within us, increases the tension in mankind; and together with the tension, suffering; and with the suffering, spiritual effort; and with the spiritual effort, joy. *Tantum relligio potuit suadere malorum* (So much evil could religion precipitate) said Lucretius of old in a formula after all amphibological. He should have added, and how necessary also is it to the very breath of humanity! And what great good it has been able to call forth, what hopes and virtues it has been able to inspire! Nothing that has been done through the substance of the centuries has been lastingly useful to human beings without religion, at least without religion in its purest forms.

It is not religion that helps to divide men and sharpen their conflicts; it is the distress of our human condition and the interior strife in our hearts. And without religion we should certainly be far worse than we are. We see today how, when man rejects the sacred traditions of humanity and aspires either to free himself from religion by atheism, or to pervert religion by deifying his own sinful blood through a kind of racist pseudo-theism or para-theism, the darkest forms of fanaticism then spread throughout the world. Only by a deeper and purer religious life, only by charity, is it possible to surmount the state of conflict and opposition produced by the impact of religion upon human weakness. To bring to an end all fanaticism and all pharisaism will require, I believe, the whole of human history. But it is the task of the religious conscience itself to overcome these evils. It alone is capable of doing so. It is the religious conscience which, by spiritualizing itself in suffering, must gradually rid itself and the world of the leaven of the pharisees and the fanaticism of the sectarians.

I believe that when we think of all these things, we better perceive the dramatic greatness of our time. As has often been pointed out, a certain unification of the world is taking place on the subhuman level of matter and technique, whereas on the human level itself, the most savage conflicts come into being. In an apocalyptic upheaval, which imperils the very foundations of life, the advent of men to a new age of civilization is thus being prepared, which doubtless will indicate not only an historical transformation of great importance, for good as well as for evil, in the forms of consciousness and culture, but also the coming of a higher state of unity and integration. In the meantime—and it is this which lies at the root of our unhappiness—technical progress has outstripped the mind, matter has gone faster than spirit. And that leaves to those who would hope—I am among them—only one hope: hope in a heroic effort of spiritualization thanks to which all progress in the material and technical order—a progress we must utilize, not condemn—can at last serve to effect a real progress in the emancipation of the human being.

All this is to say that the world itself is serving men an awful summons, and this summons is primarily addressed to those who are believers. The future will be good neither for the world nor for religion unless those who believe understand what is first and foremost required of them. If those very men who wear the insignia of the spirit allow their souls to become subject to those forces of destruction which desperately set evil against evil, and if they enlist religion—even, as some may say, in its own interest—in any undertaking whatever of domination and violence, I think that the disaster for civilization will be irreparable. What is required of believers at the outset and before everything else, even in the struggles of this world, with all the harsh means they imply, is not to dominate but to serve. It is to preserve among men confidence in good will, in the spirit of cooperation, in justice, in goodness, in pity for the weak and the outcast, in human dignity and in the power of truth. These are big words, but it is not enough to let them remain words; they must be made flesh in our lives. If we speak the truth without *doing it,* we run the risk of leading men to regard truth as an imposture. It has been said again and again in recent times, and rightly, that the believer is specially called upon to confess his God in social and temporal life, in the hard work of men. Many things which he accepts today in the earthly state of his fellows and in the conditions of human societies, will appear later to be as little worthy of acceptance as now appears to us the slavery of antiquity. The tragedy of unemployment, the tragedy of the refugee and the émigré, the tragedy of war, are symptoms of a deep disorder which we must work tirelessly to remedy.

Undoubtedly the world needs bread. It is horrible to think that there are so many millions of men on this earth who cannot satisfy their hunger. But what the world needs also and above all are the words that come from the mouth of God, words of active truth, of effective and fertile truth; it needs—I do not say solely or exclusively, but I do say primarily—the contemplation of the saints, their love and activity. And from us who are not saints it needs that in the patient insignificant acts of our everyday life, and in our social and political activities, each of us should faithfully witness, according as his state of life permits, the love of God for all beings and the respect due to the image of God in each human creature.

THE ANALOGICAL SIMILARITIES IN
BASIC PRINCIPLES AND IDEAS REQUIRED
FOR THE COOPERATION OF MEN OF DIFFERENT CREEDS
IN THE TEMPORAL ORDER

THERE IS STILL one question about which, in conclusion, I should like to say something. In the first part of this chapter, I emphasized the fact that religious division creates for believers of different denominations a fundamental plurality of points of view, and I drew attention to the illusion of seeking for the basis and purpose of good fellowship in a common minimum of doctrinal identity—a common minimum which would be seen gradually to shrink to nothing while we discussed it, like the wild ass's skin in Balzac's story.

Yet on the other hand I have just said that this fellowship, based on friendship and charity, should extend, on the level of temporal civilization, to common action (doubtless not free from a certain amount of inevitable opposition and conflict); that it should extend real cooperation for the good of temporal society. But how can such common action be possible without common principles, without a certain basic community of doctrine?

Before passing to more concrete considerations, I shall first answer this question in my own philosophical language. We are all bound together by a more primitive and fundamental unity than any unity of thought and doctrine: we all have the same human nature and, considered in their extra-mental reality, the same primordial tendencies. That sameness of nature is not sufficient to ensure community of action, since we act as thinking beings and not simply by natural instinct. But it subtends the very exercise of our thought. And the nature we hold in common is a rational nature, subject intellectually to the attraction of the same fundamental objects; this unity of nature lies at the deepest foundation of what similarities our principles of action may have, however diverse they may be in other respects. Now, in order to do the same terrestrial work and pursue the same temporal goal, there must be a *certain community* of principles and doctrine. But there need not necessarily be—however desirable and obviously more effective this might be in itself—a strict and pure and simple *identity* of doctrine. It is sufficient that the various principles and doctrines between themselves should have some unity and community of similarity or proportion or, in the technical sense of the word, of *analogy,* with regard to the practical end proposed. Besides, this practical end in itself, although subordinated to a higher end, belongs to the natural order. And no doubt it will be conceived differently according to each one's particular outlook; but in its existential reality it will be placed outside each one's particular conception. Considered thus, in real existence, it will in a measure fall short of, and, at the same time, give actual reality to, each one's particular conceptions.

Therefore, men with different religious convictions will be able not only to collaborate in working out a technique, in putting out a fire, in succouring a man who is starving or sick, in resisting aggression. All that is obvious. But—and this is the problem that concerns us here—if there really is that "analogical" likeness I have just mentioned between their principles, they can also cooperate—at least as regards the primary values of existence in this world—in a constructive action involving the right ordering of the life of temporal society and earthly civilization and the moral values inherent therein. I acknowledge this possibility at the same time—and the two things are not incompatible—as I realize even more keenly my personal conviction that a complete doctrine, based on all principles of Catholic teaching, is alone capable of supplying an entirely true solution for the problems of civilization.

I shall give an example of what I mean from the field I know best, namely Western Christianity, and an example which relates to the religious life itself. The practical problems connected with the relationship between the spiritual and the temporal, and their practical solutions, are so much alike for the Orthodox Church in the Soviet Union, for the Catholic Church and Protestant communities in Germany, that the experience and testimony of believers belonging to these different Christian families are, with their sufferings, a kind of common property. Another example can be drawn from the practical convergence which appears today, in connection with questions of civilization and the defense of the human person, between speculative outlooks as incompatible as Karl Barth's and my own. A Thomist and a Barthian will always clash in theology and philosophy; they can work together within human society.

But we must be even more precise. I have said that the basis of fellowship between believers of different spiritual families is friendship and the love of charity. I now add that it is the implications of love itself that supply us with the guiding idea we need and that make manifest for us the "analogical" likeness of practical thought I referred to earlier.

It is obvious in fact that, if I am right in what I have said, the primary and fundamental likeness between us is the acknowledgement of the fundamental and primordial ethical value of the law of brotherly love, however much this law may have different theological and metaphysical connotations for us, according to the religion or school of thought to which we belong. For the Christian it corresponds to and raises to divine levels a fundamental though terribly thwarted tendency of our nature. It is the second commandment, which forms but one with the first: the commandment to love our neighbour as ourselves. "I feel," wrote Gandhi in a note on the *Satyagraha* in 1920, "that nations cannot be one in reality, nor can their activities be conducive to the common good of the whole humanity, unless there is this definite recognition and acceptance of the law of the family in national and international affairs, in other words, on the political platform. Nations can be called civilized, only to the extent that they obey this law."[2] That, I also believe, is the truth.

Now this very law of brotherly friendship in practice has many implications. The first truth it implies, and which underlies all the rest, is that our existence is directed towards God and that, in accordance with the first commandment, we must love God above everything. How indeed can the law of love have *absolute* value, transcending all the conflicts and discords which flourish among men, unless all men, whatever their race or colour, their class, their nation, their social conditions, their natural shortcomings, receive from an Absolute above the world the bond creating between them a more fundamental and far-reaching communion than all their diversities, and unless they are created to love first and foremost this Absolute in which all things live and move and have their being? We see only too readily that, in the great contemporary movements in which God is in practice denied, whether by virtue of an atheism that refuses to admit His existence or by virtue of a pseudo-theism that blasphemes His nature, love and charity

[2]Report of the Commissioners appointed by the Punjab Sub-committee of the Indian National Congress, 1920, Vol. I, Chap. 4.

are alike rejected as weaknesses and as the worst enemies either of the State or of the Revolution. The theorists of these movements make that abundantly clear in their writings.

The second implication is on the one hand the holiness of truth and on the other hand the eminent value of good will. If man can bend the truth to his own desires, will he not also want to bend other men in like manner? Those who despise charity are also those who think that truth depends, not on *what is,* but on what at each moment serves most effectively their party, their greed, or their hate. And those who despise charity also despise good will. The word to them seems pale and dangerously liberal. They forget—at any rate the Christians among them—that the word has its origin in the Gospels. It is true enough that good will is not sufficient, and that men who mistake that will which is good will for that willingness which is weakness cheat people. But good will is necessary and of primary necessity. It is useful in everything. Real, authentic good will indicates the sacred mystery which spells salvation for men and which makes it possible to say of a man that he is purely and simply good. It enables men to go out of themselves to meet their neighbours halfway. That is why the pharisees and the fanatics, walled up in their whited sepulchres, wherein they would like to enclose the whole world, are not only suspicious of good will; they detest the very idea.

The third implication contained in fraternal amity is the dignity of the human person with the rights it implies and the realities on which it is based. I refer to the spirituality of the human soul and its eternal destiny. In the text from which I have already quoted, Gandhi also pointed out that, "It [*Satyagraha*] is called also soul-force, because a definite recognition of the soul within is a necessity, if a *Satyagrahi* is to believe that death does not mean cessation of the struggle, but a culmination." I as a Christian know very well on what my faith in the immortality of the soul and the dignity of the human person is based. I read in the Gospels: "What doth it profit a man if he gain the whole world and lose his own soul?" I read also that the hairs on each of our heads are counted, and that the angels who see the face of the Father watch over each of the children of men, who are equal in that dignity, and that we must love our enemies. And I read the story of the man who went down from Jerusalem to Jericho and whom robbers left half-dead by the roadside. A Samaritan, in other words a foreigner, with whom the Jews did not mix and whose religious beliefs were different from theirs, recognized his neighbour in that man by having pity on him; whereas a doctor of the law and a priest, going on their way with closed hearts, by so doing excluded themselves from neighbourship with men. The mysterious words of Christ on this matter mean that it is up to us really to become the neighbour of any man, by loving him and having pity on him. It is not community of race, of class, or of nation; it is the love of charity that makes us what we ought to be, members of the family of God, of the only community where each person, drawn out from his fundamental loneliness, truly communicates with others and truly makes them his brothers, by giving himself to them and in a certain sense dying for them. Nothing that has ever been said points out more profoundly the mystery and dignity of the human person. Who is my neighbour? The man of my blood? Of my party? The man who does me good? No. It is the man to whom *I* show mercy, the man to whom is transmitted through me the universal gift and love of God, who makes the rain from heaven fall upon both the good and the wicked.

The existence of God, the sanctity of truth, the value and necessity of good will, the dignity of the person, the spirituality and immortality of the soul: these, and all the other implications bound up with them which I shall not mention here, correspond to spontaneous perceptions of our reason and to primary tendencies of our nature; but they are not understood in an identical and univocal way by believers in the various religions of humanity. Thus Christianity and Buddhism have different conceptions of the human person; the survival of the soul has a different meaning for those who believe in personal immortality and in the resurrection of the body and those who believe in transmigration; the sanctity of truth appears in a different light according to the fashion in which both revelation and human reason are conceived; the value of good will has different connotations for the Catholic who believes in sanctifying grace, for the Orthodox who believes in the sanctifying uncreated Spirit but not in created grace, for the Protestant who believes that the merits of Christ are imputed to an essentially corrupt nature, for the Israelite who believes in the Law, for the Moslem who believes in salvation by the mere profession of Islamic faith; and this difference is still greater as between these religious groups and the religious groups who believe in Karma. As regards the existence of God itself, I do not think that Buddhism rejects, as is often stated, the existence of God, nor that it is in reality an atheistic religion. I believe that this apparent atheism comes from the fact that Buddhism has developed historically as a kind of mystical destruction of the Brahmanic affirmation, so that the Buddhist ascesis and Nirvana are, as it were, like a vast apophatic or negative theology, standing alone in emptiness. But this example does serve to cast light on the extent to which the idea of God may differ among believers of the various religions. It should be added that those who believe that they are non-believers may, in their practical lives, by choosing as the aim of their activity the authentic moral good, choose God, and may do so by virtue of God's grace, without their knowing God in a consciously and conceptually formulated manner.

All this goes to show that there is nothing *univocal* between the various paths travelled by men, and that practical good fellowship is not based on a common minimum of doctrinal identity. In a certain sense, *less* than a common minimum is to be found there, since ultimately no notion appears to be univocally common to all the different religious outlooks. Yet in another sense there is much *more* than a common minimum, since among those who, belonging to different religious families, allow the spirit of love to enter into them, the implications of brotherly love create, for the principles of the practical reason and of action and as regards terrestrial civilization, a community of similitude and *analogy* which corresponds on the one hand to the fundamental unity of our rational nature and is, on the other hand, not merely concerned with a minimum number of points of doctrine, but penetrates the whole gamut of practical notions and of the principles of action of each one. The coming together of such men to co-operate for the good of human society is not based upon an equivocation. It is based upon "analogical" likeness as between the practical principles, motions, and progressions implied in their common acceptance of the law of love, and corresponding to the primary inclinations of human nature.

And why should I, a Christian, according to whose faith a single Name has been given to men through whom they can be saved, even in the temporal order, why should I disguise the fact that this community of analogy itself supposes a *primum analogatum* purely and simply true; and that implicitly and ultimately everything which is authentic love, working in the world for the reconciliation of men and the common good of their life here below, tends, under forms more or less perfect, more or less pure, toward Christ, who is known to some, unknown to others?

In this philosophical attempt to solve a difficult problem, I have spoken in accordance with my faith, and I hope that I have said nothing which might offend the conscience of any of my readers. I shall be glad if I have succeeded in outlining with sufficient clarity what are, from my point of view, the foundations of mutual fellowship and understanding between believers of different religious families and of a constructive cooperation between them for the good of civilization. The good of civilization is also the good of the human person, the recognition of his rights and of his dignity, based ultimately on the fact that he is the image of God. Let no one deceive himself; the cause of religion and the cause of the human person are closely linked. They have the same enemies. The time has passed when a rationalism fatal to reason, which has prepared the way for all our misfortunes, could claim to defend the person and his autonomy *against* religion. Both against atheistic materialism and against an irrationalism drunk with inflicting domination and humiliation, an irrationalism which perverts the genuine instincts of human nature and makes of the political State a supreme idol and a Moloch, religion is the best defender of the person and of his freedom.

And finally if I am asked what I believe to be the reason for God's having permitted the religious divisions in mankind, and those heresies which "must be," according to Saint Paul—I should answer: For the education of mankind, and in order to prepare the way for final religious unity. Because on the one hand it is something above human powers to maintain purity and strength in the collective virtues of any natural community, unless it be within the particular hereditary bias of this earthly, sociologically closed social group. And on the other hand the common life of the Church, the Kingdom of God, is that of a spiritual, supernatural, supra-racial, supra-national, supra-earthly community, open to all humanity as it is open to Deity and divine and deifying blood. Much suffering and many purifications throughout human history are necessary to extricate us from any restriction and adulteration of spiritual unity brought about by fleshly unities.

On the day when all the faithful could live with men of

other creeds in perfect justice, love and understanding, and at the same time keep the true faith perfectly whole and pure, on that day men would not need actually to practice these virtues toward people of other creeds, because infidelity and religious division would on such a day have vanished from the face of the earth.

CHAPTER VI

THE MYSTERY OF ISRAEL[1]

I

I SHOULD LIKE to preface the following reflections with some preliminary remarks.

The essay which forms this chapter was written in France in 1937. At that time, certain racist publications of very low quality had already dishonoured the French press, but the eventuality of any anti-Jewish legislation in France seemed impossible. (In fact, the anti-Semitic decrees promulgated later were treason against the French spirit, imposed by the Vichy government, under German pressure, upon a defeated nation.) At that time the vast majority of French people were nauseated by anti-Semitic trends. It was possible then to consider the Jewish problem in a purely philosophical, objective and dispassionate manner. I do not know whether at the present time I could maintain this manner. I do not know whether, in the face of the anti-Semitic nightmare spreading like a mental epidemic even among some groups of democratic people, it is fitting to speak of such questions except to utter our indignation at the iniquity and spiritual wretchedness now assaulting minds and nations.

Yet the publication of these pages, written during a less

[1]My study, *A Christian Looks at the Jewish Question* (New York, Longmans, 1939), on the trials now suffered by Israel in certain countries, contains material which complements from the historical point of view the considerations of a philosophical nature set forth here.

ominous period, may still be appropriate. We must never despair of intelligence and the healing power of its dispassionate attempt toward understanding. Perhaps I may even hope that some readers who, though in good faith, are more or less affected by anti-Semitic slogans, will be able to perceive that the question does not depend on gossip arguments, anecdotal observations, drawing-room philosophies, old prejudices or instinctive temperamental feelings, but on the crucial principles that direct human history and command the Christian conscience. I wish to emphasize that the independence of judgment shown in this essay regarding what is good and what is bad in the average Jewish behaviour and the average Jewish psychology, supposes and embraces the deepest esteem and love for the Jewish people; and it must be understood as being the normal prerequisite for an examination of the problem carried on "among the mature," as Saint Paul says, and on the plane of the penetrating, arduous insights given to us by Christian wisdom. For in reality the point of view from which this essay was written is neither psychological nor sociological nor ethical, but is primarily metaphysical and religious. I did not seek to characterize the empirical aspect of events, but rather their hidden and sacred meaning. What I tried to explain has significance only if it is taken in its total unity. If any one sentence in this essay were taken out of its context and isolated in order to support or to condemn, as if it were mine, an opinion which is not mine, such a misfortune could spring only from a complete misinterpretation.

If these pages are seen by Jewish readers, I hope they will agree that as a Christian I could only try from a Christian perspective to understand the history of their people. When this essay was published in France, there were some who, guided by their prejudice, tried to see latent intentions of proselytism where only a desire for truth engaged my mind; others took as personal "reproaches" what was only a statement of the consequences of the drama of Calvary regarding the relation of Israel to the world. They were mistaken. I am perfectly aware that before agreeing with the statements proposed in my essay, it is necessary to admit, as a prerequisite, the whole Christian outlook; therefore it would be inconsistent to hope for any agreement from a reader who does not place himself in this perspective. I do not intend to try to convince such a reader, but, for the sake of mutual understanding, I think it would perhaps be interesting for him to know how a Christian philosopher considers this question.

I should like to add that such words as "penalty" or "punishment," which we are obliged to use when we seek to elucidate human matters from the viewpoint of the divine conduct of history, must be deprived of any anthropomorphic connotations, and that they become pitiably inadequate if we fail to do so. In any case, there is no more absurd abuse than to believe it to be the affair of poor creatures to foster their pride and injustice by applying to their neighbours, as if they were the police force of God, "penalties" and "punishments" which concern only the Creator in His intimate dealings of love with those who have been called by Him.

On the other hand, it is to be noted that in this essay the word "Church" is not used in the common sense that it conveys in the unbeliever's language, where it designates only an administrative organization—or the administrative organizations of various denominations—charged with the dispensation of religious matters. This word is used in the strict sense it conveys in the language of Catholic faith and theology. It designates a reality both visible and invisible, both human and divine, the mystical Body of Christ, which is itself a mystery of faith; which bears in itself the blemishes and sins of its weak members, and yet is, in its very essence, life, and inspiration—which it receives, in so far as a living whole, from its divine Head—without any blemish and rust and contamination of the devil; to which all the baptized, gathered together in Catholic faith and discipline, visibly belong, and to the vivifying soul of which all men in good faith and good will, living by divine grace, invisibly belong.

Finally, I should like to point out that the most impressive Christian formulas concerning the spiritual essence of anti-Semitism may be found in a book recently published by a Jewish writer, who seems himself strangely unaware of their profoundly Christian meaning. I do not know whether Mr. Maurice Samuel shares even in Jewish piety; perhaps he is a God-seeking soul deprived of any definite dogmas, believing himself to be "freed" from any trust in divine revelation, either of the Old or the New Covenant. The testimony that he brings appears all the more significant. Because prophetic intuitions are all the more striking when they pass through slumbering or stubborn prophets, who perceive only in an obscure way what they convey to us.

"We shall never understand," Mr. Maurice Samuel says, "the maniacal, world-wide seizure of anti-Semitism unless we transpose the terms. It is of Christ that the Nazi-Fascists are afraid; it is in *his* omnipotence that they believe; it is *him* that they are determined madly to obliterate. But the names of Christ and Christianity are too overwhelming, and the habit of submission to them is too deeply ingrained after centuries and centuries of teaching. Therefore they must, I repeat, make their assault on those who were responsible for the birth and spread of Christianity. They must spit on the Jews as the 'Christ-killers' because they long to spit on the Jews as the Christ-givers."[2]

The simple fact of feeling no sympathy for the Jews or being more sensitive to their faults than to their virtues is not anti-Semitism. Anti-Semitism is fear, scorn and hate of the Jewish race or people, and a desire to subject them to discriminative

[2]Maurice Samuel, *The Great Hatred,* New York, Knopf, 1940.

measures. There are many forms and degrees of anti-Semitism. Not to speak of the demented forms we are facing at present, it can take the form of a supercilious nationalist and aristocratic bias of pride and prejudice; or a plain desire to rid oneself of competitors; or a routine of vanity fair; or even an innocent verbal mania. No one is innocent in reality. In each one the seed is hidden, more or less inert or active, of that spiritual disease which today throughout the world is bursting out into a homicidal, myth-making phobia, and the secret soul of which is resentment against the Gospel: "Christophobia."

II

To UNDERTAKE the study of the origins and modalities of anti-Semitism, it would be necessary to treat the entire problem of Israel's dispersal. Then there would be the opportunity of pointing out that, despite the economic, political and cultural forms which this problem superficially assumes, it is and remains a mystery of a sacred nature, whose major elements Saint Paul, in a sublime summary, relates in chapters ix, x and xi of his Epistle to the Romans:

"What then shall we say? That the Gentiles who were not seeking after justice have attained to justice, but the justice that is of faith. But Israel, by seeking after the law of justice, is not come unto the law of justice. Why so? Because they sought it not by faith, but as it were of works. For they stumbled at the stumbling-stone. As it is written: *Behold I lay in Zion a stumbling-stone and a rock of scandal. And whosoever believeth in him shall not be confounded. . . .*[3]

"But I say: Hath not Israel known? First, Moses saith: *I will provoke you to jealousy against that which is not a nation:*

[3]Rom. ix:30–33. This is taken from the Douay version of Saint Paul's epistles with a few words modified to make the sense clearer. *Cf.* the remarkable commentary by Erik Peterson in *Le Mystère des Juifs et des Gentils dans l'Église,* Paris, Desclée de Brouwer, Les Iles.

against a foolish nation I will anger you. But Isaias is bold, and saith: *I was found by them that did not seek me. I appeared openly to them that asked not after me.* But to Israel he saith: *All the day long have I spread my hands to a people that believeth not and contradicteth me. . . .*[4]

"I say then: Did God cast off his people? God forbid. . . ."[5]

"I say then: Have they so stumbled, that they should fall? God forbid! But by their lapse salvation is come to the Gentiles, that they may be emulous of them. Now if the misstep of them is the riches of the world and the diminution of them the riches of the Gentiles: how much more the fulness of them? For I say to you, Gentiles: As indeed the apostle of the Gentiles, I will honour my ministry. If, by any means, I may provoke to emulation them who are my flesh and may save some of them. For if the dispossession of them hath been the reconciliation of the world, what shall the reintegration of them be, but life from the dead? For if the first fruit be holy, so is the lump also: and if the root be holy, so are the branches. And if some of the branches be broken and thou, being a wild olive, wert ingrafted among them and with them partakest of the root and of the fatness of the olive tree: boast not against the branches. And if thou boast, still it is not thou that bearest the root, but the root thee. Thou wilt say then: branches were broken off that I might be grafted in. Well: because of unbelief they were broken off. Thou standest by faith. Be not highminded, but fear. For if God hath not spared the natural branches, fear lest perhaps also he spare not thee. See then the goodness and the severity of God: towards them indeed that are fallen, the severity; but towards thee, the goodness of God, if thou abide in goodness. Otherwise thou also shalt be cut off. And they also, if they abide not still in unbelief, shall be grafted in; for God is able to graft them in again. For if thou wert cut out of the wild olive tree, which is natural to thee; and, contrary to nature, wert grafted into the good olive tree: how much more shall they that are the natural branches be grafted into their own olive tree?

[4]Rom. x:19-21.   [5]Rom. xi:1.

"For I would not have you ignorant, brethren, of this mystery (lest you should be wise in your own conceits) that blindness in part has happened in Israel, until the fulness of the Gentiles should come in. And so all Israel shall be saved, as it is written: *There shall come out of Zion, he that shall deliver and shall turn away ungodliness from Jacob. And this is to them my covenant:* when I shall take away their sins. As concerning the gospel, indeed they are enemies for your sake: but as touching the election, they are beloved for the sake of the fathers. For the gifts and the calling of God are without repentance. For as you also in times past did not believe God, but now have obtained mercy, through their unbelief: So these also have not believed, for your mercy, that they also may obtain mercy. For God hath concluded all in unbelief, that he may have mercy on all."[6]

❂   ❂   ❂

The Jews are not a "race" in the biological sense of the word. Actually, in the present state of the world, there are no pure races among groups of people large enough to have any importance, even among such groups as are, from this viewpoint, the most favored. The Jews do not represent an exception; mixtures of blood and ethnic amalgamations have in the course of history been as important for them as for other groups. In the ethico-historical sense, where the word "race" is above all characterized *by a community of mental and moral patterns, of ancestral experience, of memories and desires,* and where hereditary tendencies, the blood strain and the somatic type play a more or less important part, but only the part of a material foundation—are the Jews a race. As are the Iberians or the Bretons. But they are much more than this.

They are not a "nation" if this word means an historical community of men bound together by a unity of origin or birth (a race or a group of historically associated races, in the ethico-

[6] Rom. xi:11–32.

historical sense of "race") and *jointly leading or aspiring to lead a political life*. Yiddish has not the characteristics of a national language.[7] It is the language of misery and dispersal, the slang of the Holy City scattered into pieces among the nations and trampled by them. A small number of Jews (500,000 in 1940), gathered together in Palestine, constitute a nation, and Hebrew is their national language. They are a special and separate group bearing witness that the other Jews (there are about sixteen millions in the world) are not a nation.

The Jews of the Palestine homeland are not merely a nation; they are tending to become a state (a complete or "perfect" political whole). But the great mass of Israel obeys a totally different law. It does not tend in any way to set up a temporal society. By reason of a deep vocation and by its very essence, Israel is disinclined—at least, so long as it has not brought to completion its mysterious historic mission—to become a nation, and even more, to become a state. The harsh law of exile, of the Galuth, prevents Israel from aspiring toward a common political life.

If the word "people" means simply a multitude gathered together in a determinate geographical area and populating that region of the earth (*Daseingemeinschaft*), the Jews are not a "people." To the extent that the word "people" is synonymous with "nation," they are not a "people." To the extent that it is synonymous with "race" (in the ethico-historical sense), they are a people, and more than a people; to the extent that it indicates an historical community characterized, not, as is a nation, by the fact (or desire) of leading a political life, but by the fact of being nourished with the same spiritual and moral tradition and of responding to the same vocation, they

---

[7] It might be called a national language in a different sense; in the sense that, like Ladino, it is a criterion of Jewish nationality in several countries. It is well known that Yiddish developed in Southern and Central Germany, in the twelfth century.

are a people, the people of peoples, the people of God. They
are a consecrated tribe; they are a *house,* the house of Israel.
Race, People, Tribe—all these words, if they are to designate
the Jews, must be made sacred.

☼ ☼ ☼

Israel is a mystery. Of the same order as the mystery of the
world or the mystery of the Church. Like them, it lies at the
heart of the Redemption. A philosophy of history, aware of
theology, can attempt to reach some knowledge of this mystery, but the mystery will surpass that knowledge in all directions. Our ideas and our consciousness can be immersed in such
things; they cannot circumscribe them.

If Saint Paul is right, we shall have to call the *Jewish problem* a problem *without solution*—that is, until the great reintegration foreseen by the apostle, which will be like a "resurrection from the dead." To wish to find, in the pure, simple, decisive sense of the word, a *solution* of the problem of Israel,
is to attempt to stop the movement of history.

What made the rationalist-minded "liberal" position of the
nineteenth century intrinsically weak, despite its great historical
merit, when it was confronted with this problem, was precisely
that it set itself up as a decisive solution.

The solution of a practical problem is the end of tension
and conflict, the end of contradiction, peace itself. To assert
that there is no solution—in an absolute sense—to the problem
of Israel is to ensure the existence of struggle. There are two
methods for this: an animalistic method, which is one of violence and hate, of war that is open or covert, prudent or furious,
a war of the flesh aimed at the extermination, the riddance,
or the enslavement of the Jews, a war of the world, of the
animalis homo against Israel. This is the *anti-Semitic* method.
The other is the Christian method. It consists in entering
through compassion into the sufferings of the Messiah and

through the intelligence of charity into a spiritual struggle
aimed at accomplishing the work of man's deliverance, the
struggle of the Church and of the *spiritualis homo* for the salvation of the world and the salvation of Israel. This is the
Catholic, the Pauline way, which furthermore would have us
take part at the temporal level in the constant work of the
concrete intelligence which neither definitively resolves nor
overcomes antinomies, but at each moment in time discovers
whatever is needed to make them bearable and more supple.

III

IT IS DIFFICULT not to be struck by the extraordinary baseness
of the leading themes of anti-Semitic propaganda. The men
who claim the existence of a world-wide conspiracy of Israel
for the enslavement of all nations, the existence of ritual murder, the universal perversion of the Jews effected by the Tal-
mud; or who explain that Jewish hysteria is the cause of all the
woes suffered by the blue-eyed dolichocephalic blond (a characteristic of those superior races where brown eyes and brown
hair unfortunately are more often met with); or who explain
that the Jews are united in a scheme to corrupt morally and to
subvert politically all Christendom, as it appears in an obviously forged document, the Protocols of the Elders of Zion;
in short, who know that all Jews are excessively rich and that
the earth would prosper again if only we could once and for
all do away with this monstrous race;—such men seem to prove
that it is impossible to hate the Jewish people and at the same
time remain an intelligent being. (In this they curiously resemble those who hate priests and cite the *Monita secreta* of the
Jesuits, or the fact, well known in certain isolated districts of
the United States, that Catholic priests have cloven hoofs.) To
a mind sufficiently alert, this baseness itself seems disquieting:
it must have a mystical meaning. Stupidity pushed too far im-

pinges upon mystery and hides the demonic instinct of the
shadow world of the irrational.

It has been said that the tragedy of Israel is the tragedy of
mankind; and that is why there is no solution to the Jewish
problem. Let us state it more precisely: it is the tragedy of man
in his struggle with the world and of the world in its struggle
with God. Jacob, lame and dreaming, tireless irritant of the
world and scapegoat of the world, indispensable to the world
and intolerable to the world—so fares the wandering Jew. The
persecution of Israel seems like the sign of the moments of
crisis in this tragedy, when the play of human history almost
stops at obstacles that the distress and moral weakness of nations cannot surmount, and when for a new start it demands
some fresh horror. There is a supra-human relation between
Israel and the world as there is between the Church and the
world. It is only by taking into account these three terms that
some idea of the mystery of Israel can, even obscurely, be formulated. A kind of inverted analogy with the Church must
serve, I believe, as our guide. Through trying to perceive a
mystery of suffering by the light of a mystery of grace, we are
led to use in an improper meaning ideas and expressions properly belonging to an altogether different object.

Jewish thought itself is aware that Israel is in its own way a
corpus mysticum.[8] The bond which forms the unity of Israel
is not solely the bond of flesh and blood, nor of an ethico-historical society; and yet it is not the bond of the communion of
saints, the bond which forms the unity of the Church, through
faith in the incarnate God and through the possession of His
heritage. (Of course Israel understands the meaning of the
communion of saints and longs for it! But if it is true that its
Christ came and that Israel failed to recognize Him and thus,
on that day, failed in its own faith and in its own mission, so

[8]*Cf.* Erich Kahler, *Israël unter den Völkern,* Humanitas Verlag,
Zurich.

straightway it lost the trust of dispensing to souls, through the signs of the Ancient Law, the grace of the Christ to come, while at the same time it repudiated the office of dispensing to souls, through the efficacy of the New Law, the grace of Christ already come; in other words, it repudiated the bond which would have really made the communion of saints its unity within a mystical body.) The bond of Israel remains a sacred and supra-historical bond, but a bond of promise, not of possession; of nostalgia, not of sanctity. For a Christian who remembers that the promises of God are without repentance, Israel continues its sacred mission, but in the night of the world which it preferred to God's night. (There are many Jews who prefer God to the world and many Christians who prefer the world to God. But I am referring to the choice which the religious authority of Israel made when it condemned the Son of Man and rejected the gospel.) Blindfolded, the Synagogue still moves forward in the universe of God's plans. It is itself only gropingly aware of this its path in history.

Kingdom of God in the state of pilgrimage and crucifixion— the Church is in the world and is not of the world; and, however much she suffers from the world, she is free of the world and already delivered.

People of God famished for the Kingdom, and who would not have it—Israel is in the world and is not of the world; but it is attached to the world, subject to the world, in bondage to the world. One day Israel stumbled and was caught in a trap; it stumbled against God—and in what an encounter, never to be repeated! Israel did not know what it was doing; but its leaders knew that they were making their choice against God. In one of those acts of free will which involve the destiny of a whole community, the priests of Israel, the bad watchers in the vineyard, the slayers of prophets, with excellent reasons of political prudence, chose the world, and to that choice their whole people was henceforth bound—until it changes of its own accord. A crime of clerical misfeasance, unequalled prototype of all similar crimes.

If the concept of Karma is wrong in that it transfers punishment from the moral to the purely physical order, the Western idea of punishment is too often weighted with a juridical anthropomorphism. Penalty is not the arbitrary contrivance of some wound inflicted from without upon an unimpaired being to satisfy the law. It is—in the moral order itself—the fruit of the wound inflicted on a being through his own freedom voluntarily at fault, and this natural fruit *is* the satisfaction of the law. The penalty is the working out of the fault; our punishment is our choice. It is terrible to fall into the hands of the living God, for those hands give to each man what his will has settled on.

The Jews (I do not mean the Jews individually, but the mystical body of Israel at the moment when it struck against the rock) the Jews at a crucial moment chose the world; they have loved it; their penalty is to be held captive by their choice. Prisoners and victims in this world which they love, but of which they are not, will never be, cannot be.

The Church is universal, spread throughout all civilizations and all nations like a transcendent unity or community whereto from the depths of temporal diversity each man and all men may be lifted, in order to be made sons of God's lineage through the vivifying blood of the Son of God. The mystical body of Israel is that of a specific people; its basis is temporal and involves a community of flesh and blood. If it is to spread in the universe, it must do so disjointed from itself, broken and dispersed. The diaspora—already begun before the Christian era—is the earthly and bruised counterpart of the universality of the Church.

The mystical body of Israel is a Church fallen from a high place. It is not a "counter"-Church, any more than there exists a "counter"-God, or a "counter"-Spouse. It is an unfaithful

Church (such is the true meaning of the liturgical phrase, *perfidia Judaica,* which does not at all mean that the Jews are perfidious).[9] The mystical body of Israel is an unfaithful and a repudiated Church (and that is why Moses had figuratively given forth the *libellum repudii*)—repudiated as a Church, not as a people. And ever awaited by the Bridegroom, who has never ceased to love her.

❀ ❀ ❀

She knows that she is awaited, but knows it obscurely.

The communion of this mystical body is not the communion of saints; it is the communion of earthly hope. Israel passionately hopes for, awaits, wants the advent of God in the world, the kingdom of God *here below*. It wants, with an eternal will, a supernatural and unreasonable will, justice in time, in nature, and in the community. Greek wisdom has no meaning for Israel: neither its reasonableness nor its felicity in form. The beauty Israel seeks is ineffable, and Israel wants it in this life of the flesh, today.

A faith which would do violence to the seeming plan of the world in order to give a man today, tangibly, the substance for which he hopes and the accomplishment of the desire which God has planted in him, and hence would have him recapture everything spiritual and temporal—such is the faith of Israel. It is such a faith Israel is burning to have, and at the same time doubts it has (for if Israel had it, it would have all justice and

[9]*Cf.* Erik Peterson, *Perfidia Judaica,* in *Ephemerides Liturgicae,* 1936. The author shows that in patristic literature the word *perfidia* is used in the sense of "unbelief" or "infidelity," particularly in connection with the Jews, and that such is the original meaning of the liturgical expression, *perfidia Judaica;* it is by a subsequent change of meaning that in the Middle Ages this phrase assumed in popular usage the sense of *perfidious,* at the same time as crept in (ninth century) the omission of the genuflection in the prayer for the Jews on Good Friday. It is to be hoped that an innovation made in the ninth century can be changed again in the future.

plenitude). In modern times this faith has progressively weakened as rationalism has increased. Of such a notion of faith, which seems to me profoundly Jewish, Chestov's philosophy affords us incomparable evidence.

And Jewish charity is also a virtue fallen from a high place. I do not mean in any way that it is a false love. Divine charity can be present in it, as it may be absent from it. Nor is it Lutheran pity, nor Slavic pity. It is an active and, on occasion, a relentless love of the creature as such; it grapples the creature, torments it, never lets it go, so as to oblige it to become aware of its evil and deliver itself from its evil.

Of earthly hope the Jews have an excess; and of this virtue many Christians have not enough. The basic weakness in the mystical communion of Israel is its failure to understand the Cross, its refusal of the Cross, and therefore its refusal of the transfiguration. The aversion to the Cross is typical of that Judaism of the Exile, which does not mean Christianity's first outline and imperfect beginning, as Judaism is by essence, but which indicates the spiritual pattern which shapes Israel's severance from its Messiah. With all Jews in whom grace dwells, as with all souls of good faith and good will, the work of the Cross is present, but veiled and unperceived, and involuntarily experienced. Despite himself, and in an obscuring mist, the pious Jew, the Jew of the spirit, carries the gentle Cross, and thus betrays Judaism without realizing what he does. The moment he begins to be aware of this mystery of forgiveness and of this putting off of self, he finds himself on the road to Christianity.

In Jesus alone and in His mystical Body taken as such, the devil plays no part. He does play his part in Israel, as in the world, but Israel struggles against him. The drama of Israel is to struggle against the Prince of this world while yet loving the world and being attached to the world; and while knowing better than anyone else the value of the world.

Israel plays a dual part with regard to the history of the world and the salvation of the world. In what *directly* concerns this salvation, Israel has given the Saviour to the world; and now it remains a witness. It preserves the treasure of the scriptures (it must not be forgotten that the Church took unto herself for her own use the labour of the rabbis and the Masoretes for the establishment of the text of scripture, just as she used the work of the philosophers and of Aristotle for her theology); and Israel is itself, throughout time, a living and indestructible depository of the promises of God.

In what *indirectly* concerns the salvation of the world, Israel is obedient to a vocation which I think above all deserves emphasis, and which supplies a key for many enigmas. Whereas the Church is assigned the task of the supernatural and supratemporal saving of the world, to Israel is assigned, in the order of temporal history and its own finalities, the work of the *earthly leavening* of the world. Israel is here—Israel which is not of the world—at the deepest core of the world, to irritate it, to exasperate it, to *move* it. Like some foreign substance, like a living yeast mixed into the main body, it gives the world no quiet, it prevents the world from sleeping, it teaches the world to be dissatisfied and restless so long as it has not God, it stimulates the movement of history.

The passion of Israel is not, like that of the Church, a passion of co-redemption, completing what is lacking in the sufferings of the Saviour. This passion is not suffered for the eternal salvation of souls, but for the stimulation and emancipation of temporal life. It is the passion of a scapegoat, enmeshed in the earthly destiny of the world and in the ways of the world mixed with sin, a scapegoat against which the impure sufferings of the world strike back, when the world seeks vengeance for the misfortunes of its history upon what activates that history. Israel thus suffers the repercussion of the activation it produces, or which the world feels it is destined to produce.

⚙   ⚙   ⚙

Saint Paul assures us that God has imprisoned all men in disobedience, that He may have mercy on all. From this point of view Jews and Christians have inversely corresponding rôles. Israel failed in the spiritual and supernatural order; and when, through the breach offered by its fall, "the fullness of the Gentiles should come in," the Church, having reached its third epoch,[10] and exulting in the return of the people of God, will know the fullness of its earthly dimensions and of its heroic pilgrimage.

The fault of Christians resides in the temporal order. Obviously I am not thinking of the individual achievements of saints, but of the collective historic responsibilities of Christians. I do not refer to the "worthiness of Christianity," but to the "unworthiness of Christians." By some sort of mysterious indifference to the requirements of the Gospel with regard to earthly society and to temporal history, the collective mass of those called Christian, because it has again and again consented to the accumulated injustice of centuries, has allowed the social and political structures of the world, the body of temporal society, to escape the vivifying law of Jesus Christ, which alone is able to preserve for us human rights and dignity.

And when this historical process shall have reached its fullness, when man shall have reached the ultimate consequences of wishing through himself alone to save himself and the world, it is possible to believe that another reintegration—this time in the temporal order, and relating to the multitudes who seek life far removed from Christ—will coincide with that which we have just considered, and that this reintegration will also be, for the world, a resurrection from the dead; and that Israel reconciled will play therein a major part. We have already said that Israel is charged with activating the history of the world. And also that the abiding mission still assigned

[10]*Cf.* the second commentary on the *Canticle of Canticles,* attributed to St. Thomas Aquinas.

to Israel, since through its fault it has left to others the care of the kingdom of heaven, is, under the contrasting forms wherein good and evil are intertwined, the acceleration of the movement of temporal things, and the hastening of the world's business, in view of the account which the world must settle with God. Consider, in this connection, of what richly symbolic value is the famous fondness of the Jews for business, and the fact that, since the Babylonian captivity, commerce is their principal occupation, wherein they do not merely excel, like other oriental peoples, but wherein they find the mental stimulation which they need, and even a sort of *spiritual* satisfaction.[11]

Let us consider once more this strange inter-crossing symmetry which holds our attention. As to Christians, the Church follows her divine vocation, and it is not Christianity, it is Christendom, the Christian world, which has failed (in the temporal order) without being willing to hear the voice of the Church who, while she directs men toward eternal life, also requires them to help the development of life on earth along the lines of the Gospel. For the Jews, it is Israel as a Church, it is Judaism which has failed (in the spiritual order); and it is Israel still as the chosen people, it is "Jewdom" which pursues in history a supernatural (yet ambiguous) vocation.

IV

LIKE THE WORLD and the history of the world, the mystical body of Israel and its activity in the world are ambivalent activities, and what I have already said may permit us to under-

[11]"They feel happy in an atmosphere of risk and uncertainty, illumined by hope. . . . The Jew never foregoes hope, and it is this which permits him to adapt himself to new conditions. He is not beaten down by reverses, and always expects things to get better. . . . This frame of mind is especially useful in the uncertainties of trade. . . ." Arthur Ruppin, lecturer on Jewish sociology at the Hebrew University of Jerusalem, *Les Juifs dans le Monde Moderne,* Paris, Payot, 1934.

stand that, in the case of Israel, this ambivalence is carried to an extreme. This is what happens with all consecrated people, whose power for good and for evil is supernaturally increased.

The will to attain the absolute in the world can assume all forms. It can,—when it confines itself to what is human and contingent, or when it turns to atheism, at least in practice— create that overgrowth of activity in the handling of the goods of the earth and in money making, which finds in capitalist civilization an appropriate ambience;[12] or it can create that revolutionary impatience and that ceaseless agitation which Bernard Lazare and many other Jews liked to point out. When it becomes feverish from wounded sensibility or resentment,

---

[12]Be it a matter of free competition, or of interest on borrowed money, or of price conceived as the result of bargaining, rather than as the expression of the objective value of a thing ("fair price"), these are ideas that fit in with the Jewish economic conceptions (more generally, with the Oriental economic conceptions) which the shift from the mediæval system of guilds to the capitalist system has made predominant.

I certainly do not think that the Jews alone are responsible for the advent of capitalism. R. H. Tawney, J. B. Kraus, A. Fanfani have corrected the excessive thesis of Werner Sombart. But in this advent the Jews played a part; and whereas the Christian mediæval economy, with the guild system and the prohibition of lending at interest, was contrary to their conceptions, it has been possible to say that the "commercial practices of the Jews found themselves rehabilitated" by the advent of capitalism, "since the search after profits and free competition became the bases of the capitalist system." (A. Ruppin, *op. cit.*) "The investment of capital in commercial and industrial enterprises thenceforth took the place of usury," says the same author. In an interesting chapter he shows that the abandonment of free competition, which, before the War of 1914, had been considered as the guiding principle of the capitalist system, dealt a heavy blow to the economic prosperity of the Jews. "There is no more room for the Jew in commerce and industry while a degenerate capitalism is changing into state capitalism, and his condition once more approaches that which it was at the end of the Middle Ages, when the officially approved guild system restrained to his detriment the play of free competition. The birth of capitalism had improved the position of the Jews, its disappearance threatens them anew." "Das Judentum erreicht seinen Höhepunkt in der Vollendung der bürgerlichen Gesellschaft," wrote Karl Marx in *Zur Judenfrage.*

it may create a violent pessimism which makes out of bitterness and anger a singularly powerful instrument of discovery, a detector (itself out of gauge) of the self-deceit involved in the pleasure of enjoying a noble soul, of enjoying an orderly existence and a clear conscience. Finally, it can produce, when of the flesh but affecting spiritual things, a pharisaic trend of mind, and the blinding refinements of the harsh cult of the letter, a legal purism.

But when it is of the spirit, this will toward the absolute brings to flower seeds of true purity, the purity of soul and of morals preserved in the tradition of so many Jewish families. It produces asceticism and piety, love for the word of God and for its sensitive interpretation, uprightness of heart and subtle innocence, and that burning spirituality exemplified especially by the Hassidic mystics, and which shows us the true visage of Israel "when Israel loves God." And above all, this will finds expression in the zeal for justice and in the love of truth which is the most exalted indication of this people's election. "Behold in truth an Israelite, in whom there is no guile." The Saviour himself gave witness to the true Israel. The true sons of Zion ever feel as they did in the days of the Psalmist and of Isaiah: "How beautiful upon the mountains the footsteps of those who bear peace . . . O, never take from my mouth the word of Truth."

> "Viens étancher la soif de ta justice pure
> et de toi-même, Dieu! ô ma source, ô ma fin!"[13]

The love of truth even unto death, the will for truth, pure, absolute, unattainable since truth is that very One whose Name in ineffable,—this is what the best of the Jews owe to Israel and to the Holy Spirit and this is what makes exultant their song in the fiery furnace.

[13]Come, Thou and quench my thirst for Thy pure justice
And for Thyself, O God! O my source, O my end!
(Raïssa Maritain, *Lettre de Nuit*.)

To recapitulate: Israel's ambivalence and its destiny's ambiguity are most clearly to be seen in the double center of attraction—one illusory, the other real—which divide its existence. To the extent that Israel has quit reality for an illusory image, money (here is one of the most profound themes of Léon Bloy, and certain of Karl Marx's phrases have a similar sound) has for Israel a mystical attraction, for money among the world's most shadowy shadows is the palest and the least real image of the Son of God. Léon Bloy used to say that money is the poor man's blood, the poor man's blood transmuted into a sign. In that sign and through that sign, and the signs of that sign, man serves an inert omnipotence which does everything man wants; he ends up in a kind of cynical theocracy, the ultimate *religious* temptation of whoever refuses the reality of the gift of God.

But to the extent that Israel is ever beloved and ever relies on the promises without repentance, it is God's justice, as I have just said—and God's justice to be made manifest in this life—which is Israel's other center of attraction. It is real this time, not illusory; where others say a wise man, or a saint, the Jew says a "just" man. It is earthly hope and it is poverty,—no people know better than the Jewish people how to be poor and know better (however little they love it, however much they dislike it) the generating power of poverty.[14] Here by the waters of Babylon is the sighing for the Jerusalem of Justice, here is the cry of the prophets, the expectation and the endless desire for the terrible glory of God.

Thus, in such a complexity, in so mad a discord of typical

[14]"Yet, writing a book on the Poor Man," Léon Bloy said, "how could I not have spoken of the Jews? What people is as poor as the Jewish people? Ah, I well know, there are the bankers, the money lenders. Legend, tradition demand that all the Jews be usurers. People refuse to believe anything else. And this legend is a lie. For it pertains to the muddy residue of the Jewish world. Those who know the Jew and regard him without prejudice realize that this people possesses quite other

characteristics and inclinations, there will always be reason to exalt Israel, and reason to debase it. Those who want to hate a people, never lack pretexts; particularly when that people's vocation is extraordinary and its psychology contrasting. Tactlessness, ostentation, self-esteem, an almost artistic feeling for success and a loud bewailing of suffered injury—many defects are charged to this tenacious people and make some of them irritating. Jews are on the average more intelligent and quicker than Gentiles. They profit thereby; they do not know hòw to make people forgive them their success. The traffic of the money lender or the merchant, the various non-productive businesses and occupations which, indeed, they are not the only ones to practice, but which have become perforce for them an hereditary habit,[15] and at which they are unbeatable—are not designed to attract the favour of people, themselves as eager for gain but less expert.

When they gather in the high places of culture to worship the idols of the nations, Jews become corrupted. And as with other spiritual groups, it is only rarely that the best of them mount the stage of politics and show.

These are pretexts against the Jews; and whenever they would appear to justify hatred or discriminatory measures, such allegations are always unjust. If men could tolerate each

---

aspects and that, bearing the misery of the centuries, it infinitely suffers.

"The teaching of the Church throughout all times indicates that holiness is inherent in this exceptional, unique, and imperishable people, protected by God, preserved as the apple of His eye, in the midst of the destruction of so many peoples, for the accomplishment of His ulterior Purpose. Even the abasement of this race is a divine omen, the very visible omen of the permanence of the Holy Spirit in this so scorned a people, who must rise up in the Glory of the Comforter on the last day." Léon Bloy, *Le Vieux de la Montagne,* 2 janvier 1910.

[15]Under certain historical conditions they turn preferably to certain kinds of professions, above all the liberal professions. Under different historical conditions they turn elsewhere. The Zionist Colony is only one example, proving a "return to the land" and agriculture is possible for many Jews.

other only on condition that no one bear grievance against another, all sections of a country would constantly be at war.

And the Jews have more good qualities than defects. Those who have frequented them enough to have shared in their life know the incomparable quality of Jewish goodness. When a Jew is good, he has a quality and a depth of goodness rarely encountered among people whose natural sharpness has been less matured by suffering. They know of what virtues of humanity, of generosity, of friendship the Jewish soul is capable. Péguy made famous his Jewish friendships. It is among "grasping" Jews that one can meet the most unreasonable examples of that natural propensity for giving, which perhaps comes not so much from the wish to be a benefactor as from the utter lack of protective boundaries and defenses against pity. Nothing is more disarmed, more tender than Jewish goodness. Jews have done more in the world for Knowledge and Wisdom than for commerce and trade. A very high feeling for the purity of the family and for the virtues which follow in its wake, has long since characterized Jews. They have the fundamental human virtue of patience in work. They have an innate love for independence and liberty, the abiding flame of the ancient prophetic instinct, the intellectual fire, the quickness of intuition and abstraction, the faculty of passionate dedication and devotion to ideas. If it is true, as Psichari dared to say, that God prefers sin to stupidity, then His liking for the Jews (and for some others) becomes understandable. One is never bored with a Jew. Their nostalgia, their energy, the naïveté of their finesse, their ingenuity, their knowledge of penury are all rare tonics for the mind. I remember with what joy, in a large city of the United States, after lectures and university gatherings, I, who am a *goy,* would go to the home of Jewish friends to refresh myself in the vitality of that tireless pathos and the perpetual motion of ideas which vivified for me long centuries of painful refining of the soul and the intelligence.

But it is above all important to note that the various special causes to which an observer may attribute anti-Semitism,[16] from the feeling of hatred for strangers which is natural—too natural—in any social group, to the social dislocations created by large-scale immigration, and to the various grievances I have already described,[17] serve to hide an even deeper root of hatred. If the world hates the Jews, it is because the world is well aware that they will always be *supernaturally* strangers to it; it is because the world detests their passion for the absolute and the unbearable activation with which this passion stimulates it. It is the vocation of Israel which the world execrates— a hatred which can turn against the race bearing that vocation, or against the various forms of temporal manifestation which outwardly express and mask this vocation. *Odium generis humani.* Hated by the world, this is their glory, as it is also the glory of those Christians who live by faith. But Christians—by virtue of their Mystical Body—have overcome the world[18] and the Jews have not; that is why for a Jew to become a Christian is a double victory: his people triumphs in him. Woe to the Jew—and to the Christian—who is pleasing to men! And the time is perhaps coming, has already come in certain countries, when the witnessing of the one and the witnessing of the other being alike judged intolerable, both will be hated and persecuted together. And, united in persecution, they will together be brought back to their sources.

The Jew is lost if he settles down, and by *settling down* I

[16]A good sociological analysis of these causes will be found in the already quoted work by Arthur Ruppin.

[17]For the various shallow, half-baked or sophistic arguments commonly used in anti-Semitic propaganda, see my book, *A Christian Looks at the Jewish Question,* pp. 3–9.

[18]True Christians have overcome it for eternal life. God's commandments are not grievous, wrote Saint John, "For whatsoever is born of God overcometh the world: and the victory which overcometh the world is our faith. Who is he that overcometh the world, if not he who believeth that Jesus is the Son of God?" (I John v:4–5).

mean a spiritual phenomenon, like the loss of a stimulating disquiet and the failure of a vocation. *Assimilation* involves an altogether different problem, in the social and political, not spiritual, order. An "assimilated" Jew may be one who is not "settled." Assimilation is not the solution of Israel's problem, any more than is Yiddishism or Zionism; but assimilation, like autonomy and Zionism, is a partial accommodation, a compromise solution, good and desirable to the extent that it is possible. Assimilation took place in the past on a large scale in the Hellenistic and Hispano-Arabic periods. Yet it carries with it a risk—as does also Zionism (as a state)—the risk of the Jews becoming settled, becoming *like others* (I mean spiritually). It is the risk of losing the vocation of the house of Israel. Their God then strikes them down by the vilest of instruments. Never had there been Jews more assimilated than the German Jews. They were all the more attached to German culture for its having in part been their achievement. They had become totally Germans, which did not make them either more discreet or more humble. They were not only assimilated, but settled down, conciliatory and well reconciled with the Prince of this world. Jews who become like others become worse than others. (When a Jew receives Christian grace, he is less than ever like others: he has found *his* Messiah.)

❖   ❖   ❖

"The Jews [wrote Charles Péguy[19]] know what is the cost of being the fleshly voice and the temporal body. They know what is the cost of bearing God and his agents, the prophets. His prophets, the prophets. Then, obscurely, they hope that one need not begin anew. . . . They have fled so often, and in so many and such dire flights, that they know how precious a thing it is not to flee. They have pitched their tents, they have entered a little into modern peoples; how much they would

[19]Charles Péguy, *Notre Jeunesse.*

like there to find themselves at ease. All the Policy [the political mood] of Israel consists in not making any noise (so much noise has been made in the world), in buying peace by a prudent silence. . . . They are still bleeding from so many lacerations.

"But all the Mystic [the mystical impulsion] of Israel demands that Israel continue in the world its resounding and suffering mission. Hence incredible rendings, hence the most painful internal antagonisms that ever perhaps have existed between a Policy and a Mystic. People of merchants. And at once people of prophets. One quality knows for the other what calamities are. . . .

"I know this people well. On its skin it has no single spot which is not painful, where is not some old bruise, some old contusion, some silent woe, the memory of a silent woe, a scar, a wound, a laceration from Orient or Occident. . . ."

v

I HAVE SPOKEN of the extreme stupidity of the anti-Semitic myths, and I have said that even this stupidity conveys a hidden meaning. The hatred of the Jews and the hatred of the Christians spring from the same source, from the same will of the world *which refuses to be wounded* either with the wounds of Adam, or with the wounds of the Messiah, or by the spear of Israel for its movement in time, or by the Cross of Jesus for eternal life. Man is well off as he is; he needs no grace, no transfiguration; he will be beatified in his own nature. Here there is no Christian hope in God the Helper, nor Jewish hope in God on earth. Here is the hope of animal life and its deep power, in a certain sense sacred, demonic, whenever it takes possession of the human being who believes himself deceived by those who bear tidings of the absolute.

Tellurian racism is anti-Semitic and anti-Christian. Communist atheism is not anti-Semitic; it is sufficient that it be universally against God.[20] In both, the same absolute naturalism, the same detestation of all asceticism and of everything transcendent comes to light. Enough of God's constraint; let us now try man's,—we shall see whether it is sweeter. No more slave morality—morality of the weak, the suffering, the impotent disguised as the merciful. We shall see if the morality of blood and the morality of sweat are not the moralities of free men. The mystical life of the *world* will now blossom forth heroically; every *corpus mysticum* set apart from the world must be rejected as such.

But what has happened? History has so *intoxicated* them with Judæo-Christianity that they cannot help wishing to *save the world*. The racists remain the debtors of the Old Testament as do the Communists of the New. It is from the Jewish Scriptures that the former have taken—only to corrupt it—the idea of a predestined race; it is from the Gospel that the latter have taken and distorted the idea of a universal emancipation and human brotherhood.

✿　　✿　　✿

As much hated by the world as is the Jew, and equally out of his place in the world, but himself grafted into the olive tree of Judah, and member of a mystical body which is the Body of the Messiah of Israel victorious over the world, the Christian alone can assign its proper dimensions to the Jewish tragedy. It is with feelings of brotherly love, and not without fear for himself, that he should look at the men involved in this tragedy. From the one side and from the other, Jews and Christian answer each other. If both of them are pious and good, they know one another, they smile at meeting on the premises of the Prince of this world and on the roads of Jahveh.

[20]The Soviet régime takes pride in its radical opposition to anti-Semitism. Yet on the religious plane, Judaism has suffered as much in Russia as Christianity, and has offered far less resistance to the anti-religious campaign. Cf. *A Christian Looks at the Jewish Question*, pp. 44–46.

The reflections which make up this chapter have as their object the explanation, in some measure, of the pathos of the position of the Jewish people. Perhaps such reflections help us to understand how, often despite itself, and at times manifesting in various ways a materialized Messianism, which is the darkened aspect of its vocation to the absolute, the Jewish people, ardently, intelligently, actively, give witness, at the very heart of man's history, to the supernatural. Whence the conflicts and tensions which, under all kinds of disguises, cannot help but exist between Israel and the nations.

It is an illusion to believe that this tension can disappear (at least before the fulfilment of the prophecies). It is base—one of those specimens of baseness natural to man as an animal (be he an Arab, and himself of the lineage of Shem, or a Slav, or a Latin, or a German . . .) and a baseness of which Christianity alone can, to the degree that it is truly lived, free mankind—to wish to end the matter by anti-Semitic violence, whether it be of open persecution, or politically "mitigated." There is but one way, and that is to accept this state of tension, and to make the best of it in each particular case, not in hatred, but in that concrete intelligence which love requires of each of us, so that we may agree with our companion—with our "adversary" as the gospel says—quickly while we are with him on the way;[21] and in the awareness that "all have sinned and have need of the glory of God"—*omnes quidem peccaverunt, et egent gloria Dei.* "The history of the Jews," said Léon Bloy, "dams the history of the human race as a dike dams a river, in order to raise its level."[22]

[21]Matt. v:25.

[22]Léon Bloy, *Le Salut par les Juifs.* Among Catholic contributions to the study of the problem of Israel, I should like to mention the study by Erik Peterson already cited, *Le Mystère des Juifs et des Gentils dans l'Église;* and the penetrating pages written by Charles Péguy in *Notre Jeunesse* and in *Note Conjointe sur M. Descartes;* also Louis Massignon, *Pro Psalmis (Revue Juive,* 15 mars, 1925); Jean de Ménasce, *Situation du*

This permanent tension appears in two very different manners—one on the spiritual level, the other on the temporal.

On the spiritual level, the drama of love between Israel and its God, which makes Gentiles participate in the economy of salvation, and which is but one element in the universal mystery of salvation, will be resolved only in the reconciliation of the Synagogue and the Church. In the important text quoted at the beginning of this chapter Saint Paul says to the Gentile Christian: "See, then, the goodness and the severity of God, towards them indeed that are fallen, the severity, but towards thee, the goodness of God: if thou abide in goodness, otherwise thou also shalt be cut off." Considering the condition of the world, and the way in which the nations give witness that they *abide in goodness,* one is tempted to wonder whether tomorrow will not see the resolution. In any case nothing requires us to think that the resolution will come at the end of human history, rather than at the beginning of a new age for the Church and the world.

⚙   ⚙   ⚙

On the temporal level, even if there is no solution in the pure and simple meaning of the word, before the fulfilment of the prophecies,—no truly decisive solution for the problem of Israel, there are nevertheless *certain* solutions, partial or provisional, particular answers to the problem whose disentangle-

Sionisme and *Quand Israël aime Dieu* (*Le Roseau d'Or*); the Rev. Joseph Bonsirven, *Sur les ruines du Temple, Juifs et Chrétiens, Les Juifs et Jésus* (I hope that the lectures on Judaism given by the same author at the Institut Catholique of Paris in 1938 may one day be published); O. de Férenzy, *Les Juifs et nous chrétiens;* the article published in *Die Erfüllung* (1937) under the title *Die Kirche Christi und die Judenfrage* and signed by several Catholic writers and teachers (translated in part and published in pamphlet form by National Catholic Welfare Conference, Washington); and the periodicals, *La Question d'Israël* (a bulletin published by the Fathers of Our Lady of Zion) and *La Juste Parole* (**Paris**). See also Rabbi Jacob Kaplan's work, *Témoignages sur Israël,* Paris, 1935.

ment is the duty of political wisdom and which it is the task of various historical periods to attempt.

The Middle Ages tried a "sacral" solution, in accordance with the typical structure of the civilization of that time. This solution, which was based on the presupposition that a sacred penalty, inflicted by God, not by men, weighed on the destinies of Israel, and which gave Jews the status of foreigners in the Christian community, the solution of the ghetto,[23] was hard in itself and often iniquitous and bloody in practice. Yet it proceeded from a high concept, and was in any case better than the bestial materialism of the racist laws initiated in our own day by Germany. It was on the religious, not at all on the racial, level. It recognized the privileges of the soul, and the baptized Jews entered as a matter of right into the full fellowship of the Christian community. This mediæval solution has gone, never to return, like the kind of civilization from whence it sprang.

The emancipation of the Jews, brought about by the French Revolution, is a fact which civilized people, to the extent that they remain such, should consider definitive. If indeed this emancipation was in itself a just and necessary thing (and a thing which corresponded to a Christian aspiration) nevertheless the hopes which the rationalist and bourgeois-optimist way of thinking, forgetful at once of the mystery of Israel and of supra-individual realities, had based upon this emancipation to *extinguish* the Jewish problem, were soon to prove vain.

It looks as if the time into which we are entering is called upon to try another experiment. The régime of which I am

---

[23]The ghetto itself did not become obligatory until the fourteenth and fifteenth centuries. I use this word as the symbol of a certain politico-juridic conception. Concerning this, see P. Browe, S.J., *Die Judengesetzgebung Justinians* (*Analecta Gregoriana*, VIII, Rome, 1935). On the doctrinal controversies and mediæval *apologiæ*, see the important work of A. Lukyn Williams, *Adversus Judæos* (*A Bird's Eye View of Christian Apologiæ until the Renaissance*), 1935, Cambridge University Press.

thinking and which far from having been conceived for the particular case of Israel, answers in a general way to the kind of civilization whose historic ideal suits our age, can summarily be described as *pluralist* and *personalist*.[24] In utter contrast to the insane Hitlerian parody of the mediæval way, shamefully accepted by the unhappy rulers of a crushed France, I think of a pluralism founded on the dignity of man, and which, on the basis of a complete equality in civic rights and of effective respect for the liberties of the person in his individual and social life, would accord to the various spiritual families participating in the fellowship of the temporal community a proper ethico-juridical status for the questions described as mixed (impinging on the spiritual and the temporal). Such a pluralism would represent, along with other advantages, for the nations that might be capable of this kind of civilization, an attempt at the organic ordering of the Jewish question best suited to our moment in history. By means of direct agreements with the Jewish spiritual community—as with the different Christian churches —a community institutionally recognized, such questions as concern this community and the common good of the political whole would be resolved.[25]

[24]Cf. *True Humanism*. Chapters IV and V.

[25]It is needless to say that in such a conception which relates to the temporal and socio-political fellowship of various spiritual families in the profane community, it is the *spiritual* not the *racial* which differentiates the statuses in question. In becoming Catholic or Protestant, a Jew would thus quit the juridical status of the Jewish spiritual family: which is not to say that he would quit Israel and its vocation.

Inversely, the Zionist homeland or the eventual Jewish State in Palestine being of a profane kind and based on nationality, not on the Israelite religion, it is logical that it makes room for baptized Jews who shall enjoy the full liberty of their religious life and shall be able to found colonies. It is well known that in 1933 the "Association of Christian Hebrews" whose headquarters are in London and which is made up of converted Jews, acquired lands in Southern Palestine, with a view to establishing baptized Jews there in agricultural colonies. (A. Ruppin, *op. cit.*, p. 16.) *Cf.* Simon Marcovici-Cléja, *Le Problème juif mondial*, Paris, 1938.

The pluralism I have outlined concerns the *spiritual families* which live together in the same political community. The same régime of organization of liberties in accordance with an order truly "political," and not "despotic," to use Aristotle's words, could and should extend in the countries which include a diversity of *national minorities,* to those diverse communities living together in the same political community (in the same state). And the horrible oppression suffered in our days by many national minorities seems to demand with a special urgency a solution of this sort. But spiritual family and national community are altogether different things; to a spiritual family one voluntarily gives oneself, to a national community one naturally belongs (although one can renounce it). A pluralist régime of spiritual families is compatible, not only with political fellowship in the State, but with a very complete national *assimilation*. A pluralist régime of national communities or minorities implies by definition the renouncing of *assimilation* (although it is in no way repugnant to political fellowship in the State). As far as the Jews are concerned, it is clear that in the countries where there exists a Jewish national community or minority, an inevitable complication would arise, under a pluralist régime, from the necessary distinction between the Jewish national community and the Jewish spiritual family. A man of non-Jewish nationality can become a convert to Judaism; a man belonging to a Jewish national minority can be a Christian or a free-thinker. Jurisdictional tangles of this sort are the price of any organic conception of social life; and moreover, as between the status of the spiritual community and the status of the national community, it is obviously the former which, in the event of a conflict of rights, should be regarded as having greater weight.

As for the Zionist homeland, or the future Jewish State of Palestine, it is to be feared that, even supposing it much larger than it can actually be, it would never suffice to receive all those who will flee the lands where anti-Semitic persecution rages. This is not the place to examine the question of Zionism, to which no mind aware of the unfolding of prophecy throughout history could be indifferent. Since it may be called upon to become one day the animating centre for all dispersed Jewry, Zionism seems to me to have an historic importance of the first order. But it does not yet represent deliverance from exile: the return to Palestine is but the prelude to such deliverance. No more than individualist liberalism or than the pluralist régime we have been discussing, can the Zionist State do away with the law of the desert and of the Galuth, which is not consubstantial with the Jewish people—this law *will* come to an end—but is essential to the mystical body and the vocation of Israel in the state of separation.

VI

It is when they obey the spirit of the world, not the spirit of Christianity, that Christians can be anti-Semitic. Much historical confusion, in the works of careless or impassioned writers, arises on this score from the fact of the intertwining, in mediæval civilization, of the things of the Church and of the things of a sacrally constituted temporal community, where earthly interests and all the good and all the evil of human social life were steeped in religion. If this confusion is avoided, it is possible to see that in a temporal civilization, where the régime of the ghetto—let alone the drama of the muranos and the Spanish Inquisition—encouraged (above all in the later Middle Ages and in the decay of feudalism) the worst anti-Jewish passions and excesses, the Church herself, apart from certain of her ministers, is not responsible for these excesses. It is well known that the Popes time and again defended the Jews, especially against the absurd accusation of the crime of ritual murder, and that the Jews were ordinarily less unhappy and less ill-treated in the Papal States than elsewhere.

Moreover, as it receded from the Holy Roman Empire and the mediæval régime, Western civilization, even though deteriorating in other respects, as we well know, freed itself from powerful impurities which that régime in fact carried in its train; and it would be a strange aberration for Christians to wish to come back to these impurities at the very moment when they have lost their historical occasion for existence. Anti-Semitism today is no longer one of the accidental weeds growing in a temporal Christendom intermixed with good and evil, but it is rather a disease of the spirit contaminating Christians.[26]

From the point of view of its moral quality in Catholic eyes, and when it spreads among those who call themselves disciples of Jesus Christ, anti-Semitism appears as a pathological phenomenon which reveals an adulteration of the Christian conscience, when it becomes incapable of assuming its own responsibilities in history and of remaining existentially faithful to the high requirements of Christian truth. Instead of recognizing as God's visitation the trials and shocks of history, and of assuming the necessary burdens of justice and charity, man's conscience falls back on substitution-phantoms, involving an entire race, to which certain real and fancied pretexts lend verisimilitude. And by giving free rein to feelings of hatred

[26]Let it not be forgotten that anti-Semitism has been explicitly condemned by the Catholic Church in a document of the Holy Office dated September 5, 1928 (directed against the mistakes of a too zealous "Association of the Friends of Israel"). Racist errors, already denounced in the encyclical *Mit Brennender Sorge,* have been again and expressly condemned in a document (Letter of the Pontifical Sacred Congregation of Seminaries and Universities, April 13, 1938). "Notice that Abraham is called our Patriarch, our ancestor. Anti-Semitism is incompatible with the thought and sublime reality expressed in this text. It is a movement in which Christians can have no part whatsoever . . . Anti-Semitism is unacceptable. Spiritually we are Semites," said Pope Pius XI in September, 1938. The American Hierarchy has also expressed itself on this matter. See article by Emmanuel Chapman, "The Catholic Church and Anti-Semitism," *The Social Frontier,* January, 1939.

which such a damaged conscience believes justified by religion, it seeks for itself a kind of alibi.

In truth, we are dealing here with a sort of collective "lapse," or with a substitute for an obscure and unconscious passion of anti-clericalism, or even of resentment against God. For, do what we will—or even do what it will—the people of Israel remains the priestly people. The bad Jew is a kind of bad priest; God will have no one raise his hand against either. And even before recognizing Christ, the true Israelite, in whom there is no guile, by virtue of an unbreakable promise, wears the livery of the Messiah.

It is no small thing for a Christian to hate or despise, or to wish to treat in a debasing way, the race whence issued his God and the immaculate Mother of his God. That is why the bitter zeal of anti-Semitism always at the end turns into a bitter zeal against Christianity.

"Suppose [wrote Léon Bloy], that people around you should continually speak of your father and your mother with the greatest scorn and treat them only to insults or outrageous sarcasm, how would you feel? Well, that is exactly what happens to Our Lord Jesus Christ. We forget, or rather we do not wish to know, that our God-made-man is a Jew, in nature the Jew of Jews, the Lion of Judah; that His Mother is a Jewess, the flower of the Jewish race; that the Apostles were Jews, as well as all the Prophets; and finally that our Holy Liturgy is altogether drawn from Jewish books. How, then, can we express the enormity of the outrage and blasphemy which lie in vilifying the Jewish race?

"Anti-Semitism . . . is the most horrible slap in the face suffered in the ever-continuing Passion of Our Lord: it is the most stinging and the most unpardonable because He suffers it on *His Mother's Face,* and at the hands of Christians."[27]

[27] Léon Bloy, *Le Vieux de la Montagne,* 2 janvier 1910.

Léon Bloy also said that the "veil," to which Saint Paul refers and which covers the eyes of Israel, is now passing "from the Jews to the Christians." This statement, which is harsh on the Gentiles and on the Christian distorters of Christianity, helps us understand something of the extensive and violent persecution to which the Jews today are victim, and of the spiritual upheaval which has been going on for years among many of them, denoting deep inward changes, particularly in respect to the person of Christ.

The growing solicitude in Israel's heart for the Just Man crucified through the error of the high priests is a symptom of unquestionable importance. Today in America representative Jewish writers like Sholem Asch and Waldo Frank are trying to reintegrate the gospel into the brotherhood of Israel. While not yet recognizing Jesus as the Messiah, they do recognize Him as the most pure Jewish figure in human history. They themselves would be disturbed to be considered as leaning toward Christianity. Yet while remaining closer than ever to Judaism, they believe that the gospel transcends the Old Testament and consider it a divine flower issuing from the stem of the Patriarchs and the Prophets. Never forgetful of the conflicts of history and of the harsh treatment received by their people, the authors of *Salvation* and of *The New Discovery of America,* have long studied and loved mediæval Christianity and Catholic spiritual life. They agree with Maurice Samuel that "christophobia" is the spiritual essence of the demoniacal racism of our pagan world. Many other signs give evidence that Israel is beginning to open its eyes, whereas the eyes of many self-styled Christians are blinded, darkened by the exhalations of the old pagan blood suddenly, ferociously welling up once more among Gentiles.

"Jesus Christ is in agony until the end of the world," said

Pascal. Christ suffers in every innocent man who is persecuted. His agony is heard in the cries of so many human beings humiliated and tortured, in the sufferings of all those images and likenesses of God treated worse than beasts. He has taken all these things upon Himself, He has suffered every wound. "Fear not, my child, I have already travelled that road. On each step of the abominable way I have left for you a drop of my blood and the print of my mercy."

But in the mystical body of the Church, the surplus humanity which Christ finds in each of the members of this His body, is called upon, in so far as each is a part of the whole, to participate in the work of this body, which is the redemption continued throughout time. Through and in the passion of His mystical body, Christ continues actively to perform the task for which he came, He acts as the Saviour and Redeemer of mankind.

I have already said that Israel's passion is not a co-redemptive passion, achieving for the eternal salvation of souls what is lacking (as concerns application, not merits) in the Saviour's suffering. It is suffered for the goading on of the world's temporal life. In itself, it is the passion of a being caught up in the temporal destiny of the world, which both irritates the world and seeks to emancipate it, and on which the world avenges itself for the pangs of its history. This does not mean that Christ is absent from the passion of Israel. Could He forget His people, who are still loved because of their fathers and to whom have been made promises without repentance? Jesus Christ suffers in the passion of Israel. In striking Israel, the anti-Semites strike Him, insult Him and spit on Him. To persecute the house of Israel is to persecute Christ, not in His mystical body as when the Church is persecuted, but in His fleshy lineage and in His forgetful people whom He ceaselessly loves and calls. In the passion of Israel, Christ suffers and acts as the shepherd of Zion and the Messiah of Israel, in order gradually to conform His people to Him. If there are any in the world today—but where are they?—who give heed to the meaning of the great racist persecutions and who try to understand that meaning, they will see Israel as drawn along the road to Calvary, by reason of that very vocation as stimulus of history which I have described, and because the slave merchants will not pardon it for the demands it and its Christ have implanted at the heart of the world's temporal life, demands which will ever cry "no" to the tyranny of force. Despite itself Israel is climbing Calvary, side by side with Christians—whose vocation concerns the Kingdom of God more than the temporal history of the world; and these strange companions are at times surprised to find each other mounting the same path. As in Marc Chagall's beautiful painting, the poor Jews, without understanding it, are swept along in the great tempest of the Crucifixion, around Christ, who is stretched

Across the lost world . . .
At the four corners of the horizon
Fire and Flames
Poor Jews from everywhere are walking
No one claiming them
They have no place on the earth
To rest—not a stone
The wandering Jews. . . .[28]

The central fact, which has its deepest meaning for the philosophy of history and for human destiny—and which no one

[28]A travers le monde perdu . . .
Aux quatre coins de l'horizon
Feu et Flammes
De pauvres Juifs de partout s'en vont
Personne qui les réclame
Ils n'ont plus de lieu sur la terre
Pour se reposer pas une pierre
Les Juifs errants. . . .
Raïssa Maritain, "Chagall" (*Lettre de Nuit,* Paris, 1939).

seems to take into account—is that *the passion of Israel today is taking on more and more distinctly the form of the Cross.*

Christ crucified extends His arms toward both Jews and Gentiles; He died, Saint Paul says, in order to reconcile the two peoples, and to break down the dividing barrier of enmity between them. "For He is our peace, He that hath made both one, and hath broken down the dividing barrier of enmity. He hath brought to naught in His flesh the law of commandments framed in decrees, that in Himself He might create of the two one new man, and make peace and reconcile both in one body to God through the cross, slaying by means thereof their enmity."[29]

If the Jewish people did not hear the call made to them by the dying Christ, yet do they remain ever summoned. If the Gentiles indeed heard the call, now racist paganism casts them away from it and from Him who is our peace. Anti-Semitic hatred is a directly anti-Christic frenzy to make vain the blood of Jesus and to make void His death. Reconciliation, breaking down the barrier of enmity—these, which the madness of men prevented love from accomplishing, and the frustration of which is the most refined torment in the sufferings of the Messiah— these agony now is the way of achieving, a universal agony in the likeness of that of the Saviour, both the agony of the racked, abandoned Jews and of the racked, abandoned Christians who live by faith. More than ever, the mystical body of Christ needs the people of God. In the darkness of the present day, that moment seems invisibly to be in preparation, however remote it still may be, when their reintegration, as Saint Thomas puts it, will "call back to life the Gentiles, that is to say the lukewarm faithful, when 'on account of the progress of iniquity, the charity of a great number shall have waxed cold' (Matt. xxiv: 12)."[30]

[29]Ephes. ii:14–16 (Westminster Version).
[30]St. Thomas Aquinas, in *Ep. ad Romanos,* xi, lect. 2.

CHAPTER VII

ANSWER TO ONE UNNAMED

My essay on the mystery of Israel (Chapter VI in this volume) was criticized in a Belgian periodical by a philosopher whom I prefer, for the sake of charity, not to name (I shall refer to him as Mr. So and So). I answered his attack in La Question d'Israël, *a Catholic publication issued by the missionary fathers of Notre Dame de Sion (July 1, 1939).*

The errors into which Mr. So and So permitted himself to fall are so significant that I think it well to repeat here, as a sort of annex to the previous chapter, the more important sections of my reply.

I

ALTHOUGH the formal purpose of my essay relates to the mystery of Israel as Saint Paul states it for us, and consequently is in the spiritual order, I took pains in several passages to touch on the strictly sociological aspects of the matter, even to indicate what from this point of view would be the orderly dispositions ("personalist" and "pluralist") in my opinion best adapted to our present historical time, and to point out that in each instance the specific solutions to be sought after in a spirit of amity and friendliness relate to "political wisdom." To anyone reading my chapter whose attitude is not vitiated by certain fundamental prejudices, the accusation of proposing an "exclusively supernaturalist interpretation of the Jewish problem" and of expecting from "saintliness alone," without regard to the knowledge, competencies, powers and techniques of the natural order, "a solution of the anguished problems of our day" will seem utterly without foundation.

It is of course true that the central emphasis of my essay is on the level of the sacred, and that for me the Jewish question is *primarily* (I do not say exclusively) a mystery of theological order; it is likewise true that I assert that neither speculatively nor practically can a Christian form a judgment on the Jewish question (nor on any of the great ethico-social questions which have import for human history or civilization) without placing himself in the perspective of Christian Doctrine and without taking his inspiration from the Christian spirit. Indeed it is here that we come face to face with the fundamental prejudices to which I have just alluded, which would *separate* Christianity from life, especially from political life. If there are any special errors which poison our generation, blind our understanding, lead peoples astray, they are these prejudices. I presume that Mr. So and So is not unaware of this, for he is well informed as to principles. But in his philosophy of history and of social life, and in applications to concrete examples, it might be asked that he not show himself vulnerable to these prejudices. May he keep himself free of Averroism; may he keep himself from writing that the "political, economic and cultural aspects" of a problem "relate to the *pure and simple* order of nature and of the concrete observation of facts," and are "as such, despite any religious incidences to which they may be subject, *independent* of religion."

Here is a formula evoking Charles Maurras rather than a Catholic formula. The happy introduction of an "as such" in no way changes it. The economic and cultural aspects of a problem belong to the order of nature and of the concrete observation of facts, but not to the *pure and simple* order of nature and of the concrete observation of facts, in such sort that they would relate to principles *purely and simply* natural and would be of themselves *independent of religion*. Nature has its own reality, its own dignity, its own finalities; yet it is not an absolute; distinct from grace, it is neither separate nor independent from grace; grace is added to it not like a cap stuck on top of some professor's head, but like a divine graft which at once makes man participate in a supernatural life and exalts his natural life itself within the very order of this natural life. If one does not understand these things, let him reread the *Summa* and the papal encyclicals, which, in dealing with economic, political and cultural realities, do not deal with them merely from the point of view of *natural law*, over the integrity of which the Church is enjoined to watch, but also from the point of view of the *gospel*, of which by her own mission it is the task of the Church ever to preserve the deposit; moreover these writings would have it that these realities in the natural order be penetrated by the evangelic virtues and by *Christian charity*, which is the supernatural virtue *par excellence* (which is possible only if economic, political and cultural realities can be exalted by gospel energies within their own natural order). And let such a man take the trouble to reread also the works of contemporary Thomists, who have carefully elaborated the truths in question.

To my mind history and culture, while having their proper ends which relate to the natural order (Thomists go so far in this direction as to look upon the end of *vita civilis* or of civilization as a "final end in a given order," *finis ultimus secundum quid*), are indirectly subordinate, given the condition in which humanity is concretely situated, to the ends of eternal life (*finis ultimus simpliciter*) and to the preparations for the Kingdom of God, which is beyond history. The minute one admits in the natural order itself and in the order of temporal realities an intrinsic modification due to a supernatural ordering, Mr. So and So seems to believe that one belittles nature and that one loses sight of its own laws, even that one denies it or hates it. Yet in such case one is only considering nature in the concrete conditions of existence in which it effectively finds itself.

How could a philosopher, inoculated with *separatist* prejudices, fail to be confronted with the Jewish problem as with a matter eminently created to scandalize him? For herein, and from the beginning and before Israel stumbled and by a unique privilege, there has been a supernatural election which involved a people in its temporal history, a race in its very ethico-social destiny. Code of social life, national tradition, temporal history, race, people *set apart* for God. Priest-people. If certain Jews cultivate an exasperating racial pride (even though it is in part rendered excusable by the extraordinary succession of persecutions under which their ancestors have suffered) we must see here the effect of a naturalistic corruption of the memory of this divine election. The ingenious anti-Semites who vituperate "Jewish racism" forget that the first one responsible for the concept of an elect race, that concept being taken at its pure source, is the God of Abraham, of Isaac and of Jacob, the God of Israel—*your God,* dear Christians who turn yourselves against the chosen olive tree into which you were grafted. In any case it is to the Bible and to Moses that Mr. So and So should impute first of all the supernaturalism he has contrived. It is only too evident that he is lost before the astounding interweaving of the natural and the sacred, of the supernatural and the temporal, presented by the unique case of Israel.

Our writer is scandalized that I should regard the choice of Israel as permanent and the mission of Israel as still continuing in a certain manner, after its lapse. Let him hold it against Saint Paul and against the apostolic affirmation that the vocation and the gifts of God are without repentance. (And indeed he holds it against Saint Paul, whose words he vainly seeks to extenuate.) What Saint Paul reveals to us is precisely that Israel, even though blindfolded, and dispossessed through its lapse and its rejection of the Gospel, is ever loved as the chosen people, and this is why its dispossession will be only temporary. Then again we must add that if the Jewish people has stumbled, and must until its final reception bear the consequences of its misstep, it would be, however, nonsense to imagine that this people as such is in a state of mortal sin, for a people has not a personal and immortal soul. It is in time and in its collective destiny here below that Israel bears responsibility, in respect of his God, for the misfeasance of its priests. I said that it is a Church fallen from a high place, and that its vocation, through its fault rendered ambivalent, continues in the night of the world. And I warned that these things should be understood analogically. "A sort of reverse analogy to the Church is here, I believe, the guiding idea. Through trying to perceive a mystery of suffering by the light of a mystery of grace, we are led to use in an improper meaning ideas and expressions properly belonging to an altogether different object." Mr. So and So is not the first philosopher to take for an accumulation of contradictions the perspectives opened up by analogical intellection. This is a regrettable fact, which it is not our task to remedy. If one does not acknowledge the "reverse analogy" to which I have alluded, it is evident that one cannot understand such assertions as these: "If the world hates the Jews, it is because the world is well aware that they will always be supernaturally strangers to it. . . . Prisoners and victims in this world which they love, and of which they are not, will never be, cannot be. . . . Hated by the world, this is their glory, as it is also the glory of those Christians who live by faith."

Yet my context was very clear. Israel is not supernaturally a stranger to the world *in the same way* as is the Church: the latter is the Kingdom of God, in a state of pilgrimage and crucifixion; the former is the people of God which God ever calls and which does not listen, but which preserves the hope of God on earth and a nostalgia for the absolute, and the Scriptures and the prophecies and the promises and the faith in the divine Holiness and the longing for the Messiah. The Jews are not hated by the world *in the same way* as are the Christians: the latter are hated by the world because of Jesus Christ and because of the Cross; the former because of Moses and the Patriarchs and because of the earthly stimulation which the world takes from their spur. And because Jesus Christ came of them as concerning the flesh. The Jews are not and will never be of the world, not because they share in the redeeming life of Christ and of the Kingdom of God, but because they are *owed* to Christ, because, set apart for God by their messianic vocation, they remain, even after their misstep, separated from the world by their passion for a Justice which is not of this world.

II

BUT MR. SO AND SO, as I have just pointed out, proposes an exegesis of his own for chapters ix through xi of the Epistle to the Romans. Let us follow him a little in this direction.

He first of all points out something which is very true: that God's promises have not failed since they have been realized in the Church. But in the Jewish people, conformably with his general presuppositions, he sees only a "natural reality," like unto other sociological aggregations. And he asserts with an astounding assurance that "there is not one passage in the Epistle which could suggest the idea of some prerogative or other for Israel as the people of God since the establishment of the New Law." Then how does he read Saint Paul?

When Saint Paul exclaims that he could wish to be anathema for his brethren according to the flesh, "who are Israelites, to whom pertaineth the adoption, and the glory, and the covenants, and the giving of the Law, and the service of God and the promises; whose are the fathers, and of whom as concerning the flesh Christ is,"[1] of what Jews is he speaking if not of those who live in his own day, and of whom a part only, "a remnant according to the election of grace," has acknowledged the Saviour? The "blinded" mass has not lost its title to the privileges—now emptied for it of their salutary meaning—enumerated by the apostle. They weigh upon it with all the weight of the dead letter, they always in some fashion "pertain" to it, by virtue of the endowment originally given, the effect whereof, because of Israel's lapse, is temporarily suspended. It is the Church, Israel according to the spirit, which has inherited from them, receiving moreover the divine efficacity which comes from Christ's Passion and is proper to the Law of Grace. But when the Jewish people as such shall convert itself and pass under the law of the new covenant, it will be within its own ancient privileges, extended to all the peoples in accordance with the very universality of the Church, and transfigured in accordance with the truth of the spirit, that, in joining itself to the Gentiles in one single fold, it will find itself received anew.

And what are we to say of this famous passage: "Now if the misstep of them is the riches of the world, and the diminution of them the riches of the Gentiles, how much more the fulness of them?"[2] Erik Peterson says in this connection: "It is not possible to express the prerogative of Israel more forcibly than in this verse of an Epistle which, let us not forget, is addressed to Romans. To the extent that the misstep of the chosen people shows itself forth a riches! Riches for the cosmos, riches for the pagan world. . . . Their conversion will have a meaning even greater still than their lapse, for the cosmos and for the Gentiles."[3]

But, says Mr. So and So, "Erik Peterson deceives himself."

[1]Rom. ix:3-5. [2]Rom. xi:12.
[3]Erik Peterson, *Le Mystère des Juifs et des Gentils dans l'Église,* pp. 56-57.

And he furnishes proof: "After all it is not because the Jews have refused grace that grace was accorded to other men! Supposing the Jews were to have accepted the divine gift, will it be supposed that the Gentiles would have had no part in it, with the result that the *spiritual Israel* would have been the mere *fleshly Israel?*" This objection, which at once comes to mind, is indeed very *natural,* too *natural,* and that is doubtless why Saint Paul, who contemplated the divine plan as it has been moulded in fact, without troubling himself over the *futuribilia,* did not occupy himself with such an objection. He left to his commentators the task of resolving it. The misstep of the Jews, writes Father Lagrange, from thenceforward appeared as a cause of salvation for the Gentiles. "It is a statement of fact. Paul, seeing himself repulsed by the Jews, turned toward the Gentiles (Acts xiii: 45–48) who therefore were earlier put in the way of salvation." Moreover, and more profoundly, it must be granted that it was due to the incredulity of the Jews that the Church was able from its birth to rise up as independent of Israel taken according to the flesh, of its temporal destinies and of its theocracy, and to appear to the world with a character of absolute, supra-temporal and supra-national, universality.

The same commentator continues: "And if the Jews had been converted as a whole, would they have been willing to give up their Law? Would Christianity have become that religion freed of national observances which alone could have suited the Gentiles? The learned of today are in perfect agreement with Paul in asserting that the refusal of the Jews facilitated the entrance of the Gentiles. And even in that, God intended the salvation of the Jews, He wished to make them emulous, etc. . . ."

And as for the extraordinary promise concerning the future conversion of Israel according to the flesh, does it not indicate for this people, as God's people, an astonishing and permanent prerogative? Let Israel desist from its obstinacy, and the course of the world is changed; indescribable spiritual riches is the joy of the Gentiles. In this sense Israel holds in its hands, in the power of an act of its free choice, the "riches of the Gentiles": "If . . . the diminution of them [is] the riches of the Gentiles, how much more their fulness?" And again (xi:15): "For if the dispossession of them hath been the reconciliation of the world, what shall the reintegration of them be, but life from the dead?" Concerning this Saint Thomas writes that "their spiritual abundance or their multitude converted to God will make the riches of the Gentiles, according to the saying of Ecclesiastes: *My dwelling place is in the fulness of the Saints.* And thus if God has permitted for the utility of the entire world the misstep and the dispossession of the Jews, how much more generously will He restore their ruins to the advantage of the entire world. . . . And what will be the effect of their reintegration, if not to call back to life the Gentiles, that is to say the lukewarm faithful, when *on account of the progress of iniquity, the charity of a great number shall have waxed cold* (Matt. xxiv: 12)?"[4]

---

[4]St. Thomas, in *Ep. ad Romanos,* cap. xi, lect. 2 (on xi:12 and xi:15). Bossuet for his part wrote: "The Saviour whom Zion did not recognize and whom the children of Jacob had rejected, will turn toward them, will wipe away their sins and will restore to them that understanding of the prophecies which they will for a long time have lost, that it may go down from hand to hand unto all posterity and be never again forgotten until the end of the world and for as much time as it will please God to make it continue after this marvellous event." (*Hist. Univ.* II, 20). "When you will see us coming into the Church and approaching you," says the Abbé Lémann, "it will not be as heralds of death, but as heralds of life. We shall come, not to announce the end but to prevent it. The Apostle St. Paul, that converted Jew who saw so clearly into the destinies of our people, calls the conversion of the Jews the *riches of the world:* again he calls it a *life from the dead.* Hence it will not be with the end of the world, but rather with the most astonishing splendour of the world that will coincide the conversion of the Jews." (*Question du Messie,* p. 150).

The passages I have just cited are not the only ones to testify to a prerogative still attached to Israel as to God's people after the establishment of the New Law. There are several others. "If the root be holy, so are the branches. And if some of the branches be broken off, and thou, being a wild olive, wert ingrafted among them, and with them partakest of the root and of the fatness of the olive tree; boast not against the branches."[5] According to Father Lagrange this means that *"the Jews are always, in a certain manner, a people consecrated to God, a people owed to God,"* and that "the Gentiles can only be compared to a wild shoot grafted onto a good plant."

Above all there is Romans xi:28–29: "As touching the gospel, indeed they are enemies for your sake: *but as touching the election, they are beloved for the sake of the fathers.* For the gifts and the calling of God are without repentance." Which means, again according to Father Lagrange, that *"the election of the Jewish people as God's people was in itself irrevocable;* if it is bounded by the necessity of assuring the success of the gospel, this dispensation is only *temporary* . . . The Jews made themselves enemies of God, who permitted their attitude in the interest of the Gentiles. *They continue to be loved as a chosen people."*[6]

[5] Rom. xi:16–18.

[6] In the First Epistle to the Thessalonians (ii:14–16) St. Paul tells them that they have suffered from their compatriots that which the Churches of Judea "have of the Jews: those Jews who both killed the Lord Jesus, and their own prophets, and have persecuted us; and they please not God, and are contrary to all men: Forbidding us to speak to the Gentiles that they might be saved, to fill up their sins always: for the wrath is come upon them to the uttermost." It is to those of the Jews who, proud and wicked like the killers of the prophets and the murderers of Christ, persecuted the Christians and through their slander put obstacles in the way of the spread of the gospels that these words of St. Paul apply, not to the Jewish people as such. This is obvious since, from the very fact that "the gifts and calling of God are without repentance," this people ever remains "beloved for the sake of the fathers." Cf. Lagrange, *Ep. aux Romains,* p. 266.

To see nothing more in the destinies of the people of Israel than in the destinies of some social aggregation or other; to pretend that the election of Israel to the title of God's people was purely and simply revoked by the coming of Christ—this is to simplify things to the point of substituting an altogether *natural* kind of thought for Saint Paul's *supernatural* thought, and it is utterly to extenuate his teaching. "Hath God cast off his people? God forbid."[7]

"Brethren," said Saint Paul, "I would not have you ignorant of this mystery . . . that blindness in part has happened in Israel, until the fulness of the Gentiles should come in. And so all Israel shall be saved."[8] "There," wrote Bossuet, "the apostle lifts himself above everything he has just said, and entering into the depths of God's counsels . . ."[9] A prophecy which involves entering *into the depths of God's counsels* by that very fact relates to a supernatural mystery. The mystery of the Jews is not something of the divine life itself, like the mystery of the Redemption, but essentially it stems from that mystery, as well as from the mystery of the voice of the Father heard or rejected by a human being, when that voice calls—in time—for faith in the Incarnate Son. It belongs in the same general order. Read the verses that follow in Saint Paul's text. It is immediately after having half opened to us God's counsels regarding the economy of the world and the temporary dispossession of the Jews and the conversion of the Gentiles that the Apostle, overwhelmed with the sublimity of the divine secrets which he has been contemplating, bursts into ecstasy: "O the depths of the riches both of the wisdom and knowledge of God! how unsearchable are his judgments, and his ways past finding out!

---

[7] *Ep. ad Rom.*, xi:1.—"God has not cast away His people since a good number of them are converted (xi:2–7), and if the others have been hardened (8–10), that hardening is not more final than the punishments which have at other times stricken Israel . . ." *Cf.* Lagrange, *Ep. aux Romains*, p. 266.

[8] Rom. xi:25–26.   [9] *Hist. Univ.* II, 20.

For who hath known the mind of the Lord? Or who hath been his counsellor?"[10]

How could one more strongly express the "spiritual and substantial" magnitude of such a mystery?

III

THE INSTANT one admits in the Pauline sense that the destiny of Israel according to the flesh is a mystery, it is clear—and moreover this is a basic traditional view—that this mystery weighs upon Jewish temporal history among the nations and upon the sociological and natural implications of the Jewish question. Far from failing to recognize these implications and denying that they can be made the object of quite empirical studies, I have particularly called attention thereunto.[11] But it is upon the "sacred" aspect of the Jewish question that I have especially devoted my attention; not that that aspect suppresses the others or makes their study superfluous, but because that aspect casts light upon the others and remains itself primary. Not that I refuse the economist, the historian, the sociologist their rights, but because philosophy has also its rights. And because in the realm of the philosophy of history and of culture, a philosopher should not withdraw himself from theology. And can a Christian be forbidden to look at things from such a formal perspective when, from his own altogether sociological point of view an author like Werner Sombart, struck by the way in which Max Weber connects the success of capitalism to the Puritan religion, in turn undertakes to cast light upon the temporal activity of the Jews by means of their religious faith? That the pages devoted to this undertaking should be the least successful in his work is another matter.

Not only are laws of racial or religious discrimination funda-

[10]Rom. xi:33–34.
[11]Cf. *A Christian Looks at the Jewish Question.*

mentally unjust; they also are for the state an avowal of impotence and political immaturity. Just laws, equal for all, should suffice to check evil, whencesoever it may arise, and to promote good, whencesoever it may come.

As for some eventual pluralist organization of the commonwealth, such an organization, established upon respect for the fundamental rights of the person and upon the equality of rights, would permit the State to arrange with the Jewish spiritual community, as well as with the other spiritual communities, for the free cooperation required by the common good and suitable to peace in common life. But Mr. So and So will not hear of equality of rights nor of the emancipation of the Jews brought to pass by the French Revolution. He dislikes this Revolution. This is not a proper place in which to demonstrate that the mere condition of being *against* leads to nothing. Let it suffice to quote these words from the late Cardinal Verdier: "The three equalities proclaimed by the Revolution—political equality, the equality of all men before the law, whether that law represses or protects, the equality of opportunity of all citizens with regard to public employment—if one takes into account the vivifying current of fraternity and love which is the most deep-seated and the healthiest element therein, are in essence Christian and are sprung from the vivifying currents of the Gospel, made available to the world by Christ."[12]

Mr. So and So "is not anti-Semitic," at least in the sense that he is no advocate of pogroms nor of concentration camps nor of the savage hatreds characteristic of militant racism, and in the sense that he urges with regard to the Jews a practice of *individual charity*. But he is an advocate of the régime of the ghetto (the *isolation* of the Jews, and a refusal as far as they are concerned of complete equality of rights), and he proposes in their regard a *collective severity* which would exclude them

[12]*Christian Answers to Social Problems,* p. 62.

from their status as citizens and would have them considered as "guests." As though retrogression to a condition conceivable only (and with what consequences of abuse and injustice) in a feudal régime wherein religious unity lay at the foundation of political life could, in a régime of civilization like ours, be brought to pass otherwise than by instituting debased racial categories, and could in consequence be anything but a barbarizing process! Because it seeks shelter in theology, the hypocritical anti-Semitism of Mr. So and So is a particularly impudent and wicked form of anti-Semitism.

He sets himself up as an enemy of "logical abstractions" and of figments of the reason. But on his own account he admits the most unhealthy imaginings of racism, which he adorns with a bargain-counter theology picked up from among the bric-a-brac of Julius Streicher and the anti-Jewish caricaturists.

The doctors of Christian antiquity suffered from none of these imaginings. With whatever hardness they may have spoken of the Jews, the conception they formed of them was always noble. How does Saint Gregory figuratively interpret the running of the two apostles to the Saviour's sepulchre? "Peter went in the first; after him John enters in turn. This signifies that, at the end of the world, the Jewish people, itself also, is to be received into the faith of the Redeemer."[13] Saint Thomas, in connection with the same incident in the Gospel, also sees in the apostle John a similitude of the Jewish people: "The two peoples, the Jewish people and the people of the Gentiles are, at Christ's Sepulchre, symbolized by the two Apostles. They run to Christ simultaneously throughout the ages: The Gentiles by means of their natural law, the Jews by their written Law. The Gentiles, like Peter, who arrives second at the Sepulchre, come later to the knowledge of Christ, but, like Peter, they first enter therein. The Jewish people, the first to know the mystery of the Redemption, will be only the last converted to

[13]St. Gregory the Great, *Hom. xxv. in Evang.*

faith in Christ. *Then,* says the Gospel, *John went in;* Israel is not to remain eternally at the entrance to the Sepulchre. After Peter shall have gone into it, it will itself go in, for at the end the Jews also will be received in the faith."[14]

There is a certain apex of perfection and of supreme achievement, an acme of nature and of natural law to which the régime of grace inaugurated by the New Law is happily suited to carry nature, and to which nature left to itself could not succeed in attaining. Here is one of the essential aspects under which it is true to say that Christianity lifts up within their own order the things of culture and of the commonwealth. Thus there is a Christian honour, natural Christian virtues, a Christian law; thus there is, at work in history, and countered by powerful adverse forces, a Christian leaven which tends to cause human society to pass on into conditions of higher civilization. That Christians should consent to let this inner energy, which it is their task to maintain, waste itself—here is a great loss for nature and for humanity.

I know very well that among all the temporal, economic, political, social problems to which peoples are subject, the problems created by the Jewish diaspora take their place (and can be particularly difficult in countries having a large Jewish national minority). I have said it, specifically. And it has been brought home to all of us by the coincidence of a world-wide economic depression, and of the tormenting troubles suffered by every nation, with the additional burdens which waves of immigrants, driven out by a ferocious racist policy, today impose on the civilized community. In such a case political prudence requires that governments, taking into account the reactions of the crowd, should not show themselves *too* generous; in any case they can be fully relied on for that, and so also can a great part of public opinion be fully relied on: is it not true to

[14]St. Thomas Aquinas, in *Joan.,* xviii, lect. i.

say of the greater number of us tnat what each detests most of all after the executioner is his victim? That is indeed a very *natural* feeling. I cannot fail to appreciate at its worth this sort of inglorious necessity of the moment; I merely maintain that this is not the moment for Christians to betray the Christian spirit.

I say that in a time wherein anti-Semitic persecutions have assumed an unheard-of proportion, wherein thousands upon thousands of miserable people have been put outside the law, subjected to brutalities and humiliations beyond description, to slow death, to the "spontaneous" violence of the mob or to the horrors of concentration camps, in a time when every day we hear that the epidemic of suicides among Jews continues in Vienna and elsewhere, or that, in the winter of 1938 cold and hunger decimated entire train loads of Jews stopped at forbidden frontiers, or that, as is true at the moment of writing these paragraphs boatloads full of Jews are dying of want, as they wander about the Mediterranean Sea, from one port to another, everywhere repulsed—in such a time the only *realism* which matters, not only to a Christian, but to all men still endowed with a natural feeling for the *caritas humani generis,* is not to speak a word, not to write a word which could serve as any excuse whatever for degrading hatred, and thereby to find oneself some day accused of the blood or the despair of creatures of God.

CHAPTER VIII

THE CATHOLIC CHURCH AND SOCIAL PROGRESS[1]

I

PHILOSOPHY, being rational knowledge, is not concerned with historical data and events in time as constituting an intrinsic part of its own subject-matter. Faith is concerned with them —because faith penetrates into existence much more deeply than does philosophy, and is concerned with the most concrete and individual realities, those of *my* salvation, of the salvation of each human person. I distrust a faith which sits in comfortable ease, above every human and divine fact, despising the old-fashioned "historical" faith of ordinary believers; I fear that such a supra-temporal faith is no more than a sublimation of philosophical feeling.

In reality, faith necessarily postulates God's descent into history in order to establish communion with human beings and undertake a personal dialogue with them. And faith itself descends into the weakness and entanglements of specific, historic and contingent events in order to know them, of that particular and irreplaceable *certain day* when the Uncreated Word became flesh. Faith can achieve this, because at the same time it ascends into the absolute stability and simplicity, into the most concrete and existential individuality of the divine

[1]This text—with some additions—is a translation of the original French version of a study published in *Foreign Affairs,* New York, July 1, 1939. *Foreign Affairs* had asked the author to write on this subject for the American public.

Self, and because it knows historical events not as a process of historical knowledge, but by means of the supra-historical, eternal, prime Truth in Person, "declaring"[2] itself to us and enlightening human hearts.

Thus there exists not only the manifestation of the eternal Word without regard to time and in every man entering into the world, which is the very root of natural human knowledge, and especially of philosophical and metaphysical knowledge. There also exists the manifestation of the eternal Word as an historical event, in an individual man in time and space, in the coming of Christ and in the fact of the Redemptive Incarnation, which is the root and the object of faith. This Christ —who ever pre-existed not in relation to time but in relation to divine knowledge, because every reality contained in time is ontologically present to creative eternity—lived, died and rose from the dead at a certain given moment in time, and He left behind Him a mystical body which continues His task, and acts within time.

All this pertains to the domain of Christianity and not of philosophy. Philosophy, however, though distinct from Christianity, is in interrelation with it, and must deal with matters pertaining to religion, if it is to understand and analyze concretely the problems of human life and human conduct. Not after the fashion of any necessary requirement, but after the fashion of a concrete and existential suitability, the natural manifestation of the eternal Word, in which philosophy is rooted, in a certain sense invokes the supernatural manifestation of the Incarnate Word, in which faith is rooted. Because if it is true that the infinite Self is manifested in finite existence throughout time, then its manifestation in actual unity with the finite, and for the finite—at a given moment and through the assumption of one single human nature by the personality of the Uncreated Word—is but the free fulfilment of that same

[2]John i:18.

movement of love thanks to which the divine plenitude—doing everything "for its own glory," that is, without need of anything and not for its own sake but for the finite's sake—freely superabounds and inclines itself toward the finite. This supreme manifestation of the Uncreated Being thus produces a new Being—the Christological Being, the universe of the Hypostatic Union and of divine grace—in which the infinite diversity between the Infinite and the finite, and their opposite properties, are not suppressed or cast away, but conquered and overcome. Since the new Being appears within and under the conditions of created existence—within and under suffering—it has the character both of liberation and of anticipation. Christ the liberator suffered and died. Afterwards He is seated in glory. Liberated souls suffer in time, and after time they will enter peace; yet even now they participate in divine life. Eternal life is already begun, and it is to come.

I consider it good to make these observations, which may be useful with respect to Chapter V, but more particularly to the present Chapter. Here I deal with religious data of fact, especially with the attitude of the Catholic Church toward social progress. My point of view, however, remains philosophical. What I attempt is the analysis of the diverse lines of finality and of action which human conduct follows in the midst of the entanglements of spiritual and temporal realities.

II

THE AUTHOR of this study is a Catholic. By way of introduction he will indicate briefly within what general perspective are found the ideas he wishes to set forth and which otherwise would remain insufficiently clear. He does not forget in any way the work accomplished in the social field by Christians of other denominations. On the contrary, he highly esteems their work and he wishes to pay tribute to the generosity manifested by many of them, in Europe as well as in America. Particularly the efficacious cooperation developed in Great Britain, during the second World War, between the diverse Protestant churches and the Catholic Church, in order to defend threatened civilization, to awaken the Christian spirit in its way of thinking of temporal matters and to outline the principles of a new social and international order, seems to him an important sign for the future. Then again the admirable activity displayed in the world by the Quakers appears to him especially significant, not as belonging to the social and temporal domain, but as evincing how a merely religious and charitable activity may impose respect on political powers, even the worst ones, because it is free from any political or national motive, and transcends any earthly interest. Yet, knowing better what concerns the Catholic Church, and believing in her as in the true Church of Christ, the author prefers to treat his subject with respect to her alone. Moreover the considerations he proposes regarding Catholicism can be applied, *mutatis mutandis,* to the other Christian bodies in their own way.

The distinction between the things which are Cæsar's and the things which are God's is fundamental for the Catholic conscience. This distinction guarantees the freedom of the spiritual with regard to the temporal, and the freedom of the Church with regard to the State. Yet this distinction is not a separation: divine things should operate in common with human things. From this point of view it should be remembered that the sudden appearance of the gospel in history did not simplify human affairs. But it did accelerate the movement of history and gave it its direction.

On the other hand, the Church, according to Catholic belief, is a true *civitas* of divine origin—the Kingdom of God in a state of pilgrimage—a "perfect society" organized in accordance with its own appropriate laws and its own appropriate hierarchy, in which authority comes from above to teach souls and lead them to salvation. This community, one and universal, extends throughout the nations and communities of the world whose nature and diversity it respects.

Finally, the end toward which this community leads its members is a supernatural end: entrance into the life of God; its common good is eternal life. Its own special concern is not the earthly life of man, not conflicts, disagreements and problems of a temporal order, not political and social progress, not the organization of happiness here below. Yet it is not disinterested in all these matters; it cannot be disinterested in them. For, on the one hand, by reason of the connections between the natural order and the supernatural order, it is a part of the Church's mission to guard the integrity of the principles of natural reason, of natural law, and of social ethics as well as of individual ethics; and on the other hand, by virtue of a superabundance which is a consequence of the law of the Incarnation, that which the Church brings to the world is a good which reverberates in the earthly life of man, and—although suprapolitical—is of prime importance in his political and social progress and in his accession to a happier existence in the world. As concerns earthly matters, the action of which I speak is the only one that men may expect from the Church without running the risk of being disappointed—a merely spiritual action, which from the realm of things divine overflows into the temporal realm.

This action of the Church—transcendent, respectful of the autonomy of temporal things, "maternal" with regard to them —is clearly indicated in Saint Paul's Epistle to Philemon. Saint Paul does not ask Philemon to free his slave Onesimus; he is not concerned with breaking the social framework of the ancient world; he accepts this framework made by men. But he cuts an opening in it so that the power of the gospel will seep through and, working from within the world, will burst little by little the social bonds of slavery. Onesimus, who is Philemon's slave, is to Philemon "much more" than his slave; he is a "most dear brother." Paul calls him "my own bowels."—The slave, as well as the master, is an "heir of God" and a "joint heir of Christ."[3]

Saint Paul requires those under authority to obey those above. For him it is a duty of man's conscience to have respect for legitimate authority, because all legitimate authority has its primary source in God, Author of nature. Indeed, the early Christians, in preferring the *corona martyrum* to the *corona militum,* preferred to run the risk of an unjust death rather than revolt against the tyrannical power of the persecuting emperors. And yet, again, the ideas and desires which Christian revelation caused to rise up in the soul of man, ceaselessly exert their influence at the very heart of society and transform it gradually. As far as the Church herself is concerned, it is not her task to descend to undertakings directly temporal in the ebb and flow of political activities. Hers is the treasury of energies of another order, more hidden and more powerful. It is justice and love, and Christian revelation, that she must keep alive. Once they have been conveyed into the substance of history, these energies have their own action which unfolds in a measure of duration quite different from the rhythm of time.

❖ ❖ ❖

These introductory remarks will serve to make clear that for Catholics the relation between the Church and the world is not simple, but is in itself very mysterious. No static equilibrium can be found in this relation capable of satisfying a mathematical imagination or the neat ideal of a textbook writer. The relation we speak of is dynamic—like one which exists in a *concerto* between massed forces whose very interpenetration is antinomic and whose harmony is unstable—lasting until the final moment when time is over.

Some anti-clericals reproach the Church with being on the

[3]Rom. viii:17.

side of the rich and the powerful and with social stagnation. Some apologists, in an attempt to magnify the Church's work in social progress, insist, on the contrary, on the "revolutionary leaven" which she brings to the world. They describe the Church as having no other end or mission than that of transforming the earthly conditions of peoples' lives and of creating peace, prosperity and happiness in the world. In the opinion of Catholics, both these schools of thought are suffering from illusions, even if both are able to cite specific facts in support of their theses. The key to the problem is to be found on a different level.

Pascal said that signs and miracles are sent—in accordance with the dispositions of men's hearts—to blind some and enlighten others. A young Hungarian writer, Odon de Horvath, who died tragically in Paris in 1938, pointed out in his novel, *Jeunesse sans Dieu,* an impressive testimonial against totalitarian régimes—that the State represents a natural necessity and that it is, therefore, willed by God. Consequently the Church is duty-bound to collaborate with the State. But what State, he added, is not governed by the powerful and the rich? and how can anyone collaborate with the State without being obliged at the same time to collaborate with the powerful and the rich? The Church must above all fulfill its own special task, and endure. It is beside the point if the Church takes on the appearance of cynicism when she accepts the State for what it is, with injustices and impurities marring it, and tries only to make the State less unholy. This is a constraint the Church undergoes, and the difficulties which arise therefore for her can be diminished only if she deals with a weak State or with a State which is itself Christian, and I mean vitally (not decoratively) Christian. To such considerations a Catholic will add that the special help which, according to his faith, the Church receives from God, is evidently less rigid when it is a question of establishing a *modus vivendi* with a government than when it is a question of defining a dogma. In the former case, this help can be limited to preventing irremediable errors as regards her own merely spiritual destiny. Finally, it is precisely in the realm of secular matters that the human weaknesses of individuals can most easily lead them astray. Often the temptation to link religion with the cause of the rich and powerful, or of a political party or of a State, in order to make use of their resources—and even their injustices—in the interest of churchmen or of the social classes which support churchmen, has given birth to more or less serious abuses and to a "clericalism" altogether opposed to the spirit of the Church and to her true welfare. On the other hand, the temporal behaviour of the *Christian world* (which is something altogether different from the Church) is often far from being Christian. This is enough to create an *appearance* which hides the reality from many people.

As a deeper historical investigation confirms, the reality is, that by her very mission, the heart of the Church is always with the poor, and she always finds in them her real source of strength. According to the great French philosopher, Henri Bergson, history shows that whatever lasting good was accomplished in human society during almost two thousand years, was accomplished under the influence of Christianity.[4] Le Play had arrived at the same conclusion regarding the moral conditions necessary for the progress of civilized life. The gospel and the Church taught men respect for the human person and respect for human life, respect for conscience and respect for poverty, the dignity of woman, the sanctity of marriage, the nobility of work, the value of freedom, the infinite worth of each soul, the essential equality of human beings of all races and of all conditions before God. When the Church affirms that political, economic, social and international life intrinsically depends upon ethics (that is, upon that special branch of

[4]In a private conversation with the author.

ethics which is political ethics), and that there is no peace or prosperity possible among men, without justice and respect for law; when the Church insists that even in the temporal order life cannot withdraw itself from the primacy of charity and brotherly love, it is the very foundations of all human progress which the Church is eager to assure. In our times it seems that to new needs the Church answers with new undertakings of great breadth. As formerly, when the Church contributed, in the mediæval fashion, to the political moulding of Europe, it seems that today she is aware of her duty to contribute, after the fashion of our own modern age, and thanks to the moral authority which is everywhere recognized as being hers, to the salvation of our threatened civilization, to the social shaping of the world and to the advent of a new order. As to the actual result, the efficaciousness of such a task depends in large measure both on the living faith and the political enlightenment of the Christian masses. Indeed we do not overlook what deep renewal and large educational undertakings are necessary in this regard for the present time.

Much space has been devoted to these preliminary observations, but they indicate how social problems in general are seen from a Catholic perspective. They will permit us to approach more easily the specific questions which arise with regard to Christianity and social progress.

III

CHRISTIANITY is at work in the social life of people according to two very distinct modes of action which, for the sake of brevity, we shall call the movement from below and the movement from above.

What we call the *movement from below* consists in the germination naturally produced in the depths of the profane, temporal conscience itself under the stimulus of Christian leaven. The philosopher of history sees that this leaven itself developed in the world in very diverse forms and conditions. The believer who belongs to a Church careful of orthodoxy—especially the Catholic—thinks that in this Church alone the gospel leaven has been preserved unchanged. But in a pure or impure form, orthodox or heretical, it is that leaven which in fact (for good or for evil) raised up the history of the secular world. If it is true that Jean Jacques Rousseau is the "father of modern times" and that he started our age along bad paths, in search of good things disfigured by errors, it is equally true that this *naturalization* or laicization of the gospel, as also revolutionary Messianism, are themselves inconceivable without that Christian element from which sprang Western civilization.

With regard to the spiritual and social conflicts of our day, the tragedy of the modern world consists basically in this: that in the nineteenth century—at the very moment when many Christians made themselves, in practice, accomplices of social injustice and set themselves up against the normal movement of history—many enemies of Christianity devoted themselves to the furthering of social justice, while distorting their idea of the latter by the errors of a disastrous materialism and being led astray by the myth of the Revolution-Saviour, not seeing that whatever was just and fruitful in their actions derived in fact from Christian (even though "bewildered") truths and from Christian sentiments (even though secularized). Thus took place what Pius XI described as the greatest scandal of the nineteenth century: the fact that the working classes had been separated from Christianity and the Church, and believed that, in order to hope for a better life on earth, they must necessarily turn away from Christ. The immense task which in our time is imposed upon Christian thought and upon Christian activity is to save the efforts of the last century toward social progress—while purifying them of the errors which are now causing their collapse.

As far as Catholics are concerned, it is for them a well-established belief that the Christian religion does not tie up its lot with any one temporal régime; it is compatible with all forms of government legitimate and worthy of man; it holds none up for the preference of Catholics. Nor does the Christian religion (assuming that a certain set of higher principles are protected) require a determinate system of political philosophy. But if the Church takes care not to bind herself to any temporal ideal, still, believers, acting not *as* believers and in the name of the Church, but *as* members of an earthly community and in their quality of citizens, are required to struggle for a temporal ideal and are required to take part, at their individual risk, in the struggle for freedom, social justice and for the progress of civilization. Many Catholics today are beginning to understand this necessity; they have put an end to the remissness of the nineteenth century.

To the extent that we are concerned here with the *movement from below,* which derives from Christian initiative at the roots of the secular conscience, it is clear that this movement does not engage the Church herself. Consequently, such a movement usually gives rise among those who participate in it—even when they are equally orthodox believers—to highly diverse attitudes, conformable to the social connections and habits of thought of each participant (without mentioning the varyingly serious obstacles which the spirit of the gospel can encounter in one place or another). It is perhaps more important to point out that social progress thus accomplished presupposes at once certain technical possibilities and a more or less protracted period of moral maturing. Such was the case with the abolition of slavery in ancient times. First, this abolition was conditioned by certain technical developments. It has been shown that the discoveries which permitted the substitution of animal motive power for human motive power, notably for the transportation of freight, played in this matter a considerable part.[5] (In the modern world the development of the machine seems called upon to play an analogously liberating rôle.) Secondly, as we have already seen, it was not by virtue of a law which the Church promulgated in the social-temporal sphere, it was rather by virtue of a slow, vital development that Christianity gradually freed the moral conscience of the necessity of slavery and, at last, freed the world of its existence.

If he takes this point of view, the philosopher of history can assert with Bergson—and without causing in any way adherence to a democratic political system to be a requirement of Christian faith—that, in fact, the leaven of the gospels dirècts human history toward that ideal of respect for the rights of the person and of brotherly love which is basic to the "democratically-minded temper" when errœneous metaphysics do not vitiate it; and that this leaven will continuè to work until the end of time in human history, in order to eliminàte, to the extent that technical progress shall make it pōssíble, évèry form of servitude.

❂   ❂   ❂

The *movement from above,* mentioned a few pages back, has its source in the official doctrine of the Church, especially in the teachings and practical instructions of the papal encyclicals, which stimulate, or consecrate, direct and control the "movement from below."

Particularly in the last half-century the Catholic Church has accumulated an extremely rich store of doctrine where the principles governing the ensemble of social questions and problems relating to the temporal life of men, are gathered together and coordinated. It has been explained that the Church herself does not undertake to participate in the administration of temporal matters. But she does recognize her responsibility to in-

[5]Commandant Lefebvre-Desnouettes, *La Force Môtrice animale à travers les âges,* Paris, Alphonse Picard.

tervene in whatever involves moral law. In this she fulfills a
function in practical wisdom.

A lengthy study would be needed to sum up these teachings
and this chapter cannot attempt it. The important undertakings accomplished by Leo XIII are well known. The titles of
some of his encyclicals are: *Inscrutabili* (1875) on the evils of
society; *Arcanum divinæ sapientiæ* (1880) on marriage; *Diu-
turnum* (1881) on the origin of civic power; *Immortale Dei*
(1885) on the Christian constitution of the state; *Libertas præ-
stantissimum* (1888) on human liberty; *Sapientiæ christianæ*
(1890) on the principal civic duties of Christians; *Rerum no-
varum* (May 16, 1891) on the condition of the working class.
This last encyclical is of special importance. Many people, at
the time of its publication, were almost scandalized and imagined that the Pope "was becoming a socialist." The Pope was
not becoming a socialist; he was merely recalling to a world
rotten with egoism the laws of Christian ethics in social matters. If all Christians had listened to him, many great evils
would have been averted. "We do not hold the encyclicals
against you," said the Communist Rappoport to a Catholic
speaker some ten years ago, "but we reproach you for scorning
the encyclicals." In a recent encyclical Pius XI wrote: "There
would be neither Socialism nor Communism if the leaders of
the nations had not scorned the teachings of the Church and
Her words of maternal warning."[6]

In many documents Pius XI and Benedict XV likewise
touched on social and political problems and completed the
teachings of Leo XIII. But Pius XI, with solid doctrinal understanding and boundless energy, carried the Catholic synthesis
in social matters to a state of precision which was the most
appropriate to our age and produced the decisive condemnation of the worst errors which today threaten civilization. The
major document was the encyclical *Quadragesimo anno* (May

[6]*Divini Redemptoris,* 1937.

15, 1931) on the restoration of social order, in which the Pope brought to light the moral and social roots of present evils, and, after criticizing individualism, Manchester liberalism, Socialism and Communism, outlined in principle the program of a social renovation founded on the organization of professional "bodies" and on the emancipation of the proletariat by supplying it with property. It must be noted that the "orders" or "professional bodies" of which this encyclical speaks are entirely different from the "corporations" of the totalitarian States. The latter are organs of the State, and the State itself in this case is said to be corporative. On the contrary, it is merely a functional *economy* which the encyclical recommends, and both the vocational group and the trade union are conceived as being essentially established on freedom of association, and provided with all the autonomy compatible with the requirements of the common good. Then came the encyclical *Non abbiamo bisogno* (May 29, 1931) where the totalitarian statolatry of the Fascist ideology is condemned; the encyclical *Mit brennender Sorge* (March 14, 1937) on German National Socialism; the encyclical *Divini Redemptoris* (March 19, 1937) on atheistic communism.[7] At the end of this volume, in Appendix I, appear some characteristic passages from these encyclicals and from Pius XII.

❂   ❂   ❂

The Catholic Church does not set out merely to teach theoretical lessons. She wants them to apply to daily living. From this point of view, how do the teachings of the encyclicals affect social problems? Despite the opposition and neglect of which I have spoken and of which the Popes have often com-

---

[7]Two other important encyclicals of Pius XI should be mentioned: *Quas primas* (1925) on the kingship of Christ; and *Casti connubii* (1930) on Christian marriage. These encyclicals do not directly concern the subject of this essay.

plained,[8] it can be said that the practical efficacy of their teachings appears as powerful as any *unarmed* teaching in the world can be—unarmed and nevertheless respected. To answer this question with greater precision, the historian is forced to distinguish what might be called differing *zones of realization.*

To a first zone of realization belong the attempts undertaken by certain Catholic state leaders to make out of the precepts of the encyclicals an immediate program for a political or national reconstruction, to be brought about by means of the State's authority. By a seeming paradox, this first zone of realization, which is the most obvious (for often the papal encyclicals are then expressly invoked as basis for a political platform) is that which involves the greatest risk of failure. Indeed such attempts, since they are not the result of a slow maturing of historical forces, very often assume dictatorial form and henceforth share in the fragile quality of such a form. Moreover, the universal and highly conceived precepts of the Church's doctrine are therein applied to the contingencies of social material without the preliminary elaboration of a more particularized political philosophy which is closer to the concrete; and hence, they are in danger of appearing to be abstract patterns, without existential force, or even at times a decorative apparatus covering realities which are in practice very little Christian. Also, the danger of making an artificial superstructure is all the greater in so far as, contrary to the nature of things, one has used Catholicism as a means of replacing a political ideal naturally

[8]"What is to be thought of the action of those Catholic employers who in one place succeeded in preventing the reading of Our Encyclical *Quadragesimo anno* in their local churches? Or of those Catholic industrialists who even to this day have shown themselves hostile to a labour movement that We Ourselves recommended? Is it not deplorable that the right of private property defended by the Church should so often have been used as a weapon to defraud the workingman of his just salary and his social rights?" *Divini Redemptoris.* The workers' movement to which Pius XI here referred is that of the Jeunesse Ouvrière Chrétienne (JOC).

temporal and a principle of unification naturally temporal, which fail as a result of circumstances. (Such was the case with Austria before the Anschluss. The good will of Chancellors Dollfuss and Schuschnigg was of no avail against this fact. Not to mention the achievements of Franco or Pétain.)

A second zone of realization—in my opinion, far more important—is that of the influence exerted on the legislation of various states either by men directly inspired by the encyclicals, or by the indirect influence of these documents. In many countries a Catholic school of social thought has grown up from which have come various movements and forms of activity, notably the "Semaines Sociales" and the movement of Christian labour unions. Before the present war there existed an International Confederation of Christian Labour Unions with headquarters at The Hague. In France the Christian Labour Unions represented a far from negligible body of workers. From the time of Leo XIII, Catholics of the school of La Tour du Pin and Albert de Mun became the parliamentary proponents of social laws which, had they been adopted, would have averted many grievances. In 1936, when the Blum government passed—in a too mechanical and rigid manner—certain social reforms which had become urgently necessary, it could well have been pointed out that this labour legislation (vacations with pay, collective bargaining, conciliation and arbitration, readjustment of pay, regulation of hours and free time) was, in fact, a return to proposed laws introduced many years before by Catholic deputies, or to measures which Catholics had urged, on an international basis, as arising from the proposals of the International Labour Office.[9] In other

[9] In this latter category is the forty-hour week. The economic competition between European nations made it impossible to apply this measure effectively if it was adopted by only one of the states. It is also true that the Catholic school of social thought has always favoured not only the living wage, but the *family* wage as well. The French laws of June, 1936, disregarded this idea and, from this point of view, were impeded by an outmoded individualism.

countries a more complete system of labour laws, at least as far as the first three points listed above are concerned, has long since been in force. And if the stubborn insistence of the working masses and the hard fight which they fought in the name of socialism, have played the preponderant rôle, surely the influence and effect of papal teachings on men's minds, and even on non-Catholics', have put forth a vast indirect action. Indeed, Pius XI was able to say that "Catholic principles of sociology gradually became part of the intellectual heritage of the whole human race." He added: "As a result of these steady and tireless efforts, there has arisen a new branch of jurisprudence unknown to earlier times, whose aim is the energetic defense of those sacred rights of the workingman which proceed from his dignity as a man and as a Christian. These laws concern the soul, the health, the strength, the housing, workshops, wages, dangerous employments, in a word, all that concerns the wage-earners, with particular regard to women and children."[10]

Finally, a third zone of realization, which is closely attached to the second, can be defined. It relates to the action which the teaching and guidance of the Church exercise on the mass of Catholics throughout the world—and indirectly on Christians not Catholics and even on non-Christians—in order to bring about in them the "movement from below," discussed a few pages back, and illuminate it doctrinally. This zone of realization is the largest of all and the least determinate. The penetration of the Church's action is here slower and more deeply rooted in the substance of the world. As far as the historical process of preparation and as far as the evolution proper of social-temporal realities are concerned, one may well believe that here also is the most fertile of the zones of realization, the zone where the deepest and most secret labour in the secular order is carried out.

[10] *Quadragesimo anno.* For the social action of the Church, notably in the nineteenth century, the reader may consult with profit Professor Chénon's *Le rôle social de l'Eglise,* Paris, Bloud et Gay.

In the *movement from below* the secular conscience itself, worked upon by the leaven of the Gospel, moves forward through suffering and contradiction—at times inspired by sane doctrine, at times blindly and hesitantly—toward a higher state of civilization. If it is true that not only among Christians themselves—for instance, in the nineteenth century and to speak only of France, among orthodox Catholics like Ozanam or Lacordaire, or among Catholics who had deviated from orthodoxy, like Lamennais—but even among "infidels" and in the innumerable currents, more or less erratic, which were interpenetrating in modern history;—if it is true that in all this it was Christian energies which were at work: both pure energies and worldly ones (even, corrupt ones), it is easily understood that to have a complete idea of the part played by Christianity with regard to social progress and the internally conflicting movement of history, it would be necessary to take into account both the power Christianity exerts *from above* (beginning with the initiatives of the teaching Church) and the power it exerts *from below* (beginning with the initiatives of the secular conscience).

Ideally—if Christianity ruled all hearts and if in the human elements in the Church herself human weaknesses had no place; in short, if everything moved as it should in the world—these two actions—from above and from below—ought to join and continually act in concert. But there is often distance and discord—and even opposition—between them. The secular conscience may take a wrong direction, or the movement from below may be in advance of the other. Here is some part of the price we must pay for a state of the world of whose constitution stress and conflict are elements, where, moreover, religious differences exist and evil plays its rôle. Generally speaking, strict fidelity to pure truth and passionate efficiency in the struggles of this world and in its great temporal victories are rarely to be found in the same men and the same provinces of human activity.

IV

THE WORLD CRISIS which has been raging for several years and
which is due, in its immediate causes, to the unleashing of two
sets of revolutionary-totalitarian phenomena, each opposed to
the other, the one issuing from a class-socialism (communism)
and aiming to set up the world dictatorship of the proletariat;
the other proceeding from a socialism of racial community or
political state (fascism and national socialism) and aiming to
set up a world empire of the "proletarian-nations"—this crisis
is so serious that it may well announce the night of Western
civilization. In my opinion, it represents the liquidation of
several centuries of error. According to the philosophy of history which I consider true, there is ground for thinking that
in the social-temporal order, the only happy outcome—for the
present or for the future—lies in the establishment of a new
political philosophy and of a thoroughly revivified commonwealth of free men.

The Church is not enlisted in any political school or party.
As I have tried to explain in this chapter, she is, because of
her central vocation, above such temporal patterns.

But in the present historical moment, it appears evident that
she regards totalitarian idolatry, under whatever form or colour
it chooses to appear, as presenting the most serious possible
threat to the exercise of her spiritual mission and to the deposit
of truths which she is intrusted to teach. The very freedom of
the word of God and the dignity of the human person as well
as the roots of any Christian civilization, are at stake. In the
years 1939–1941, it was not difficult to perceive that the fortunes
of religion, like those of natural law, and of international good
will, paralleled those of freedom.

If the world-conquering power of Nazism is finally defeated,
and if the democracies, cruelly beset by ancient materialistic
errors and by disorders due to the primacy of money, have the
strength and time to purify themselves and renew themselves—

as the Church has exhorted them to do through all the teachings which this chapter has treated,[11] and whose necessity their leaders have recognized[12]—the danger of a catastrophe for civilization can still be averted. If not, we can always hope that, after some centuries of night, a new human commonwealth will arise from the ashes of the old.

I have already indicated that the Catholic Church, who has time on her side, and who is accustomed to the turns of fortune and to the catastrophes of history, seems today to be applying herself to the task of taking up again, under forms basically different from those of mediæval Europe, her work of moral guidance and spiritual inspiration with regard to civilization. The means of action upon which she seems to rely mainly, in order to accomplish this task, is that which Pope Pius XI instituted and promoted under the name of "Catholic Action." Catholic Action does not operate on the political level and does not play politics. It restricts itself to the spiritual and apostolic realm.[13] But as it works to infuse a Christian vitality into the lives of individuals and the communities where they gather together, it prepares from within—from the soul—the first conditions necessary for a renewed social and political life. The most characteristic example of the movements set up by Catholic Action is the *Jeunesse Ouvrière Chrétienne* (Young Christian Workers) which before the second World War united in Belgium and France thousands of young workers and which has as its object the restoration, in Christ and in the spirit of the gospel, of the dignity of the working class. Such movements point toward advanced forms of social progress and toward the advent of a new city. What conditions and means will Christian action in temporal civilization be able to find

[11]The pastoral letter of the American Hierarchy in favour of Christian democracy (October, 1938) is especially significant in this connection.

[12]We have in mind the speech delivered by President Roosevelt on January 4, 1939.

[13]*Cf.* "Catholic Action and Political Action," in my book *Scholasticism and Politics*.

in the devastated post-war world? Through lack of understanding, selfishness, fear and social prejudices of the ruling classes, the Catholic world missed the opportunity of assuming the guiding rôle, before the war and during it, in the struggle against barbarism and enslavement. Yet the spiritual resources of the Church's doctrine and of faith and love within the hearts of men always remain in reserve for humanity. Let us hope that they will inspire the work of reconstruction which will need first of all men of good will and courage and of deep social and *political* understanding.

I close this chapter with two additional observations. First, if it is true that in political life and in a just understanding of politics, honesty of instincts and inclinations is most important, then it is clear that what a democracy most profoundly needs is the development, in the mass of its citizens, of Christian instincts, both intellectual and emotional, with regard to their social and political life. The historical rôle to which Catholic Action is called appears from this viewpoint tremendous. Secondly, if it is true that politics is by its essence a special branch of ethics, as in its natural wisdom the ancient Chinese civilization has for centuries recognized, it is apparent that the fundamental problem for which a Christian civilization must find a solution (and after four centuries of Machiavellianism this would be a singularly profound revolution for the modern world) is the problem of the establishment of a Christian politics. And I mean a politics truly and vitally, not decoratively, Christian. I quote here two sentences which have far-reaching applications. One is from Pius XI: "There will be no true peace until the day when states and peoples make it their sacred duty to follow the teachings and the precepts of Christ in their political life, both interior and exterior."[14] The other is from Benedict XV: "The law of love in the Gospels is not different for states and peoples from what it is for individuals."[15]

[14]Encyclical *Ubi arcano* (1922).   [15]Encyclical *Pacem Dei* (1920).

CHAPTER IX

SIGN AND SYMBOL

THERE ARE no more complex problems, no problems of wider bearing on psychology and on culture than those pertaining to the sign. The sign involves the whole extent of moral and human life; it is in the human world a universal instrument, just as is movement in the physical world.

A treatise on the sign and on the symbol, such as I hope some day may be written, would on the one hand endeavour to winnow out what is essential in the extensive intellectual elaboration to which mediæval thinkers subjected this matter, above all in logic (theory of concept and judgment) and in theology (theory of the sacraments). On the other hand, it would endeavour to link up with this, making use of the conceptual procedure thereby established, the scientific investigations of our own day and that vast assemblage of problems of whose importance various contemporary schools of thought, in particular that of Warburg, have been so well aware, and which relate to the symbolic, its rôle in primitive civilizations, in magic, in the arts and sciences, in the social life of our more developed civilizations, etc. The project for such a treatise, it seems to me, should include (i) a philosophical theory of the sign (general theory of the sign: the speculative sign; the practical sign); (ii) reflections and hypotheses with regard to the magical sign; (iii) reflections on art and the sign, science and the sign, social life and the sign, religion, ethics, mysticism and the sign. The present study will attempt only to clear the ground for the subject by suggesting certain very incomplete notions on a few of the themes which arise from the first two parts of the project outlined above.

THE THEORY OF THE SIGN

"SIGNUM EST *id quod repræsentat aliud a se potentiæ cognoscenti.*" For scholastics, the sign is that which makes present for knowledge something which is other than itself. The sign *makes manifest,* makes known: and it makes manifest or makes known something distinct from itself, of which it *takes the place* and with regard to which it exercises a ministerial function, and on which it *depends* as on its measure. It is essential to the sign that it be: infravalent with regard to that which is signified; measured by it; and related back to it as a substitute to a principal.[1][1]

The philosophers of old distinguished between the natural sign (*signum naturale*) and the conventional sign (*signum ad placitum*). For them, each sign is constituted as such by the typical relationship of notification of another thing in virtue of being a substitute or a vicar for this other thing. Taken precisely as such, this relationship does not belong to the class of transcendental relationships (*relatio secundum dici*), but to that of relationship as a special entity (*relatio secundum esse*).[2] And in the case of the natural sign, it is a *real* relationship: because the natural sign is naturally "more known" to us than that which it makes manifest; and to be *more knowable*— and that relative to another thing thereby also made knowable—is a real property, it is not a purely ideal relationship (*relatio rationis*), existing as such only in thought.[3] That

---

[1]In this chapter all notes citing Latin texts *in extenso* have been included in Appendix II at the back of the volume. Such notes are indicated in the text by an arabic figure in brackets, thus: [1].

smoke should make us know fire rather than water, that the spoor of the bullock should make us know a bullock rather than a man, and that the concept horse should make us know a horse rather than a stone—all that is based on a really intrinsic proportion between signs and that which they signify. This realist idea of the natural sign definitively rests upon a metaphysics for which intelligibility is consubstantial with being (*verum et ens convertuntur*).

This real relationship is not a relationship of efficient causality. Everything here is kept within the order of the "objective causality," or formal causality of knowing, not within the order of efficient or productive causality. When a sign produces an effect, it is never in so far as it is a sign. The sign does not even produce as an efficient cause the knowing of the signified; it produces knowing only because, in the cognitive faculty, it takes the place of the object, and thus makes the object present to that faculty, and because, to this extent, it keeps itself within the same line of causality as the object (formal causality).[4]

Every image is not a sign and every sign is not an image. For the image (which "proceeds from another as from its principle, and in the likeness of that other") can be of the same nature and the same ontological degree as that from which it proceeds (the son is the image of the father, but he is not the sign of the father). And many signs are not images (smoke is not the image of fire, nor is a cry the image of suffering).[5] We would define the symbol as being a *sign-image* (at once *Bild* and *Bedeutung*): something sensible *signifying* an object by reason of a presupposed relationship of *analogy*.

The sign is bound up with all knowing, even animal knowing. In the psychic life of animals not endowed with reason signs play a great part.[6] (In this connection one could advert to the well-known experiments with conditioned reflexes which in my opinion must be given a psychological explanation.)[7]

The external senses make use of signs (I see Socrates when I see his statue, my eye sees him in it). For the use of the sign does not necessarily involve inference and comparison. There is thus a certain presence—presence of knowability—of the signified in the sign; the former is there *in alio esse,* in another mode of existence. Here is a point of capital importance from which flow many great truths, and which must be noted in passing as absolutely characteristic: *"Quid est illud in signato conjunctum signo, et præsens in signo præter ipsum signum et entitatem ejus? Respondetur esse ipsummet signatum in alio esse.*[8] "What may be that element of the signified which is joined to the sign and present in it as distinct from the sign itself and its own entity? I answer: No other element than the very signified itself in another mode of existence." Hence the content of significance with which overflowed the statues of the gods. The god did not exist; but all the cosmic and psychic forces, the attractions, the passions which took shape in him, the idea which the artist and his contemporaries conceived of him—all that was *present* in the statue, not in a physical sense but *in alio esse,* in another mode of existence, and after the manner of the presence of knowability. For the statue had been made precisely to make all that known, to communicate it. In our museums, this pagan content is asleep, but it is always there. Let some accident take place, an encounter with a soul itself sensitized by some unconscious content: contact is established; the pagan content will be awakened and will unforgettably wound that soul.

The birth of idea, and hence of intellectual life in us, seems bound up with the discovery of the value of meaning of a sign. An animal employs signs without perceiving the relationship of meaning. To perceive the relationship of meaning is to have an *idea*—a spiritual sign. Nothing could be more suggestive in this connection than that kind of miracle which is the first awakening of intelligence in blind deaf-mutes (Marie Heurtin,

Helen Keller, Lydwine Lachance): essentially it depends upon the discovery of the relationship of the meaning of some gesture with regard to a desired object.[2] The sign is the keystone of intellectual life.

[2]Compare Louis Arnould, *Ames en prison* (Paris, Oudin, 1910). In his work, *La Pensée* (Paris, Alcan, 1934), Maurice Blondel with good reason draws attention to these facts, which he discusses with profundity.

For the very genesis, for the first stirring of the idea as distinct from images, the intervention of a *sensible sign* is necessary. Normally in the development of a child it is necessary that the idea be mimicked by the senses and lived before it is born as an idea; it is necessary that the relationship of meaning should first be actively *exercised* in a gesture, a cry, in a sensory sign bound up with the desire to be expressed. *Knowing* this relationship of meaning (signification) will come later, and this will be to have the *idea,* even if it is merely implicit, of that which is signified. Animals and children make use of this signification; they do not perceive it. When the child begins to perceive it (then he exploits it, he plays with it, even in the absence of the real need to which it corresponds), at that moment the idea has occurred.

Language properly so called (*conventional* sensory signs) develops out of this "language" of natural sensory signs.

Well then, in "imprisoned souls," among blind deaf-mutes, the first stirring of an idea cannot spontaneously produce itself for lack of natural sensory signs. These latter require the convergence of the senses; a cry which is not heard, a gesture which is not seen—how can these poor walled-in souls actively make use of such to express a desire? With them there can be no natural and spontaneous exercise of a relationship of signification, preceding the knowledge thereof, and hence preceding the birth of the idea.

In order to *put into practice* the first relationship of signification of which they are to make use, they must *know* this relationship; it is necessary that the idea, that the knowledge of the signification come to life at the same time as its first practical use! That is why some external help is indispensable. The miracle of awakening to the life of thought will come to pass precisely when—thanks to the patiently repeated attempts of the teacher who refuses a desire and suggests a sign, an *artificial, conventional* sign, intended to obtain the satisfaction of the refused desire—the child suddenly will *discover* by some sort of sudden eruption of the idea, the signification of this conventional sign (for example of some gesture or other in the language of the deaf), and from that moment on progress proceeds with astonishing rapidity. A Marie Heurtin, a Helen Keller achieved the higher levels of intellectual life.

In the order of social life the sign plays no less important a part. Just as the individual advent into consciousness depends on it, so also does social advent into consciousness. A city, a class, a nation becomes conscious of itself by means of its symbols.

In God alone intellectual life makes no use of signs. He knows Himself, and everything, by His own essence. That is the privilege of the pure Act.

The philosophers of old divided the sign into the *speculative sign* and the *practical sign,* and this by reason of the fundamental division of the functions of the intellect into the speculative and the practical. The good proper to the speculative intellect, is purely and simply the true; the good proper to the practical intellect is the true as leading to right action. In one way or another—that is to say, for reasons and to degrees which differ greatly with cases—the practical intellect presupposes the will; its object, in so far as it is known object, is something to be put into existence, something to be made concrete in action.

Another distinction deserves attention; it is that between the *instrumental* and the *formal* sign.

Sometimes the sign is something which, *itself known beforehand,* thereafter makes known another thing: a ribbon of smoke which we see going up in the air, a portrait which we see in a museum are objects on which our knowledge has its impact beforehand, later passing to other objects known by means of the former, to the fire of which the smoke is the effect and the sign, to the model of whom the portrait is the image and the sign. Such are *instrumental* signs (we could also say "sign-things"), and this is the case with all the signs which we experience, *save* for a privileged category consisting in the mental signs which intervene in the act of knowing; an image, in imagination or in memory, a concept.

Such signs the scholastics called *formal* signs[3] (we could also say "pure signs"); they are mental forms whose *entire essence* is to convey meaning (to signify); before being themselves known as objects (by a reflexive act), such signs are known only by the knowledge itself which by their means brings the mind to the object; in other words, in order to exercise their function as signs, they are known not by "appearing" as an object but by "disappearing" before the object. Mnemonic image, the mental form preserved in memory, is not *that which* is known when we remember, it is purely the means by which we know directly an event lived in the past; the concept is not *that which* is known when our intelligence is at work, it is purely the means by which we seize directly an intelligible aspect of things. Such signs are pure *élans* ("intentions," urges) of the mind toward the object. In an entirely and irreducibly original universe which is the universe of knowledge, they realize in an altogether special manner, the ideal of the perfect sign and of the perfect image; they are natural signs, natural images, and are also *pure* signs and *pure* images.

I have just said that by a single act of knowledge, when the eye sees the statue of Hermes, it sees Hermes in that statue. That is true; in such a case there is an immediate transition from the statue—a thing seen (a thing seen at a first moment not of time, but of nature), a thing which receives the extrinsic qualification of being seen—to Hermes seen in it. But in the case of *pure signs* there is not only an immediate transition; we must add that at the instant when the sign is first known (by priority of nature, not of time) it is not a *thing known,*

[3] *Cf.* my work *Les Degrés du Savoir,* Paris, Desclée de Brouwer, 1932, Chapter III and appendix i; English transl., *The Degrees of Knowledge,* London and New York, 1938, Chapter III. The English edition is not as complete as the French and does not include the reference cited in the appendix. *Cf.* John of Saint Thomas, Log. II. P., q. 22, a. 1 to 4.

but a *form of knowing,* an internal cause or determination to know, *"ratio intrinseca cognoscendi." Formaliter constituit rem ut cognitam.* It formally or definitely constitutes the thing as known; in other words, to be known is for it an intrinsic qualification because all its essence and all its "known being" is to make that which is signified present to the mind—something which is not the case with any instrumental sign, with any statue, with any portrait.

The *practical sign* must be distinguished from the mere expression of a sentiment (although often it is joined to such). In order that there may be a practical sign there must be a manifestation of an intention of the intelligence and of the will. Of such sort are many natural signs (gestures of supplication, of command; smiles, glances laden with some intention or other) or conventional signs (signals employed for the control of traffic or to aid navigation, gestures and formulas for taking oaths, military insignia, religious rites, etc.).

Let us say that the practical sign is the sign used by the practical intellect and which derives from it.[9] In order to be practical, the intellect does not need to be drawn outside its proper limits as intellect; it is within these limits, remaining intellect and without passing over to nervous motor influx, that the intellect exercises its practical functions and deserves to be called practical. So also in order to be practical the sign does not need to be drawn outside its proper limits as sign, and thus become an efficient cause; it is by remaining within the category proper for signs (*formal* causality) that it exercises a practical function and deserves to be called practical: as making manifest not precisely a thing but an intention and a direction of the practical intellect. It is not as itself causing or operating something that the sign is active; it is as conducting or directing the operation by which is produced or caused the thing signified.

At the highest point in the category of the practical sign, as a pre-eminent and unique case, is found the *sacrament*.

What is the generic idea of the sacrament? It is a practical sign ordered to interior sanctification, *signum practicum significans rem sacram prout nos sanctificat.* Being something external and sensory which signifies an effect of interior sanctification to be produced, it is a conventional sign founded in fact on a certain analogy (a practical symbol).[10] Theologians explain that every sacrament has a character at once social and religious. Its meaning (signification) is determined by social authority (that is to say, either human authority under the inspiration of God as was the case under the law of nature, or immediately the transcending authority of God itself, as under the Mosaic Law or under the Law of the Gospel). In the historical situation described as "the state of nature" (not, certainly, in the sense of a state of pure nature, for grace was there, as were the wounds of the first sin, but in the sense of the state of mankind *before the Law*) there were, say the theologians, sacraments, and these were instituted by the civil community as acting by virtue of the internal inspiration of God, and exercising a religious function sanctioned by God;[11] in the state defined by the Mosaic Law and by the Law of the Gospel, the institution of the sacraments of the Old Law and of the sacraments of the New Law, refers back immediately to God Himself, in the (supernatural) society which He has with men: whether this promulgation took place by means of a mediator, as in the Old Law, or whether it takes place, as in the New Law, by means of the Incarnate Word Himself.[12]

Saint Thomas Aquinas teaches that the sacraments of the Old Law, for example circumcision, the eating of the Paschal Lamb, expiatory actions, the priestly anointing of Aaron, were true sacraments, and as such ordered toward internal sanctity: practical signs signifying sanctification—but not effecting it themselves.[13] The realization of this effect of interior purity sprang from the disposition of the subject, from his contrition, from his love; just as in the oath-taking of a knight it is the disposition of the subject and the stirrings of his soul which produce in him the virtues of chivalry.

The sacraments of the New Law involve an additional perfection; not only are they sacraments, but they are sacraments in a super-eminent manner: they effect that which they signify (if the subject does not put obstacles in their way by his contrary disposition). This comes to be by virtue of a superabundance coming forth from Christ's passion, and because the major thing in the New Law is the grace of the Spirit operating from within.[14] The sacramental sign is no longer merely a *practical sign,* it then becomes an *instrumental cause* of which the very Cause of being makes use to produce grace in the soul, just as an artist makes use of the violin or flute to produce beauty. And to be thus a cause (instrumental) is extrinsic to the idea of the sign, even of the practical sign.

According to Catholic doctrine the greatest of the sacraments is the sacrament of the Eucharist. In his study on the symbol (1887) quoted by Warburg,[4] Friedrich Theodor Vischer sought therein an eminent example of one of the poles which his theory attributes to the symbol. Yet in reality we do not in any way find here an example of an identity between the sign and the signified. The sacred words, "This is my body" in no way assert an identity; they operate (as an instrumental cause) a change (transubstantiation). Far from resting upon an identity between the sign and the signified, the sacrament of the Eucharist adds to the relationship of sign to signified that of cause to effect and implies the intervention of the First Cause producing the most radical change of which we can conceive, a change which affects being in so far as it is being.

[4] *Cf.* E. Wind, *Warburgs Begriff der Kulturwissenschaft,* Fourth Congress for Aesthetics, 1930. (*Zeitschrift für Aesthetik und allgemeine Kunstwissenschaft,* Band 25, Supplement, Stuttgart, 1931.)

THE MAGICAL SIGN AND THE NOCTURNAL KINGDOM OF THE MIND

IN CONNECTION with the problems relating to the practical sign, a new division of capital importance should, I believe, be introduced: that between the *logical sign* and the *magical sign*. Everything which has been said above had to do with the logical sign, or with *the state* of the sign in a more evolved human régime (dominated by the intelligence).

In giving to the word "logic" a very broad and rather infrequent usage, but a usage which seems to me justified, I describe sign as a "logical sign," or a sign in the sphere of the Logos, when it is located in a certain functional status, wherein it is a sign *for the intelligence* (speculative or practical) taken as the *dominant factor* of the psychic régime or of the régime of culture. Whether the sign in itself be sensory or intelligible, it is then definitively addressed to intelligence: in the last analysis, it relates to a psychic régime dominated by the intelligence.

I describe sign as a "magical sign," or as a sign in the sphere of the Dream,[5] when it is located in another functional status,

[5]"But, to aid him to resolve about Cyrus, he [Astyages] called to him the same Magians who had interpreted his dreams. . . ." Herodotus, I:120.—". . . and with that he took the Magians who interpreted dreams and had persuaded him to let Cyrus go free, and impaled them. . . ." *Ibid.*, 128 (transl. A. D. Godley).

In several of the Australian and Papuan languages, the terms which designate the mythical era, or that term which pertains to this era, are likewise used to indicate a *dream*. (A. P. Elkin, "The Secret Life of the Australian Aborigines," *Oceania*, III, pp. 128–29.) Also the Yuma Indians suppose a strict relationship to exist between the myth and the dream. "'As Kroeber points out (*Handbook of the Indians of California*, p. 857), myth-dreaming is a common cultural feature of the Mohave and the Yuma. Joe Homer, who was fifty-six years old in 1921, had become a Methodist. . . . When I reminded Joe Homer that he no longer dreams about Awikwame Mountain, the home of the gods, he replied that it was too big a place to dream about more than once. "You would not go to Washington every year," he said. The potency of dreaming as a means of properly learning a myth was emphasized on one wherein it is a sign *for the imagination* taken as a supreme arbiter or *dominant factor* of all psychic life or of all the life of culture. Whether the sign in itself be sensory or intelligential, it is then definitively addressed to the powers of the imagination; in the last analysis, it relates to a psychic régime immersed in the living ocean of the imagination.

My hypothesis, therefore, consists in introducing here the idea of a *situation,* a *state,* or functional status, and in establishing a deep distinction between the state of our evolved cultures and another state wherein, for all psychic and cultural life, the final instance belongs to the imagination—wherein the law of the imagination is the supreme law. The intelligence is present, indeed, but it is not set free. Such a state under my definition constitutes the magical régime of psychic life and of culture.

As we have seen above, animals make use of signs. Animals live in a kind of magic; biologically united to nature, all the

---

occasion by Joe Homer. An Akwa'ala informant from Lower California had related an imperfect origin tale. Joe said that the informant's not having'dreamed it was the cause of the imperfections.'" E. W. Gifford, "Yuma Dreams and Omens," *Journal of American Folk-Lore,* XXXIX, p. 58, 1926. Cited by Lucien Lévy-Bruhl, *La Mythologie primitive,* Paris, Alcan, 1935, pp. xxiii–xxvi.

The etymological meaning of the words magian and *magic* is not known. The interpretation of dreams was only one of the functions of the Magians; their principal function was that of offering sacrifices. It seems that it was by reason of a Semitic influx (Babylonian) that the practices called "magical" penetrated into Persia to such an extent that the word which was to describe them in our language was precisely that. In the present study I am using the word magic in a very broad sense and as designating not only the operations and beliefs of magic themselves, but, from the point of view of the philosophy of culture, a whole régime of (primitive) psychic life and civilization. Magic itself above all seems to aim at seeking power over beings. And, in my opinion, in the kingdom of the primacy of the dream or of the imagination, it was natural that the highest value recognized by man should have been precisely that of Knowledge-Power, of *Magic.* Whereas in the régime of the primacy of the Logos, it is in Knowledge-Knowing, in *Wisdom,* that is naturally acknowledged the highest value.

signs of which they make use relate to a psychic régime which is exclusively imaginative.

The intelligence of primitive man is of the same *nature* as ours; it can even be keener in him than in some civilized men. But that with which we are here concerned is a question of *state,* of the conditions of the use of the mind. The whole mental régime of primitive man is contained under the primacy of the imagination. With him the intelligence is altogether bound up with and subordinate to the imagination and to its savage universe. Such a mental régime is a régime of experimental and lived connection with nature, of whose intensity and breadth we can only form a picture with difficulty.

Here is an inferior condition but one in no way to be scorned. It is a human state, but a state of the childhood of humanity; a fruitful state, and a state through which it was necessary to pass. In this régime humanity enriched itself with many vital truths, of which perhaps a great number were lost when it passed on to an adult state; these truths were known by means of the dream or of instinct and living appreciation, just as if, in the knowledge that a bee has of the world of flowers, the light of the intelligence were diffused, before becoming focussed in stars and in solar systems which separate daylight from shadow.

Herein we meet with a difficulty analogous to that which we meet when we seek to penetrate the psyche of the animal. Everything which *we* picture to ourselves is bathed in the intelligence and in an intelligence set free. We have great trouble in depicting to ourselves what another mental régime can be like. (And if we are Cartesians, such a procedure is strictly impossible for us.) Let me say in summary that in our logical state, sensations, images, ideas, are bathed *in sunlight,* bound up with the luminous and regular life of the intelligence and of its laws of gravitation.

In the magical state, all these things were *of the night,* bound up with the fluid and twilight life of the imagination, and with an experience which was of an amazingly powerful impact, but entirely lived and—to the extent that it was an object of reflection—dreamed.

The same is true of the sign and of the relationship between the sign and the signified.

Truth being a relationship of the cognitive faculty to the thing, and being possessed only by the judgment of the intelligence which seizes upon it as such, it must be said that among primitive men this relationship is lived, but is not winnowed out for its own sake. Doubtless it is known, since the intelligence is there present, but known in a nocturnal fashion, since the intelligence is there immersed in the powers of the imagination.

Reflecting upon primitive man, we can say that in him the relationship of the mind to the thing is ambivalent. The same relationship is "false" (in the eyes of our evolved consciousness) to the extent that it, for instance, asserts the existence of composite ancestors for the tribe: duck-men or kangaroo-men. It is "true" to the extent that it asserts the living union of man with nature, whereof this myth is the symbol. But for primitive man such a distinction has no meaning. It is because his very consent to truth is not the same as ours (the idea of truth not having for him been winnowed out for itself).

He adheres *en bloc,* at the same time and indistinctly, to the symbol and the symbolized: here is for him, in indivisible fashion, an image or a likeness of truth, an equivalent, an *als ob* of truth, without his having winnowed out the idea of truth for its own sake. In similar fashion a child believes in a story, in the adventures of Alice in Wonderland; awaken the child, withdraw him from the world of the imagination and he knows very well that a little girl cannot enter a rabbit hole. But primitive man does not wake up, he is not yet withdrawn from the motherly bosom of the imagination, which for him makes all nature familiar and without which he could not face the dangers, whereby he feels he is surrounded on all sides, and (if we are dealing with true primitive man, with man of prehistoric times: today's homonym thereof is doubtless merely a distorted reflection of the original) the pitiless hardship of his existence as a dweller in caves, struggling among the wild beasts. He inhabits the land of *seeming truth*.

Bergson has admirably shown that what is to be found at the source and basis of magic as a primordial element is the relationship of causality.

". . . [man] realized at once that the limits of his normal influence over the outside world were soon reached, and he could not resign himself to going no further. So he carried on the movement, and, since the movement could not by itself secure the desired result, nature must needs take the task in hand. . . . [Things] will then be more or less charged with submissiveness and potency: they will hold at our disposal a power which yields to the desires of man, and of which man may avail himself. . . . [The workings of Magic] begin the act which men cannot finish. They go through the motions which alone could not produce the desired effect, but which will achieve it if the man concerned knows how to prevail upon the goodwill of things. Magic is then innate in man, being but the outward projection of a desire which fills the heart."[6]

That which I believe to be lacking in Bergson's theory is that it does not take into account the indispensable instrument of magical activity—the *practical sign*. It is surely true that magic implies an appeal to some cosmic power which brings the desire of man to a happy outcome, an appeal which itself pre-

[6]H. Bergson, *Les Deux Sources de la Morale et de la Religion,* Paris, 7e Ed., Alcan, 1932, pp. 175–77; *The Two Sources of Morality and Religion* (Tr. by R. A. Audra and C. Brereton), New York, Holt, 1935, pp. 155–57.

supposes some sympathy, some compliance in things. But it must be added that magic makes use of signs. Here the relationship proper to the sign, and to the practical sign, necessarily intervenes. Man does not merely outline some causal action, he *makes a sign* (to semi-personal cosmic elements). It is needful that we insist upon the mental characteristics of these practical signs, subject as they are to the nocturnal régime of the imagination.

(1) First of all, in my opinion, we here find ourselves confronted with a refraction in the world of imagination, or with a nocturnal deformation, of the practical sign in its quality as sign, or considered in the order of the *relationship itself of signification,* that is to say, in the order of *formal* causality, wherein the sign is, by its essence, the vicar of the object. Let us not forget that this relationship of sign to signified is, in its own order, singularly close. The motion toward the sign or the image, says Saint Thomas after Aristotle, is identical with the motion toward the object itself. *"Sic enim est unus et idem motus in imaginem cum illo qui est in rem."* [15] In the formal-objective order the sign is thus something most astonishing, whereat the routine of culture alone prevents our wonder. And this marvellous function of containing the object—with respect to the mind—of having present in itself the thing itself *in alio esse,* is fully exercised in primitive man. Words are not anemic or colorless, they are overflowing with life—with their life as signs—for primitive man. But that in itself sets a snare for his imagination. Thanks to the condition of experienced and lived participation wherein is established his whole mental life, the presence as to knowledge of the signified in the sign becomes for him a presence as to reality, a physical interchangeability, a physical fusion, and a physical equivalence of the sign and the signified (invocation of mythical names;[7]

---

[7]"When a man thus employs a name to help him in his purpose, we might at first sight be inclined to think he was actually calling on the bearer of the name for help . . . [this] does not represent the con-

magic objects, spells, idolatry). Primitive man is intoxicated with the excellence of the sign; yet the sign never altogether loses its genuine relationship of signification (to some *other* thing). The idol is god and yet is never altogether god.[8]

(2) Then again a slurring takes place from formal-objective causality to *efficient causality*. The creation of signs is a mark of the pre-eminence of the mind, and the instinct of the intelligence quickly informed man that symbols make him enter into the heart of things—in order to know them: at once, in a psychic régime wherein the imagination is dominant, this slurring will take place, man will think that symbols make us enter into the heart of things in order to act physically upon them and in order to make them physically subject to us and in order to effect for us a real and physical union with them. Moreover, are not the signs in question first and foremost practical signs? At once the imagination will take a sign directive toward an operation as an operating sign. And why should we be astonished that the imagination of primitive man cannot distinguish between formal causality and efficient causality, when the intelligence of philosophers so often confuses them?

The sign, then, not only makes men know, it makes things

struction which the magician himself here places on his action . . . he is rather applying the mythical names to himself or to this or that feature of his undertaking. In short, he is himself impersonating a mythical character or identifying some feature of his undertaking with a corresponding feature of a mythical undertaking which reached a successful close. A man told me that whenever he went fish shooting he pretended to be Kivavia himself." He did not implore the favour and help of this mystical hero; he identified himself with him. F. E. Williams, "Trading Voyages from the Gulf of Papua," *Oceania*, III, pp. 164–65 (cited by Lévy-Bruhl, *Mythol. prim.*, pp. 161–62).

[8]We are furnished with a remarkable specimen of this order of ideas by tantrism. Here thought magically creates symbols which themselves become living and powerful. Tantrism thus *creates* the gods which it *adores;* by means of the activity of the pious magician these gods actualize universal psychic forces, directed in their very intentionality toward some ideal object conceived by the man, forces from the symbolization of which they are born, and of which—even though they are gods, and are adored—they yet remain symbols.

be, it is an efficient cause in itself. Hence all the procedures of sympathetic magic. In order to make rain, the sorcerer waters the ground. In order to obtain abundant tubers, he buries in the ground at seed time magical stones of the same shape as the desired tubers, which shall "teach" the yams and the taro to grow big, to reach the same size as the stones.[9] The stones make them a sign, they are pattern-symbols. The theory of *mana* among the Melanesians (*avenda* among the Iroquois, *wakonda* among the Sioux), the theory of a force spread throughout nature wherein all things participate in differing degree, seems to be the fruit of a later reflection upon this use of the sign. To the extent that reflection will be intensified, the idea of this semi-physical, semi-moral environment will become more materialized.

(3) But the sign, in spite of everything, remains a sign. Inevitably there will take place a return of the order of causality to which it belongs, that is, of formal causality and of the relationship of signification—which with primitive man becomes

[9]Lévy-Bruhl, *Mythol. prim.*, pp. 157–58.
Then again, in central Queensland, in Australia: "It was necessary to bring the drought to an end. They do not simply turn to a specialist, to a professional rainmaker. A great number of natives take an active part in the operation. 'On the Georgina River, at Roxburgh Downs, a piece of quartz-crystal, the rain-stone which has been obtained from somewhere out in the ranges is crushed and hammered to powder. Some very straight-stemmed tree is chosen—. . . with the butt for a long way up free from branches—and saplings, from fifteen to twenty feet in length are ranged all round it in the form of a bell-tent, forming a sort of shed. Outside, in front of this erection, a small space of ground is cleared; a portion scooped out, and some water placed in it. The men, having been collected within the shed, now come out, and dancing and singing all around the artificial water-hole, break out with the sounds and imitate the antics of various aquatic birds and animals, *e.g.,* ducks, frogs. All this time the women are camped at about twenty to twenty-five yards distant. The men next form themselves into a long string, in Indian file, one behind the other, and gradually encircle the gins, over which they throw the crushed and pulverized stone: the women at the same time hold wooden troughs, shields, and pieces of bark over their heads, and

a relationship of fusion and of physical equivalence—upon the relationship of efficient causality and of operation. And the imagination will oscillate from one way of thinking the sign to the other. In the perspective of efficient causality (as well as in the perspective of the relationship of signification understood in accordance with its true nature) there is a *distinction,* a difference, between the cause and the effect (as well as between the sign and the signified). In the perspective of formal causality denatured by the imagination, and of that intoxication with the sign induced in primitive man by the relationship of signification, there is a physical *interpenetration* and fusion of the sign and the signified.

Since we are by hypothesis dealing with the nocturnal régime of the imagination, and since for the imagination as such (as dreams bear witness) the principle of identity does not exist; and then again, since the intelligence is still present, bound

---

pretend that they are protecting themselves from a heavy downpour of rain.'" (Dr. W. E. Roth, *Superstition, Magic and Medicine. North Queensland Ethnography.* Bulletin 5, p. 10, 1903.)

"The procedure consists essentially in imitating what happens when it rains. A hole is filled with water. Frogs croak, ducks and other water birds beat their wings and cry out; the women protect themselves as best they can against the shower which soaks them (the crystal powder which the men threw on them). By this 'imitation' of that which habitually accompanies it, rain is invited, is called upon, to fall. It is almost falling already; surely it will fall.

"This realization of the circumstances which always accompany rain should, it seems, act upon rain as a suggestion, which its magic nature makes irresistible.

"Similarly on certain days the Nagas of the northeast frontier of India come down the path which leads from their rice fields, with slow steps, their backs bent, as though they were doubled up under the burden of their harvest. By 'imitating' the journey they will have to make if the harvest is fine, they persuade it to be so, they insure that it shall be so. One remembers the Papuans of the island of Kiwai, the Kanakas of New Caledonia, and many other primitives who bury in their gardens magic stones charged with 'teaching' the yams, the sweet potatoes, the taro, to become as large as they are themselves." (L. Lévy-Bruhl, *Mythol. prim.,* pp. 190–92.)

up with and clothed in the imagination, it is easy to understand that for primitive man the identity of things is constantly unmade and made again. It is altogether too hasty for us to say that with him there is simply an identity between the sign and the signified. No, there is an oscillation, there is a going and coming from distinction to identification. When children play by building sand castles, these castles are truly castles for them. If you trample them, the children will cry with rage and indignation. But once their play is at an end, what were castles are only sand. Primitive man believes to be identical (through the living power of the imagination) that which he obscurely knows to be different (through his intelligence, bound up in the imagination). It is impossible to understand anything about his thought if it be conceived from the point of view of the logical or daylight state of the intelligence, taken as the rule and measure of all thought. It is the thought of an awakened dreamer, wherein the rôle of *play* (and the allowance of *play*) is tremendously great.

I believe that the preceding considerations can help to resolve certain difficulties. Bergson,[10] Olivier Leroy[11] with reason insist upon this truth, which is of major philosophical importance: that there is no difference in *nature* between the intelligence of primitive man and our own intelligence. The structure of the intelligence of the Papuah or of the Yuma is the same as that of a civilized European; and, when the principles and laws of his reasoning are considered in their own properly logical texture, his is the same logic as ours.

But if the intelligence is—with its principles, its logic, its curiosities, its virtualities, its intuitions, its great primordial inclinations—the *same intelligence* in primitive man as in us, yet it sets to work in altogether different fashion and after an alto-

[10]H. Bergson, *The Two Sources of Morality and Religion,* notably p. 85.
[11]Olivier Leroy, *La Raison primitive.*

gether different manner, because with primitive man it is not working *at home,* in its *own environment,* but rather in the environment of the imagination, in the huge, fluid, fertile world of the imagination, to whose laws it is subject and wherein are prepared the living materials and the great energizing themes on which rational life, properly so called, will labour, but which have not yet reached the rational state. There is no difference in *nature* between the intelligence of primitive man and our own intelligence, but between them there is a fundamental difference of *state.* And from the very fact that, in this nocturnal state of primitive man, the intelligence—with its laws of logic in themselves identical with our own—is, as I have said, *bound up,* the concrete functioning of his thought, that is to say of his imagination-infused-with-intelligence, is typically different from the concrete functioning of the thought of civilized man. Here, and to reduce his thesis to the affirmation of such a difference of *state,* Lévy-Bruhl is right.

Whenever primitive man is dealing with the understanding of the immediate concrete, with the interpretation and practical use of the data of the senses, in short, with the world of *animal experience,* primitive man's imagination-infused-with-intelligence displays qualities properly intellectual: qualities of observation and perspicacity, of discernment and of reasoning, of grasping the real in accordance with its typical diversities, in accordance with its concrete quiddities and differences—qualities often highly superior to those in civilized man—and qualities wherein is sovereign the vigilance of the external senses.[12]

But whenever he is dealing with the world of *abstract thought* and of intelligible linkages, with the immensity of that which is to be known beyond the experience of the immediately concrete—the moment primitive man steps into that world, which is as important for him as it is for us, since he is a man—at that moment he makes his intelligence labour under the law of the internal senses and of their dream activity. And

[12]*Ibid.,* pp. 82 ff.

how could he do otherwise? Hence it comes about that his imagination-infused-with-intelligence enters into a régime of thought dominated by that *lived participation* on which ethnologists with good reason insist.[13] For the intelligence—having indeed obscurely grasped the fact that a certain characteristic is a sign of a certain nature, but having in no sense disengaged the idea itself, the abstract idea of nature—the intelligence will readily admit that the most differing subjects share, while remaining themselves, in a same (transcendent) nature. Such is the case of the totem animal, which the members of the tribe *are*, even while remaining men, in such sort that all things, in accordance with sacred laws which the ritual sets in motion, are in communication and are vitally interpenetrated in the primitive man's universe.

Still *causæ ad invicem sunt causæ,* "causes of diverse genera exert causality upon one another": if the thought of primitive man is thus altogether bathed in the idea of participation, which conditions the idea that he forms of the sign, on the other hand it is the idea which he unconsciously forms of the sign, and which I have tried to analyze by transposing it philosophically, that gives form and consistency to the lived metaphysics of participation in his thought. Professor Lévy-Bruhl rightly insists that there is an identity for the Bororo between the members of their totem group and an arara with red feathers; for the Huichols of Mexico between a stag and wheat or the Hikuli plant.[14] But Lévy-Bruhl does not see that this identity is not

[13]*Cf.* Émile Caillet, *Symbolisme et âmes primitives,* Paris, Boivin, 1936.

[14]Lévy-Bruhl, *Les Fonctions mentales dans les Sociétés inférieures,* pp. 77–78; 121–125. (*How Natives Think,* New York, Knopf.) M. Olivier Leroy is not mistaken when he points out: "The logic of a Huichol would be deficient only on the day when he would prepare a wheat porridge while he thought he was making a stag stew." (*La Raison primitive,* p. 70.) But, for his own part neglecting the typical state of the function of the sign among primitive men, he seems to go to the opposite extreme and excessively rationalizes their thought.

complete, that there is in it an element of play and, if I may
put it so, of *irony,* for he does not see the essential part played
therein by the sign and the symbol, and the very special character in which is invested the function of the sign for a thought
dwelling in the nocturnal realm of the imagination. It is in a
symbol and according to the law of the symbol—above all, I say,
of the practical symbol which is the magical sign—that everything which goes beyond the experience of the immediately
concrete is attained by primitive man. And there can well be in
all this many truths: they will be masked by dreams.

From the point of view of a positivism doubtless more subtle
than that of the "law of the three states," but still faithful to
the spirit of Auguste Comte, and above all of Littré, one would
be led to say that, mathematical and physico-mathematical
science, together with its related sciences, representing the only
function of truth (or of verification) in human thought, religion, mystical experience, metaphysics, poetry are in the civilized mentality as it were an inheritance from the primitive and
"pre-logical" mentality. They are varying metamorphoses of
ancient magic, perhaps justifiable in the practical and emotional order but directly opposed, as is magic itself, to the line
of science and truth. The era of science has succeeded to the era
of magic. And magic and science are essentially inimical and
incompatible.

For Bergson, magic and science are similarly inimical and
incompatible. There is nothing in common between magic and
science. . . . "Magic is the reverse of science." It is because, for
Bergson also, science consists entirely in the mathematical ex-
plication of matter and the utilization of universal mechanism.
Yet in his view science (at least a science in process of being
born, implied in daily life) has always co-existed with magic.
And science does not exhaust—far from it—the function of
truth in human thought; it is only the most superficial applica-

tion of that function. Other functions, above all the mystical and, on their own level, metaphysics and poetry, are functions of truth, and more profound functions of truth. But for him, as for the positivists, these things are at right angles to the line of science, and they spring from the same vital centre as magic. Magic and religion have a common origin, starting from which they developed in opposite directions, magic in the direction of illusion, of myth-making and of laziness, religion (dynamic religion) in the direction of heroism and of truth.

The interpretation which I should like to suggest differs at once from both the preceding ones. To my mind our physico-mathematical science is only one of the possible forms of science and one of the degrees of knowledge, knowledge which at its high point is called metaphysics, and, higher still, theology and mystical knowledge. Moreover, both science and metaphysics, like religion and mysticism, and like poetry—each of them in its own fashion functions of truth—are created to grow up together, and, if man will expend on them the necessary pains and effort, to blossom forth in harmony. In the nocturnal state of the primacy of the dream and of the imagination, they were inchoate, more or less fused or confused; once the threshold of the daylight state (primacy of the intelligence and of the Logos) has been passed, they more and more become differentiated from each other. But if it is not true that "the era of science has succeeded to the era of magic," on the other hand we must admit that the state of Logos has succeeded—for all the mental and cultural functions of the human being—to the state of magic. And for religion as for science, there is an incompatibility between the nocturnal state and the daylight one. But science, like religion, itself existed in the nocturnal state before it existed in the daylight state; thus in that sense one cannot say there is nothing in common between magic and science, and that magic is the reverse of science; one can say only that the magical state of science is in opposition to its logical state.

Thus all human thought, with its great and at first undifferentiated primordial ramifications, passes, I believe, through a diversity of *conditions,* or of *states of existence and practice.* As it is progressively diversified, human thought passes from the *condition* of magic to the *condition* of logic. The science of primitive man was science, and it was such in the state of magic; it made use of certain connections of physical causality, but blindly, without knowing it, without withdrawing these connections from the sacral empiricism wherein they were immersed, and in thinking them and signifying them in magical fashion.[15] Science left this condition when it passed over the threshold of the daylight psychic life dominated by the intelligence—a thing which could not have taken place without crises and struggles. It is then that magic puts obstacles in the way of science: and the residues of magical knowing, together with whatever element of truth they may still contain, are then taken over, by virtue of a process of abnormal integration and of paradifferentiation, by a "parascience"—the occultism of civilized man—utterly different from the magic of primitive man, and which will carry with it certain pathological characteristics for intellectual life (as happens for affective life in certain cases of infantile retrogression among adults).

In similar fashion the religion of primitive man (not differentiated, or scarcely differentiated from his science) was religion, and it was such in the state of magic. His myths have a character which is above all practical. "There is no doubt about the reason why the meaning of myths must remain secret, even if their text is known. To possess this meaning is not only a knowledge, but confers a power which is dissipated when the myths are profaned. And the tribe cannot get on without them.

[15]*Cf.* the story of Jacob's lambs, Genesis xxx:37–42. It is possible that in this procedure of a magical type (situated in an epoch of advanced civilization, far removed from primitive times) there may have been used some psychophysiological power, as yet unknown to our science, of visual prenatal influence.

This power alone permits the tribe to enter into community with its ancestors of the mythical period, in some way to participate in them, to make actual their presence, and to insure that their action is renewed periodically. The recital of these myths is thus something altogether different from a simple rite. It is equivalent to an act; it concerns to the ultimate degree the very life of the group."[16]

Here we once more find, therefore, and very clearly marked, one of the already-mentioned characteristics of the practical sign in the magical state: it has, by itself, a causal action. The myth, from the very fact that it makes known the origin of things, *recalls* to them their origin in order to induce them to act, it *signifies* to them their origin, and at the same time their destination and their efficient office.[17] And who knows? Thus

[16]Lévy-Bruhl, *Mythol. prim.*, p. 115.

[17]For the Cuna Indians of the Isthmus of Panama, "each magical chant must be preceded by an incantation which relates the origin of the remedy employed; otherwise it does not work. . . . The chanter first of all thinks of the origin of the *nuchus* (spirits of the wooden statuettes) that is to say, of the fashion in which God created them. If he does not know this, the chant will produce no effect. . . ." "In a Cuna village, Tientiki, there is a fourteen-year-old boy who can pass through fire with impunity, solely because he knows the charm of the creation of fire." Er. Nordenskiold, "La Conception de l'âme chez les Indiens Cuna, Journal des Américanistes," N. S., XXIV (1932), pp. 6, 16; "Faiseurs de miracles et voyants chez les Indiens Cuna," *Revista del Instituto de Etnologia, Tucuman,* II (1932), p. 464. (Cited by Lévy-Bruhl, *Mythol. prim.*, pp. 117–118.) "Thus to know the origin of animals, of iron, of fire, etc., is equivalent to acquiring over them a certain power, which one exercises through incantations. Moreover, it is the myths which supply this knowledge." (*Ibid.*, pp. 118–119.) The same belief exists among the farmers of Timor, in the Netherlands Indies. Here Lévy-Bruhl cites the observations of A. C. Kruyt (*ibid.*, p. 119): "Whenever the plants in some field look sickly or are not prosperous, someone well acquainted with the traditions and legends relating to the rice goes to that field. There he passes the night, in the plantation cabin, reciting the legends which explain how man came to possess rice (origin myths). . . . Those who do this are not priests. . . . It is hoped by this means to induce the spirit of the rice, which is believed to have gone far away, to return."

to speak to things in order to make them propitious is perhaps also, without his being aware of it and with all the ambiguities one might find in it, a way for primitive man to stammer out to Him who made things, and who is present in them by His immensity.

However it may be, observers report that for the Australian natives the "very life of nature and therefore of the human race itself depends on these rites and sites [local totem sites]. The aboriginal totemistic philosophy binds man to nature in a living whole, which is symbolized and maintained by the complex of myths, rites and secret sites. Unless the myths with their sanctions are preserved, the rites performed and the sites maintained as spirit sanctuaries, that living bond is broken, man and nature are separated, and neither man nor nature has any assurance of life in the future. This does not mean that man thinks he has a magical control over natural species, but that he has a sanctified method of expressing that mutual need which man and nature have, the one for the other. And he does his part at the appropriate seasons towards maintaining the life and regularity of nature by means of ritual which is standardized and sanctioned by myth, and by preserving continuity with the past, through these same rites and sacred sites and symbols."[18]

Thus it appears that the practicality of the myth does not relate directly and before everything else to some empirical utility, as some pre-Benthamite might understand it, but to a (transcendent) efficacity of propitiation. The same may be applied to images and their efficacity. "It is true, as the current hypothesis has it, that prehistoric man believes in the magical efficacity of the images he draws, paints or carves. But it is not at all certain that he thinks that he can thus directly cause animals to come under his power. On the testimony of the Karadjeri [a tribe of northwestern Australia whose rock-

---

[18]A. P. Elkin, "The Secret Life of the Australian Aborigines," *Oceania,* III, pp. 132–33 (cited by Lévy-Bruhl, *op. cit.,* p. 128).

paintings resemble prehistoric pictures], the mystical virtue of images is of the same nature as that of ceremonies. It insures the fertility, growth and permanence of animal and vegetable species through the presence and with the help of their mythical 'creators.' In this fashion, at every season the tribe will find, as always, the wherewithal to nourish itself. This will be one consequence of the action exercised by the image. It is not its immediate object. The mystical level conditions and in this case dominates the utilitarian level. It is not confused with it."[19]

Transcendentally practical, but still practical—such then is generally the basic character of the primitive myth, of the myth in the state of magic. I do not forget that the myths known as "etiological" already respond to a need for *knowing;* but if they are examined closely, it is seen—a remarkable circumstance —that they still remain *reductively* practical, in the sense that they are built upon the *model* of the practical signs used in rites or in magical procedures. They thus exemplify an extraordinarily curious passing-over of the practical sign of magic

[19]Lévy-Bruhl, *Mythol. prim.,* p. 147.

It seems proper to add, concerning prehistoric art, that if in many cases magic seems indeed to have imposed upon it its particular finalities, nevertheless the primordial rôle of this art seems to remain with the finality proper to art itself, with the joy of creating or recreating forms, with æsthetic pleasure. The civilization of the Reindeer age bears witness that the instinct which is properly artistic is in man a tendency of the spirit certainly more primitive than the tendency for magic. *Cf.* G. H. Luquet, *L'Art et la Religion des Hommes Fossiles,* Paris, Masson, 1926. "It is only," concludes M. Luquet, "in the Magdalenian that the convergence of purely geometric ornamental art with figured art without ornamental intent brought about the decorative use of figured motifs, and that perhaps figured art acquired a magical purpose. But this latter can only have been added to art by virtue of the creative character which it possessed from its own essence. Moreover, even in the figures which have a seemingly magical rôle, the execution was carefully wrought with a view to an æsthetic effect. Thus, even in the utilitarian use of art, which is only a later development, there remains a primitive disinterested character." (*Op. cit.,* p. 229.)

into a speculative (explicative) sign conceived after the same type. On Pentecost Island

"Children were angry with their grandmother who gave them nothing to eat.

"So, tired [of asking], they proceeded to cut down a tree and carved it in the shape of a shark and drew it along behind them singing:

'Shark, Shark, whom shall you carry off?
Carry off our grandmother.
Why carry her off?
Carry her off because of our cocoanuts' [which she refused to give them].

And they continued to drag along the wooden shark and to sing. When they had come home, they let go the wooden shark; and it jumped into the house, seized the grandmother and plunged into the sea. And that is why sharks eat men."[20]

It seems clear that this etiological shark was constructed on the model of the magical sharks and magical crocodiles which a sorcerer sends to devour men. It would be most instructive to analyze from this point of view other examples (more or less elaborated and recast) of etiological myths.[21] By explaining

[20]P. E. Tattevin, "Mythes et Légendes du Sud de l'Ile Pentecôte, Anthropos," XXVI, p. 873; quoted in Lévy-Bruhl, *Mythol. prim.*, p. 285.

[21]Cf. *ibid.*, pp. 168–173. Let us cite a few episodes from the myth of To Kabinana and To Karvuvu.

"In the peninsula of the Gazelle, Father Meier has gathered a cycle of myths, the heroes of which were two brothers, To Kabinana, reflective and intelligent, and To Karvuvu, awkward and stupid. To Karvuvu was roasting breadfruits. To Kabinana, who was taking a walk, saw him (and asked):

" 'You are cooking?'
" 'Yes.'
" 'Why are you doing it in secret, hiding from our mother? Go and take her half a fruit.'

"To Karvuvu went and took it to their mother; she had become a young girl again, for she had shed her skin.

"To Karvuvu asked her: 'Where then is my mother?'

the facts and the particular circumstances which have aroused
human curiosity by means of an historical, or more precisely,
a meta-historical (in the mythical period) *precedent*—(for example, by explaining the colour of the crow by saying that the
crow and another bird agreed to tattoo each other, that the
crow finished his task first and that the other bird, finding the
work boresome, at a stroke emptied the paint pot on the crow's

---

" 'I am she.'

" 'Oh, no,' he replied. 'You are certainly not my mother.'

" 'Yes, I am she.'

" 'But you do not look like her.'

" 'Yes; but I have changed my skin.'

"Whereupon he began to cry heartbrokenly, for under this new skin
of his mother he could not recognize her.

" 'I don't wish to have anything to do with the appearance you now
have. Where have you left your real skin?'

" 'I threw it in the water,' she replied, 'and the tide has already carried
it away.'

"To Karvuvu kept on crying.

" 'I can't bear this skin of yours; I am going to look for the old skin.'

"He got up, went away, sought for it and ended by finding it caught
up in a bush. . . . He took it and came back with it.

"He clothed his mother in it once more.

"To Kabinana came to the house where they both lived and asked
him:

" 'Why did you have put back on our mother the skin which she had
taken off? Indeed, you are an idiot. Our descendants forever will die.
Whereas snakes, both great and small, will change their skins.'

"Each time To Karvuvu is guilty of a foolishness or of a bad act, his
brother cries without fail: 'You are not more than an animal. You are
working evil on our descendants!' For example, when To Karvuvu
carved out the shark: 'You are really a strange fellow! You are making
our mortal descendants absolutely miserable! This fish [the shark] will
devour all the other fish and will also attack the mortal race.' And a
little further on: 'Your bird is a thief. Thus you work evil upon our
mortal descendants; they also will be thieves.' In another situation:
'You are truly a fool! We are going to suffer hunger and our descendants
also will have to suffer it.' And finally: 'You are dragging down into
misery the mortals who are our issue.' " The Reverend Jos. Meier, *Mythen
und Erzählungen der Küstenbewohner der Gazelle-Halbinsel*, Münster,
1909, pp. 37–39, 61, 65, 79. (Cited by Lévy-Bruhl, *Mythol. prim.*, pp.
169–72.)

feathers, "and from that time on all crows are black"),[22]—the etiological myth constructs for beings a sign which has caused them to be what they are in the nature of things, in the same fashion as the magical sign causes the effect desired by the rain-maker or crop-maker. Thus it comes about that in order to re-endow things with the efficacity of an Archtypal-sign, which is their origin and from which they derive and in which they participate, the pseudo-Platonism of primitive man accounts for them, not by a supra-temporal Idea, but by a story (which reverts to a pre-temporal event). It has been said that the etiological myth *justifies* things, it *"validates"* them.[23] Already, in a nocturnal fashion, it assigns to them a "cause"— however different that cause may be from the "causes" of our science. Already it corresponds to a seeking after knowledge, to a magical rough sketch of knowledge. But all this while making manifest its practical origin and its dependence with regard to the practical sign.

The "absurdity" of the myths of primitive man should not make us forget how much truth—in the state of magic—was contained in their religion. It seems that, for what are very different reasons, Bergson as well as the "sociologists" altogether too much neglect the body of sound apperceptions, however much they be mixed with error, wherewith this religion was still charged, under the influence of primordial traditions and by virtue of the natural élan of the reason. It has often been pointed out that the further back one goes into the authentically primitive past, the more one finds dominant henotheism and a viable idea of the Supreme Spirit.[24] A prayer that is truly worthy of the name, and which can be substantially at a very

[22]Lévy-Bruhl, *Mythol. prim.,* p. 174.
[23]R. F. Fortune, *Sorcerers of Dobu,* London, Routledge, 1932, p. 262, quoted in Lévy-Bruhl, *op. cit.,* p. 179.
[24]*Cf.* Guillaume Schmidt, *L'Origine de l'Idée de Dieu,* Vienna, 1910.

high level, remains discernible in primitive man.[25] And, from the general climate of *als ob,* from the night of "seeming-true," wherein, as I have pointed out, is built the primitive's intellectual régime, it is not merely the mass of errors, it is also the mass of truth which a philosophical ethnology ought to disengage and carry over into our own climate, for a complete and correct analysis.

That there is more truth—masked truth—in the religion of primitive man than in the *Religion innerhalb der Grenzen der blossen Vernunft*—that is something which we willingly grant to the Chestertonians. Yet it was more necessary for religion than for any other function of human life to pass over into another psychic régime. The religion of civilized humanity has crossed the threshold of the state of logic, has entered into the daylight régime of the intelligence, be it by a transformation in mythology itself (as in Greece), be it by a process of metaphysical elaboration (as in India), be it by forms of revelation adapted to such a state (as in Judæo-Christian monotheism). The residues of magical religion will then be taken over, by virtue of a process of abnormal integration and of paradifferentiation, by superstitious thought and imagery—wherein the part played by pathology is far greater than in magical religion itself.

The sacramental sign is bound up with religion in the state of logic.[26] It differs essentially from the magical sign. Both are practical signs, but the latter is a practical sign in the nocturnal régime of imaginative thought, the former in the daylight régime of intellective thought. None of the characteristics proper to the magical sign (physical fusion of the sign and the

[25]*Cf.* G. Horn, *La Vie Spirituelle,* April, 1931.
[26]The conception here proposed of the "nocturnal" state of the psychic life and of culture preceding their "daylight" state makes it seem likely that in the primitive cycles the "sacraments of the state of nature" could themselves have existed under a magical form (as the vestiges of primitive revelation could exist under a mythical form).

signified, efficient causality of the sign in itself, oscillation between distinction and identity; reference to a physico-moral
environment) are to be found in the sacramental sign. The latter does not operate as sign; it is operative (in the sacraments
of the New Law) as an instrument moved by the divine omnipotence, the principal causality of which entirely and absolutely subordinates to itself such an instrument.

The magical sign has as its end the exercise of a power over
nature or over the powers on which nature is dependent; the
sacramental sign has as its end the interior sanctity to be produced in the soul. The magical sign has as its field of action
the whole extent of human life, the sacramental sign is of an
order strictly religious and divine.

THE FATE OF MAGICAL THOUGHT

HERE ARISES an opportunity to discuss the fate of magical
thought. I limit myself to indicating—and it is here that my
position differs from that of Warburg and of his school, whose
researches, moreover, seem to me so fruitful—that since, as I
believe, religion, metaphysics, art, poetry and all the vital
powers of the spirit other than the power of pure scientific
thought are as well founded in truth as is science in the modern
sense of the word, and since they are ever to endure, while
changing their condition when the human soul passes over
into the daylight régime wherein the intelligence is dominant,
then, in the final analysis, the fact that they remain and will
always remain in culture as essential elements thereof does
not imply the continuance, under one form or another, of magical or nocturnal thought. Magical thought and the magical
sign are destined to be cast aside *in so far as they are magical*
(in so far as they imply the nocturnal state of culture and the
régime of the primacy of the imagination). They continue, it is

true, in a *virtual* state, and as though cut off, and purposeless, in the immense subterranean reservoir of the imagination and of the passions and the emotions.

There, be it to serve as the unconscious or preconscious preparations for discovery, for invention, for artistic creation; be it to serve as the background of our animal relations with nature, be it to serve as the affective charge which is needed for the putting into action of every practical sign (for in the practical domain the reason must carry with it toward the act everything that is human and everything that is animal), there it can be said that normally, in the daylight régime of the primacy of the Logos, whatever was *vital* in magical thought remains—what was *magical* as such disappears. This is because the latter was bound up with the magical *sign,* thanks to which alone the régime of the dream and of the imagination can be dominant and regulative, and now the whole value of meaning (signification) is taken over by the *logical* sign. But to the extent that the signs whereof human beings make use will again be seized upon by the psychic life which is proper to the imagination, to the dream and to instinct, to that extent magic will live again. This often comes to pass with the effects of love. Love, in being born, tends to excite at the same time a resurgence of magical thought and of magical signs.

Nothing is clearer than the importance of the sign in social life. I note by way of parenthesis that from this point of view it would be possible to work out an apology for social rites and social formalism, for etiquette, for marks of distinction, for protocol, for differences in dress, for wigs, and generally for the whole of worldly ceremonial. This whole business, which in the eyes of a "naturist" or a "hyper-spiritual" would seem inhuman or frivolous, and which so easily turns into the hatefulness of pure show and into the letter which kills, is deeply rooted in human as well as intellectual nature (and even, one might say, in animal nature as it is capable of seeing and hearing, especially when one thinks of the nuptial display of certain birds and when one recalls that an animal makes use of signs). For all this invests human affairs with *meaning* (*signification*) and fills them with something more than they physically are, makes out of men and their gestures a mirror, a sign, a symbol through which passes *another thing,* and to this extent gives social life an intellectual and indeed a poetical *quality.* That is why every society—even a "classless" society in the contemporary meaning of the word—since it must have in it internal differentiations and diversities (and hence inequalities) of function, must also have in it rites and formalities. A new society inspires a new protocol; it does not suppress all protocols. Like the dances and solemnities of folk-lore, the ceremonial of the community is the poetry of the people, of the people gathered together in the community. It is, moreover, of little importance that the significance of the sign be forgotten in the course of time, or else transformed, or else remain obscure and indistinct. The essential thing is that there should be a sign and signification. Not knowing precisely what a given sign signifies, I am free to have it signify *everything* for me. In a sense, poetical joy and affective exaltation will then only be more vast and more indeterminate.

But let us leave this digression. Under all the signs of social life there remain subjacent the strongest affective and instinctive charges (on which depends any operative efficiency). If an uprush (in the Freudian sense) takes place, if the imagination makes subject to itself the function of the sign, deforming it in accordance with its own law, a return of magic will take place. It can happen that magical thought should thus reappear in our evolved cultures under a diseased form; certain contemporary collective myths easily supply us with a proof of this fact.

Such cases are at times described as noxious returns of

primitive mentality. I believe that there are grounds on which to defend primitive men against parallels unjust to them. In general terms the disintegration of a higher structure is a quite different process from some simple retrogression leading back to the condition of primitive indifferentiation. The former, as I have already pointed out, is accompanied by abnormal integrations and paradifferentiations: von Monakow has drawn attention to this in the field of neurology, Roland Dalbiez in the field of psychology. A pathological return to childhood is altogether different from the state of childhood; it is indeed upon such a return that are based many of the perversions. The mythologies which today capture whole peoples and contaminate even science itself as well as the critical functions of the reason are in reality something very different from a "noxious return of primitive mentality"; they represent a pathological process, and it would be doing primitive men an injury were one to seek therein an equivalent to their mythology.

On the subject of art and poetry I shall limit myself to a few brief remarks. There is obviously something kindred between magical thought and poetry—if only for the fact that poetic thought and poetic creation are bathed in the waters of the imagination, whose riches and purity hold an essential importance for this thought and creation. Then, too, when certain experimentalists would seek, not poetry itself, but the psychic mechanisms of which it makes use and from which they ask a sort of ecstatic liberation (such was the case with surrealism in France), they naturally land on the magical side. Of course the sources of poetry are far deeper than the imagination; and in a state of culture which I call daylight or logical (not in the sense that therein everything would be reduced to rational discourse—far from it!—but in the sense that the light of the Logos is therein dominant), poetry finds its true nature and manifests itself for its own sake by bringing to life its own world of images from the abysses and wounds of the spirit, or from the creative intuition-emotion, which belongs to a quite supra-imaginative order.

Be it furthermore noted that in a work of art are found the speculative sign (the work makes manifest something other than it is) and the practical sign (it communicates a stimulation, an appeal); not that the work of art is formally a practical sign [16]; it is rather a speculative sign which by superabundance is *virtually* practical. And the work of art itself, without wishing it and on condition that it does not wish it, is also a kind of magical sign (it seduces, it bewitches).

In the work of art, finally, we meet with what can be called the *direct* sign (indicating an object) and the *reverse* sign (making manifest the subject). All the signs with which we have been concerned in this study are direct signs. The letter *A* signifies the sound A, mourning signifies death. But the sign can also act in a reverse sense: while making manifest an object, it can—by an inverse or retroverse signification—denote the very subject who makes use of this sign: his conditions, his dispositions, his secrets which he does not even admit to himself—the subject being then taken as object by some observer. It is in this sense that Freud and his disciples understand the word *symbol,* wherein they no longer give consideration to direct signification but only to reverse signification. The Freudian symbol is a conscious content caused by unconscious psychic states whereof it is the symptom. Thus Minerva springing from the brow of Jupiter is no longer the symbol of the divine origin of wisdom; it is the "symbol" of the physiological idea of birth *ex utero* pushed back into the unconscious, and even the idea of the divine origin of wisdom becomes the "symbol" of this unconscious representation.[27] As Roland Dalbiez has very well

---

[27]"Those conscious contents which give us a clue, as it were, to the unconscious background, are by Freud incorrectly termed *symbols.* These are not true symbols, however, since, according to his teaching, they have merely the rôle of signs or symptoms of the background processes." C. G. Jung, *Contributions to Analytical Psychology,* New York, Harcourt, Brace, 1928, pp. 231–32.

shown in this connection,[28] it would be better to say "psychic expression," and this concept is above all useful for the products of "dereistic" thought (dreams, hallucinations, neurotic symptoms).

But even in normal thought the signs of which a man makes use to signify things (direct signs) also signify him (reverse signs). It is the province of poetry to signify the world by signifying and in order to signify the creative soul itself. For the substance of man is obscurely grasped—by a knowledge which will have its word in the work of art—only at the same time as the reality of things is, so to speak, pierced by connaturality and emotion. Every work of art is an avowal, but it is by uncovering the secrets of being (divined by force of suffering the things of this world) that the work of art confesses the secret of the poet.

The distinction between the true sign and the reverse sign is of great utility for the *Kulturwissenschaften*. It is above all with the reverse sign that investigations are concerned wherein the work of art is, for example, studied as sign of the cultural backgrounds which engross the psychic life of the artist and of his epoch, and as sign of the forces which clash in him without his even being aware of them.

[28]*Cf.* Roland Dalbiez, *La méthode psychanalytique et la doctrine freudienne,* Paris, Desclée de Brouwer, 1936.

CHAPTER X

THE NATURAL MYSTICAL EXPERIENCE AND THE VOID[1]

CLASSIFICATION OF KNOWINGS BY CONNATURALITY

THIS STUDY is in the philosophical order. I have attempted to arrange in some sort of synthetic *schema,* the principal elements of interpretation and of classification which it seems possible to me to propose concerning the difficult subject of the natural mystical experience and of the void. The background for this study consists of the historical and experimental data which seemed to me the most significant in my random reading over many years and of reflections which I have long since pursued concerning the discrimination of the typical forms of knowing by means of connaturality. First of all I shall sum up the results at which I have arrived from these reflections. I think it better not to weigh this exposition down with the texts and documents which might illustrate it, since this matter is amply familiar to all those who have followed the subject. I trust that the obviously skeletal aspect of this study will be forgiven me, in consideration of the fact that in my own thought it merely *proposes* certain lines of investigation, and far from pretending to supply exhaustive solutions, belongs rather to the realm of inquiry and of hypotheses for research.

May I add, in order to give precision to my language in a manner which I believe conformable to reality, but which in

[1]Based on a communication to the Fourth Congress of Religious Psychology, Avon-Fontainebleau, September 21–23, 1938 (*Études Carmélitaines,* "Nuit Mystique," October, 1938).

any case may be granted me as a convention of speech, that in general by the phrase "mystical experience" I mean a *possession-giving experience of the absolute?*

With these preliminary warnings, I shall first set forth in a few words the manner in which I believe it is proper to classify the various types of knowledge by means of connaturality. We are here dealing with a classification which is not empirological, but ontological and metaphysical.

1. I should like in the first instance to single out that type of knowledge by means of *affective connaturality* which in the most general and the most common fashion concerns human life, because it is in the practical and ethical order. It is knowledge by means of an affective and tendential connaturality *with the ends of human action*—a knowledge which is at the heart of *prudential* knowledge. For the moral virtues being conjoint with one another and a prudent man being prudent only if he is also temperate, just, etc., such a man will form his prudential judgments not only in the mode of pure knowledge, after the fashion of a moral philosopher, but also in the mode of instinct or inclination and guided by his interior leanings—those very *habitus* of temperance or of justice which are present in him and which are himself or something of himself. This knowledge of the things of human life by means of instinct or of inclination covers an immense territory. By the very fact that it is in the practical and ethical order and specifically concerns action, it does not belong to the world of contemplation. And if it can be integrated with the mystical life properly so called (to the extent that human action itself, among those who have entered into the mystical state, is dependent upon the gifts of the Holy Spirit, particularly the gift of counsel), nevertheless this prudential knowledge by means of connaturality remains as such on an altogether different level from that of mystical experience, understood as being a pos-

session-giving—and hence contemplative—experience of the absolute. But here is the *basal* type, the type best proportioned to human beings, of knowledge by means of affective or tendential connaturality, and you will observe that Saint Thomas, in order to explain how the mystic "suffers divine things rather than learns them," refers to the case of the chaste man who knows the things of chastity, not by means of knowledge, but by means of inclination.

2. In contrast to this fundamental type of knowledge through affective connaturality, and to all knowledge of this sort, I must now call attention to knowledge through a connaturality which is not affective but intellectual, which is due to the *habitus* proper to speculative man as such, philosopher or scientist. Every *habitus* creates a proportion to the object, as well as a connaturality. But it is the intelligence of the mathematician or of the metaphysician which is thus connaturalized with the things of mathematics or metaphysics, and this intellectual connaturalization acts only to perfect and facilitate the play of knowledge in the mode of pure knowledge, by concepts and by notions. We have here a knowledge through *intellectual* connaturality with reality as *possible of conceptualization* and made proportionate in act to the human intellect. It goes on an even footing with the development of the *habitus* or proper virtues of the intelligence, and it is here that belongs the intellectual intuition—abstractive and eidetic (concept-forming) and capable of expression in a mental "word"—of the philosopher or the scientist, of him who knows in the mode of pure knowledge.

Is it possible that by following this road a metaphysician can arrive at a *natural contemplation* of divine things? I believe so. Is this natural contemplation of divine things a *mystical experience* in the natural order? I believe not.

Certain thinkers, who in my opinion somewhat dramatize

and push to the extreme Aristotelian tendencies and the *nihil est in intellectu quod non prius fuerit in sensu,* would like to say, with Father Thomas Philippe,[2] that metaphysical effort, far from preparing us in some fashion for union with God, would rather make us despair of such a union, and throw us back to earth, broken rather than unified, after having caused us to cast ourselves against the barrier of the steely sky which cuts off divine transcendence from every means of human knowing. The philosopher as such cannot contemplate divine things; he is, as it were, an Icarus of contemplation, and the movement proper to him hopelessly casts him down into the realm of the multiple and the created. Others, on the contrary, follow Platonic tendencies, even if they do not go so far as to admit that there is in the soul a door other than the senses whereby the soul naturally opens out over the real by an immediate existential contact; they believe with Father Rousselot and his school or with Father Festugière (author of a recent and much praised study on Plato) that metaphysical effort can lead (exceeding itself, but moving always in the same direction—the direction of the intelligible reality to be conquered—and by virtue of the same initial eros) either to a mystical experience in the natural order, a natural mystical union with that One or that Good which Plato placed above being, or else at least to a contemplation which, by its specific dynamism and in order to satisfy its constituent desire, demands that it pass over the threshold of supernatural realities and that it become, by means of the gifts of grace, the supernatural mystical union, conceived above all as an intellectual intuition of the absolute Being.

If we turn to Saint Thomas, we find that he is less pessimistic with regard to philosophy than is Father Thomas Philippe.

---

[2]*Cf.* R. P. Thomas Philippe, "Spéculation métaphysique et Contemplation chrétienne," *Angelicum* (*Strena Garrigou-Lagrange*), vol. XIV (1937), fasc. 1-2.

And indeed how should ananoetic or analogical intellection, set in motion by the natural movement of metaphysical thought toward the cause of being, and well aware, although welded to human means of knowing, that the divine reality infinitely exceeds these means and is not circumscribed by any of our concepts—how should this intellection not seek to make itself more stable in a more and more simplified and in a better and better savoured meditation of that prime reality? Have we not here a normal effect of the intensive increase of the *habitus* of natural wisdom, especially if, with regard to the conditions of its exercise, it dwells in a climate of grace's strengthening? Doubtless such a contemplation is more speculation than contemplation, and its fixity remains very imperfect with respect to the superior fixity of supernatural contemplation. "It flies, it is not at rest," whereas of mystical contemplation one must say: *Et volabo et requiescam.* Yet on its own account it merits the name of contemplation, albeit in an *analogical* fashion. Saint Thomas admits the existence of such a philosophical contemplation, and he admits that it has God for its object. "For, according to the Philosopher in the Tenth Book of the *Ethics,* this contemplation consists in the action of the highest power there is in us, that is to say the power of the intellect, and in the most noble *habitus,* that is to say wisdom, and also in the most worthy object, who is God. This is why the philosophers used to set aside the last days of their lives for the contemplation of divine things, employing their earlier days in the other sciences, in order to become thereby more capable of considering that which is divine."[3]

On the other hand this natural contemplation of God is not a mystical experience, even in the natural order. It is not a possession-giving experience, it occurs at the summit of the powers of the abstractive ideation of the intellect, it knows God by means of things, at a distance, and in an enigmatic fashion;

[3]In III *Sent.,* dist. 35, q. 1, a, 2, sol. 3.

doubtless an eidetic intuitivity can develop there by means of the habit of meditation, of recollection, and of metaphysical serenity, and receive from the natural love of God an affective and experiential colouring, and in some sort mimic a true experience thanks to a high intellectual taste and to a certain simplification; this intuitivity remains, however, far removed, either from an intellectual intuition of the *esse divinum* which is possible only by means of the illumination of the light of glory, or from the unitive experience of the depths of God which is possible only by means of the gifts of grace. Of itself the philosopher's contemplation stops short at a feeling of presence which, however exalted, however powerful, however illuminating it may be, so far only concerns God the Cause of things, attained from a distance in the mirror of things and as present to them. It is not the hidden God attained in His uncommunicable life by the experience of union. Knowledge through intellective connaturality with reality as capable of conceptualization, knowledge *per modum cognitionis,* this knowledge remains such even when it makes use—dialectically and notionally—of the *via negationis.*[4] In short there is no natural intuition, as Plato would have had it, of the supersubstantial One. And the philosophical contemplation of divine things doubtless corresponds—albeit in an extremely imperfect and deficient fashion, which merely makes one's thirst the greater —to that natural desire to see the First Cause, which, although conditional and inefficacious, is at the deepest depth of spiritual creatures.[5] But this desire itself is essentially distinct from the natural tendency of the created intelligence toward its proper and specifying object, which is being *in communi,* not the Cause of being. The natural desire to see the Cause of being

[4]Cf. *Les Degrés du Savoir,* Paris, p. 470, note 1; *The Degrees of Knowledge,* New York, p. 292, note 3.

[5]*Ibid.,* Paris, pp. 527–32; New York, pp. 327–31. Also see *ibid.,* Paris, p. 562, note 1; New York, p. 350, note 1, which is not complete.

derives from the natural desire of knowing being; it is a corollary thereof; it is in no way identified therewith. From this it follows that every great metaphysic is indeed pierced by a mystical aspiration, but is not built thereon. By an at least theoretically normal effect, the philosophic contemplation of God indeed implants in the soul a longing which mystical union alone will satisfy. In this sense it aspires to such a union, as a lower thing aspires to a higher, but it does not seek to pass into mystical union by virtue of its specific dynamism and of its own constitutive desire.

That there could exist in the proper sense of the word a natural mystical experience, which prolongs and consummates a metaphysical élan is what I shall undertake to show in the second portion of this chapter. But—and this is the point which in my opinion the school of Father Rousselot does not sufficiently stress—this philosophic overreaching of philosophy, this metaphilosophical contemplation does not continue the natural movement of philosophy in its own direction, which, according to Aristotle, and according to the truth of our nature, is a movement toward things and toward reality to be grasped by eidetic intuition; on the contrary it inevitably presumes a kind of reversal, a reversal against the grain of nature; and hence the bursting forth of a desire which is surely not the constitutive desire of philosophy itself, the intellectual desire of knowing being, but a deeper desire suddenly set free in the soul and properly religious, a desire which is no longer that of the intellect wishing to see the first Cause, to which I referred a moment ago as a sequel of the intellectual desire of knowing being. The desire of which I am now speaking is one more radical than the natural desire of the intelligence for being and than its natural desire for the Cause of being, for this is the natural desire not of a special faculty, but of the whole man, body and soul. This is, I believe, the desire essential to every creature to join again *its* sources and the principle of *its* individual being, in other words, that natural love of the part for its Whole—for the divine and separate Whole—which Saint Thomas[6] finds in every creature: in a stone, a rose, a bird, as well as in a rational creature, and which implants in the heart of all things, tending toward their principle and toward the good of the whole even more than toward their own specific action and their own good, a sort of hyper-finality.

3. A third category of knowledge by means of connaturality is that of *poetic* knowledge, or knowledge in the mode of creation. I believe it to consist in a knowledge by means of *affective* connaturality with reality as *non-conceptualizable,* because awakening to themselves the *creative depths of the subject.* Stated in other words, this is a knowledge by connaturality with reality according as the latter is embowelled in subjectivity itself in so far as intellectually productive existence, and according as reality is attained in its concrete and existential consonance with the subject *as subject.*

Raïssa Maritain and I have tried, in a recently published essay,[7] to characterize this sort of knowledge and its relationship to mystical knowledge; therefore I can here treat the matter very briefly. Let it suffice to note that poetic knowledge is indeed, and pre-eminently, an experience, and is more an experience than it is a knowledge. But on the one hand let it be noted that, being placed within practical lines, like knowledge by means of prudential connaturality (not in the lines of *agibile,* but in those of *factibile*) it doubtless disposes the mind to contemplation, and it is full of contemplative flashes, but it is not properly contemplative nor possession-giving; it is situated at the minimum of knowledge and the maximum of germinative power; it does not have its goal and its fruit in itself, it does not tend toward silence, it tends toward utterance *ad extra,* it has its goal and its fruit in an external work in which it objectifies itself and which it produces. On the other

[6]Cf. *Sum. theol.,* I, 60, 5.   [7]*Situation de la Poésie,* Paris, 1938.

hand that which is typically *grasped* or *apprehended* in this experience is not the absolute but rather the intercommunion of things with themselves and with the subjectivity they reveal to itself, in the spiritual flux from which existence derives. Thus poetic knowledge is truly experience, but it is not mystical experience, it is not possession-giving experience of the absolute, even though we are justified in recognizing "the proximity, in the same divine source, of the experience of the poet and of that of the mystic."[8]

4. I come now to the fourth sort of knowledge by means of connaturality, and it is this sort which interests us here. It takes place by means of connaturality with reality as *non-conceptualizable* (and in this it is in the same case as poetic experience). But, and here is the distinguishing feature, this reality grasped according as it is non-conceptualizable is at the same time grasped *as the ultimate goal of the act of knowing in its perfect immanence,* an interiorized goal in which knowledge has its fulfillment, its fruit and its living repose. In other words, this is a knowledge by means of connaturality with reality as *non-objectivable in notions,* and yet *as goal of objective union.* Here is the mode of knowing which to my mind characterizes the mystical experience in general; knowledge of contemplation in the strongest sense of the word contemplation (the philosophic contemplation to which I referred earlier in this chapter being the inferior analogue of contemplation, and mystical contemplation, under present discussion, the superior analogue, itself hierarchically diversified). Knowledge not in the mode of practical inclination, like prudential experience; not in the mode of pure knowledge, like the natural contemplation of philosophers; not in the mode of creation, like poetic experience; but in the mode of nescience, of possession-giving not-knowing.

[8]Raïssa Maritain, "Magie, Poésie et Mystique," *Situation de la Poésie,* p. 67.

This sort of knowledge is in turn divided, I believe, into two essentially distinct types, according as the connaturality which it involves is itself either *affective* or *intellectual*.

It must be noted that, as I have sought to explain elsewhere, supernatural charity alone is capable of connaturalizing the soul with the divine. Therefore in the first instance—affective connaturality—we are dealing with supernatural mystical experience, with a supernatural contemplation which, by means of the union of love (*amor transit in conditionem objecti*) and of a specific resonance in the subject itself, becomes an instrument of knowing, attains as its object the divine reality, of itself inexpressible in any created word. The problems relating to this supernatural contemplation are not germane to the subject of this chapter. The short formulas which I have just used in their connection sufficiently indicate that while I have a high regard for the researches of Father Maréchal,[9] researches which supply us with so much precious data on comparative mysticism, I think that the truer theology of supernatural contemplation is to be found less in a theory of the *intuition* of God than in the substantially converging views of John of Saint Thomas and of Saint John of the Cross regarding divine experience by means of the union of love.

In the second case—intellectual connaturality—we are dealing (I come to the subject at last!) with a natural contemplation which by means of a supra- or para-conceptual intellection attains a transcendent reality, of itself inexpressible in any human mental word. There we have the typical mode of knowing in the natural mystical experience.

Before concerning myself more closely with this natural mystical experience, I must make two more digressions.

In the first place I should like to make myself clear concern-

[9] J. Maréchal, *Études sur la Psychologie des Mystiques,* 2 vol., Desclée De Brouwer.

ing the words *object, objective union,* of which I have made
use in connection with the knowledge of contemplation and
with the mystical experience in general. These words have the
disadvantage of bothering a certain number of philosophers
from the outset, be they idealists or existentialists (existentialists formerly idealists) and I am afraid that these words will be
disapproved by Hindu thinkers, whose evidence is particularly
important in the present discussion. Why is this the case? Because in the eyes of an idealist the object is a product of the
mind which separates the being from the subject, and in any
case object signifies duality of the known and of the knowing,
whereas in the mystical experience there is a sovereign unity.
With perfect exactitude Saint John of the Cross says: "Two
natures in a single spirit and love"; and the teachers of the
Vedanta might like to say; "Identity pure and simple," using
a language which is doubtless monist only for lack of ability
better to conceptualize the experience in question. Well, then,
what I merely wish to point out is that I am herein using the
words *object* and *objective union* in a strictly Aristotelian and
Thomist sense and that under these conditions the difficulties
and anxieties to which I refer lose their reason for existence.
For in this case the object is only reality itself, according as it is
present in act to the soul, and abolishing all separation in
such a manner that the soul *is* intentionally the known reality,
and that, while being specified by the object, in this very fact
the soul indeed itself specifies itself. Objective union is the very
consummation of the unity between the knowing and the
known, according as the latter is the goal in which the knowing flowers forth in its own specific actuality, and rests therein.
For Thomists the intentional identification of sense and of its
object is so strong that pure sensation is in itself an unconscious
process, so strongly does it absorb the sentient in the sensed;
and the notion of object so little implies duality that God, the
subsistent Simplicity (but a transcendent and infinitely rich

Simplicity) is to Himself His own object, in an intuition which is His very being and the triumph of most perfect unity.

My second digression relates to the existence of a great zone of natural pre-mysticism—in the intellectual as well as in the affective order—which is not to be confused with the natural or supernatural mystical experience; this zone of natural pre-mysticism is the province of the intuitions, warnings, forebodings, premonitions, divinations which bear on the individual and the concrete and whereof the noetic world of practical affectivity supplies us with so many examples. The province, again, of certain metaphysical intuitions vouchsafed after the fashion of natural illuminations or revelations;[10] and the province of certain exalted states of philosophic contemplation. Here also is the province of other states of contemplation which have a strongly affective hue and which, without being poetic experience itself, are very common with poets (I am here thinking of Keats, Shelley and many others) and which poetic experience induces or presumes. Here is finally the province of the numerous cases of "religious experience" of which William James has collected so many examples, and of the luxuriance of "religious phenomena," often more or less aberrant, in which the Orient seems even richer than the Occident. Moreover, all such are not typical and specific forms, but rather accidental manifestations or general and inchoate dispositions of natural spirituality.

THE POSSIBILITY OF AN INTELLECTUAL (NEGATIVE) EXPERIENCE OF THE SUBSTANTIAL ESSE OF THE SOUL

I HAVE JUST said that the problems which concern supernatural contemplation are foreign to the subject of this chapter. Nevertheless, it is necessary that I summarily refer to these problems

[10]Cf. *Les Degrés du Savoir*, Paris, p. 552; *The Degrees of Knowledge*, New York, p. 343.

in order to find an easier introduction to the ideas which I should like to propose.

The supernatural mystical experience, by means of affective connaturality with the deity, not only finds a natural analogy in the prudential experience of the things of human action, in the knowledge in the mode of inclination, for example, which the chaste man has for everything which concerns chastity. This experience has many another natural analogue, especially poetic experience. But that which I should like to point out is that, being at once a contemplative knowledge and a contemplation by means of love, the typical value of this experience as contemplative *knowledge* will prove deficient the best natural analogies one can find with it in the world of inclination and of affectivity, while, inversely, the essential rôle which *love* plays in this same experience will prove deficient the best natural analogies one can find for it in the world of contemplative knowledge.

The love of the creature for the creature is thus a natural analogue of the most obvious sort for the supernatural mystical experience. Bergson, in his lectures at the Collège de France, liked to refer to this sentence: "I have suffered enough from my friend really to know him"; and he would also invoke the intimate knowledge which a mother has of her child. If the child, he said, stirs in its cradle, she wakes up, whereas the discharge of a cannon might perhaps not even half waken her. The experience of profane love is of the same sort; suffice it to remember that the *Song of Songs* is the supreme image, consecrated by Scripture—and also largely used in the annoying rhetoric of mystical platitudes—of the trials and progress which pertain to supernatural mystical experience. But whatever incidence the love of the creature for the creature may involve as regards knowledge, its own proper constituent element is not contemplation and contemplative fruition, its specifying object is not a reality to be contemplated.

In the world of contemplative knowledge there is another natural analogue, pre-eminently valuable, which Father Gardeil has admirably expounded in his great book, *La Structure de l'âme et l'expérience mystique*. It is the knowledge of the soul through itself, the inner and obscure experience of myself, through myself. But if this analogue makes us experience better than any other that value of unitive contemplation and obscure intellective transparency which is characteristic of the supernatural mystical experience, such an analogue in itself alone, however, tells us nothing of the part played by love as proper means of knowledge in this experience. Moreover, in the last analysis, this analogy enlightens us by means of a sort of *as if* rather than by means of a fact, and it presents us only with a virtual image of the supernatural mystical experience: because the specific case to which it relates—the even partial actualization of the latent self-intellection of the soul reflecting upon itself—cannot, in fact, be realized in the present life.

John of Saint Thomas, in fine sentences of which Father Gardeil has made use,[11] indeed tells us that the soul, to the ex-

[11]John of Saint Thomas, *Curs. phil.*, t. III, q. 9, a.1; *Curs. theol.*, t. IV, disp. 21, a.2, n. 13.

The human intelligence, in emanation from the substance of the soul, is in a radical and latent fashion objectively informed by the soul, for the intelligence radically considered is but one indeed with the very soul, as the properties radically considered are but one with the essence. If, in the state of union with the body, this radical and latent informing of the intelligence by the very substance of the soul cannot proceed into act, it is obviously not because the substance of the soul would thus find itself "materialized" and obscured by the fact that it informs matter. It is rather that with regard to the functioning and the activity of powers, it is connatural to the soul united with the body to be turned outward in order to accomplish the work of intellection, in other words to accomplish the work of intellection by means of the senses and sense-images. This makes of the intelligence a *tabula rasa* to the extent that the *intellectus agens* does not inform the intelligence thanks to abstraction.

This *diversion* or *progression* outward is required by the human intelligence because of its specific imperfection and weakness. For it is to be placed on the lowest level in the scale of intellectuality, and its intentent that it is a spirit, has an habitual or latent knowledge of itself—because the intellect, emanating from the substance of the soul, is intelligibly informed by the latter as by a *species intelligibilis:* here is the permanent privilege of spirituality which the human soul has in common with other spirits. But John of Saint Thomas at once adds that the actualization of this latent auto-intellection is impeded and prevented by the state of union with the body. Besides it could not be actualized except as an intuitive vision of the essence of the soul, a vision whereof it is clear that the soul is lacking in this world.

These objections are opposed to certain elements of the conceptualization proposed by Father Gardiel, not to the substance of his thought and of his views. Concerning both the structure of the soul *ut mens,* and its latent intellection of itself through itself, the recognition of the obstacle which the state of union with the body offers for their intuitive actualization is not enough to warrant our considering them as of slight account

---

sive power (*vis intellectiva*) is naturally so weak that it needs, in order to enjoy a sufficiently distinct and illuminated knowing, that *multiplicity* of concepts and of representative particles with which abstraction alone, working from the sensible, can supply it. The human intelligence needs ideas incomparably more divided and particularized than those required by the least of the angels; this is true to such an extent that if the knowledge of which it is capable when it is separated from the body were merely the intuitive knowledge of the existence of the soul, which is natural to the state of separation, that knowledge would be too indeterminate to inform suitably the human intellect concerning the world and God.

Hence it can be seen that it is *ad melius animæ,* for the good of the soul, and in order that its work of knowing and of intellection may be suitably accomplished, that the human soul is united to a body. One can also understand that if the soul's manner of knowing in the state of separation is "natural" with regard to that which is generally suited to the *spirit* as such, it is "preternatural" with regard to the *human intelligence* taken at its own proper degree of intellectuality. Moreover, in the souls of the blessed, the vision of the divine essence and the light of glory supernaturally compensate for the natural imperfection which the state of separation involves, and which will disappear only with the resurrection of the body.

and no longer being concerned with them. These data, on the contrary, are something fundamental, and it is impossible that so important an ontological privilege should not have a primordial significance for human psychology, especially for everything which touches upon natural spirituality. And here especially we have the metaphysical condition and the first foundation for the faculty of perfect reflection upon its own acts which the soul enjoys by title of its spirituality, and which is the proximate reason for the experience which the soul has of itself through reflection upon its own acts. For in this reflection we are dealing with a true experience, attaining in its singular existentiality the principle of *my own* singular operations.

In accordance with the most natural exercise of our faculties and the most natural leanings of the soul and of the "communings of common life," there is a universal, a daily experience of the soul through itself, thanks to reflection upon its own acts. "Such an experiential apprehension of the soul, not through its essence but through its acts, can be called immediate, in the sense that the reality it attains is known by means of no other intermediary than its own actuation."[12] Here, then, is for each man a true experience of the singular *existence* of his soul, through and in its operations.

But concerning *what is* our soul, concerning its essence, or its quiddity, this experience tells us nothing. The existence which it grasps is indeed the existence of something, but of a something of which we are made aware only through the glimmer-

[12]*Les Degrés du Savoir*, Paris, p. 861. This reference not included in English edition. "Here the object of direct knowledge is merely like the necessary condition for the reflection of the mind upon itself; and its *species*, which as Father Roland-Gosselin properly observes, does not prevent the object being immediately known, no more prevents the soul, having become intelligible in act thanks to this species, from being immediately known in so far as it knows. We thus have a true *experience* of the singular existence of our soul, that is to say, through and in its operations, and the concept which we form of ourselves is an *experiential* concept."

ing of the phenomena which emanate therefrom; it is the existence of the principle, unknown in itself, of the operations and psychic states grouped together in the conscious synthesis. In short, my experience of myself has, in the order of *suchness* or of essentiality, no other content than my own operations, the flux of more or less profound phenomena grasped through reflection. It is of altogether central importance to understand that my experiential knowledge of my soul (or rather of my substance, which is soul and body, but which is grasped by means of a spiritual activity, of an activity of the soul alone) thus remains in an order *purely existential* and implies no other *quid* offered to my mind than my own operations, grasped reflexively in the emanation of their principle. My soul (or my substance) cannot be experienced by myself in its essence; a *quidditative* experience of the soul is possible only for a separated soul, wherein, from the very fact of the state of separation, the latent self-intellection to which I have already alluded proceeds into act. Doubtless, the more my attention comes to bear upon the *existential* experience of my soul, the more shall I tend to neglect the diversity of objects and of operations the reflexive grasp of which is nevertheless the very condition for such an experience. Yet it remains true that as long as we go in the direction of nature, the experiential folding back of which I speak, however powerful it may be in certain "interior" souls, leaves the soul prisoner of mobility and multiplicity, of the fugitive luxuriance of phenomena and of operations which emerge in us from the darkness of the unconscious —prisoner of the apparent ego, if we agree thus to describe the phenomenal content which occupies the stage and indeed is the only set of qualities to be grasped in the existential experience of ourselves. Then, too, concern with the external world is a natural condition of mental equilibrium, and it often appears that the more man observes himself (observes himself psychologically, which is an altogether different thing from descending into himself metaphysically or mystically thanks to a disciplined and purified procedure) the more he runs the risk of dispersion or of *acedia,* if he does not indeed become a victim of schizophrenia and of the illusions of some pathological introversion.

Well then, let us suppose for a moment that the soul be by force constrained decidedly and absolutely to have reflexivity set the pace, but this time by means of an ascesis and a technique appropriate to a radical stripping of oneself, and by going deliberately against the grain of nature: supposing all this, would it not be possible—even risking all the dangers—to pass over from the common experience of the soul's existence (of which I have just been speaking) to an exceptional and privileged experience leading into the abyss of subjectivity? Would it not be possible to escape the apparent ego to attain the absolute *self?* Modified as we have sought to modify it, reworked and developed, Father Gardeil's *schema* could thus explain what I here set up as the typical case of natural mystical experience—Yoga mysticism—at least of the sort the best Hindu witnesses have lived and expressed. This mysticism, reduced to its essential kernel, would above all be a metaphysical experience of the substantial *esse* of the soul by means of negative, or rather annihilating, intellectual connaturality. I remember having put this question to Father Gardeil a few months before his death. He had not thought of such an application of his views. I, for my part, believe that this application is possible and is required by reality and that Father Gardeil has opened here an extremely valuable line of thought. For it would be an inestimable advantage to be able, at least in the classical case, to give to the natural mystical experience, and especially to that which we associate with India, an interpretation that respects its authenticity and its truth and that circumscribes with precision its proper domain.

I readily grant that the various recipes of Yogism can lead to all sorts of illusions and psychological extrapolations. But counterfeits, however swarming, must be counterfeits of something authentic. Moreover, it does not seem to my mind possible to reduce to a psychological aberration—however respectfully one does it—the age-old and manifold testimony, the testimony in the last analysis concordant, and very intelligent, of men who, in order to achieve a certain deliverance, have sacrificed everything else, and whom we have no reason either to consider sick or unbalanced. In all this there must be, at least for certain unexceptionable personalities (whatever may be the case with the camp followers and their repetitious verbalism, or even trickery), a real, not a misleading experience. I know very well that the economy of causes is a good principle, but it is such only on condition that with the explanatory material at our command we in no way warp the data of experience. It is also a principle of sound method not to challenge the integrity of testimony such as is here in case, unless we are constrained and forced to do so. It would be singularly unreasonable for us to refuse to non-Christian mystics the rules of objectivity upon which we properly insist in the study of Christian mystics. What do the men we are discussing themselves say? They say that they have experience of the absolute. And what name do they give to this absolute? They call it atman, that is to say, the Self.

I do not mean to say, of course, that these Hindu ascetics achieve a realization of that which I have just said was metaphysically impossible—an actualization, however imperfect, however partial, of the latent self-intellection of the soul. That possibility is excluded by reasons I have already stated.

What I am inclined to believe is, on the contrary, that these ascetics so thoroughly rid themselves of every image, of every particular representation, and of every distinct operation of the mind that they themselves in some fashion reduce, always by

means of an act but of a negative act, an act of supreme silence
—their souls and their intellects to such a latent, not-actualized
auto-intellection. In short, the idea I am proposing is that they
attain not at all the *essence* of their souls, but the *existence*
thereof, the substantial *esse* itself. And how do they do this?
They do it by drastically purifying and pushing to the extreme
limit that ordinary experience of the existence of myself to
which I have alluded. This ordinary experience, taking place
by means of operations and acts, usually remain immersed in
their phenomenal multiplicity; and it remains veiled because
of this multiplicity. Now, on the contrary, risking everything
to gain everything, and thanks to assiduous exercise revers-
ing the ordinary course of mental activity, the soul empties
itself absolutely of every specific operation and of all multiplicity, and knows negatively by means of the void and the
annihilation of every act and of every object of thought coming from outside—the soul knows negatively—but nakedly,
without veils—that metaphysical marvel, that absolute, that
perfection of every act and of every perfection, which is *to exist,*
which is the soul's own substantial existence.

Thus to drain oneself of every image, is this not rather
to end with pure and simple nothingness? Doubtless this is
often the case, whenever the operation involved misses fire,
and then calls upon some illusion or other to substitute itself
for the missing authentic result. But in itself such an operation,
by the very fact that it starts from the normal activity and the
immensity, in some fashion infinite, of the universe of psychic
multiplicity in order actively to reduce and concentrate all this
immensity (to an extraordinary degree exalting, through this
very death, the vitality of the soul and the intellect), must, it
seems to me, ends up in something altogether different from
pure and simple nothingness, I mean in a negation, a void, and
an annihilation which are in no sense nothingness.

We are here, then, in the presence of a negative and apophatic experience—I do not say of a dialectic and conceptual

via negationis, as is the case with philosophers, but rather a lived *via negationis,* aneidetic and para- or supra-conceptual—which no more attains (for if it did it would not be negative) the intuitive vision of the essence of the soul than does supernatural mystical contemplation the beatific vision, but which makes use of the void and of abolition in order to know as unknown the substantial existence of the soul (which is the existence of the subject as a whole, for man exists through the existence of his soul). In like fashion supernatural mystical contemplation makes use of the connaturality of love in order to know as unknown the Godhead—*in finem nostræ cognitionis Deum tamquam ignotum cognoscimus.* It is necessary to point out, as I have indicated in passing, that the words void, abolition, negation, riddance, in reality signify an act which continues to be intensely vital, the ultimate actuation whereby and wherein the void, abolition, negation, riddance, are consummated and silence is made perfect. Coming at the end of a very long ascetic process in which the intellect more and more connaturalizes itself with silence and negation, it can happen that in certain instances this actuation finally surges up after so spontaneous a fashion that it seems altogether a gift from without and passively received; and that it can from the psychological point of view lose every active and voluntary appearance. Nevertheless, it in reality finds its source in an ascending movement which is fundamentally active [13] and in a supreme tension of the forces of the soul. Even from the psychological point of view the active and voluntary aspect must therefore remain predominant;[14] and furthermore, here is ontologically, of itself, an act, an ἐνέργεια, a vital and sovereign immanent

---

[13] *Science et Sagesse,* Paris, Labergerie, 1935, pp. 24–27; *Science and Wisdom,* London and New York, 1940, pp. 7–10.

[14] As Marcel De Corte points out in his report (*Études Carmélitaines,* Oct., 1938) the Plotinian void is "entirely active." . . . "Obtaining the vision of God is the proper work of whoever has desired to obtain it." (*Enneades,* VI, 9; 4 and 7.) Such also, I believe, is the common doctrine of the Hindu samnyasin making exception of the school of bhakti.

act. Hence the principle which asserts that the soul knows itself by means of its acts is still herein preserved—paradoxically, since the act in question is the act of abolition of all act. Properly speaking, it is this act of abolition and of annihilation which is, I believe, the formal means of the experience under discussion. And it is in this sense that the void is the goal to which this experience tends, is not merely its condition but its proper medium, thanks to which the deep, fathomless "to exist" of the subjectivity is—negatively—transferred into the status of an object, not indeed of an object expressible in a concept and appearing before the mind, but an object entirely inexpressible and engulfed in the night wherein the mind engulfs itself in order to join it. Instead of saying: *amor transit in conditionem objecti,* in this case we should have to say: *vacuitas, abolitio, denudatio transit in conditionem objecti.* Here is the most purely existential experience possible, and it is an experience by means of not-knowing.[15] In the supernatural mystical experience, the void is a *condition* of contemplation (a condition actively prepared by the soul and, much more, passively received from divine influence) but its *formal means* is sovereignly positive: it is the union of love under the inspiration of the Holy Spirit. In the case under discussion, the void is not only a condition but also the formal means of the experience.

I should like to indicate three other characteristics among the ontological notes of this experience.

In the first place, and as I have already hinted, the way of

[15]Neither in conceptual and abstractive knowledge nor in any experience of a positive sort (as, for example, poetic experience) is it possible to isolate existence by perfectly "prescinding" it from the essence. But the experience here under discussion being negative and by means of not-knowing, it can attain—as unknown—existence alone, without moreover knowing anything, precisely because it attains existence by means of the act of abolition of everything else.

the void deliberately works against the grain of nature—hence
the host of techniques. It requires the soul to forswear every
movement toward things, which amounts to leaving the world.
Whereas in poetic recollection the world is drawn into the subjectivity and awakens it to itself, here, on the contrary, the subjectivity separates itself from the world, in order to seek within
itself alone a sleep more intense than all awakenings. Then
again it may be pointed out that the mystical experience of the
Self requires the soul to leave the world after an altogether
different fashion from that required by Christian ascesis and
contemplation. In both cases the crucial step must be taken, as
Father Lallemant used to say, but in the natural effort against
the grain of nature, it is to satisfy the demands of an ascesis
entirely ordered to gnosis[16]—demands at once more negative
and less profound than those of evangelic perfection. More
negative demands: for that which is required of the Christian
is the utter detachment of the heart from a world for which he,
more than ever, continues to exist, a world which he continues
to know and to love and for the salvation of which he suffers;
but that which is required of the soul in the other case is that
it purely and simply suppress the world, that it no longer exist
to the world, at least until it reaches the state of deliverance
and of "realization." Demands less profound: for a detachment which goes to the very roots of freedom itself and which
causes man not only to leave the world but even leave himself
(I do not mean merely egoism, the passions, etc.; I mean the
supreme governance of self) is deeper than a detachment which
goes to the roots of the intelligence. And a void and a dispossession which take place through the Holy Spirit and through
grace should create suppleness and abandonments and a plia-
bility toward that Spirit which bloweth where it listeth, and

[16]That love for the supreme Lord or for lesser lords should be joined
among Yogis to this intellectual contemplation is not extraordinary, but
it is not the formal means of their experience, and the latter remains
essentially gnosis.

a real passivity with regard to God, and a freedom, which are altogether different from the burning immobility, the unbending confidence in the techniques of heroism, the victory over the attractions of multiplicity which result from the most tenacious of active tensions, from that concentration and liberation of which nature is capable at its own highest point.

In the second place we are here dealing, indeed, with a metaphysical experience in the strongest sense. The effort of the Oriental contemplatives seems indeed from this point of view to be an effort to follow the line proper to philosophic intellection over and beyond philosophy itself: but by means of that reversal of which I spoke at the outset and of the intervention of a natural desire, deeper and more total than that of the philosophic intelligence for the intellectual conquest of being. The proof of this is that many Yogis—such as Râmana Maharshi, of whom Olivier Lacombe wrote a few years ago[17] —did not begin with philosophy, but with a first experience of a metaphilosophical character. The metaphysical effort against the grain of nature which is thus required is a slow labour of death, which Plato also knew, but in which India particularly excels, an art of entering while living into death, into a death which is not evangelic death, intended to give place to the life of Another, but a metaphysical death, intended to winnow spiritual activities away from the body.

In the third place and finally—and this is a major matter, but one difficult to express in a few words—from the very fact that the experience here discussed is a (negative) purely existential experience, and from the fact that existence is transcendental and polyvalent, and is limited only by the essence which enjoys it, of which in this case we indeed know nothing, it is comprehensible that this negative experience, in attaining the existential *esse* of the soul, should at the same time attain,

[17]Cf. *Études Carmélitaines,* "Illuminations et Sécheresses," Oct., 1937, p. 173.

indistinctly, both this same existence proper to the soul and existence in its metaphysical amplitude, and the sources of existence. All this, according as the existence of the soul, taken concretely and to the extent that it is an act of effectuation *extra nihil,* is something emanating from and suffused by an influx wherefrom it obtains its all. This influx is not experienced in itself, of course, but rather in the effect which it produces, and itself in and through this effect. This is why the experience we are discussing in a certain way answers (as much as that is possible in the natural order) to the desire of all things to return to their sources and the principle of their being. Man thus attains to the sources of being in his soul, thanks to the techniques through which nature reverts toward the spirit against the grain of nature and in a certain way disjoints its own proper metaphysical texture. The Hindu experience appears therefore to be a mystical experience in the natural order, a possession-giving experience of the absolute, of that absolute which is the existential *esse* of the soul and, in it and by it, of the divine absolute.[18] And how could this experience,

[18]In terms of our own philosophic vocabulary and in accordance with distinctions which Hindu thought does not know, let us indicate more precisely that we are here concerned with the divine absolute as the cause of being, not as giving Himself as an object of possession. In the experience here analyzed, the divine absolute is not, Himself, properly speaking an object of possession. It is the substantial *esse* of the soul which is the object of (negative) possession; and by this negative experience of the self God is attained at the same time, without any duality of act, though attained indirectly. God being, then, not known "by His works," that is to say by His effects as by things known beforehand and which discursively make us pass to the knowledge of their cause, but God being known (1) by and in the substantial *esse* of the soul, itself attained immediately and negatively by means of the *formal medium* of the void; (2) in the negative experience itself of that substantial *esse* (just as the eye, by one and the same act of knowing, sees the image, and in the image the signified)—all this being the case, I think it is permissible in such an instance to speak of a "contact" with the absolute, and of an improperly "immediate" experience (that is to say, one wrapt up in the very act of the immediate experience of the self) of God

being purely negative, distinguish one absolute from the other? Inasmuch as it is a purely negative experience, it neither confuses nor distinguishes them. And since therein is attained no content in the "essential" order, no *quid,* it is comprehensible that philosophic thought reflecting upon such an experience

---

creator and author of nature. To explain this we must fall back on considerations *analogous,* on an essentially different level, to those considerations which make it possible in the supernatural order—and without falling back on a partial or transitory *intuition* of the divine essence—to speak of a truly "immediate" experience (in this case, by the union of love) of God, author of grace and dweller in the soul as in His own temple. (Cf. *Les Degrés du Savoir,* Paris, pp. 509-12, page 652, note 2; *The Degrees of Knowledge,* New York, pp. 317-19, page 403, note 4.)

In natural mystical experience we do not have an experience of the *depths of God,* an experience of the Godhead, and *in this sense* I still insist upon everything I wrote in the above cited work (pp. 532-34) against the possibility of an authentic mystical experience in the natural order. But here we have an experience of God *inquantum infundens et profundens esse in rebus,* indirectly attained in the mirror of the substantial *esse* of the soul; and in this sense the case of the negative experience of this *esse,* obtained by means of the void and against the grain of nature (and wherein God, without being Himself an object of possession, is attained by this same act of the experience of the self), brings further matter and correction to these pages in my book, for it seems to me this constitutes an authentic mystical experience in the natural order. I had not taken this case into account in Chapter VI of the *Les Degrés du Savoir,* because at that time I had in mind only the mystical experience of the *depths of God,* and I considered the word mystical only in this major meaning. I now believe that a sufficiently careful reflection upon Hindu contemplation requires us to recognize the possibility, under the conditions herein analyzed, of a negative mystical experience of the *presence of immensity* itself.

May I here point out the distinction established by Ramanuja, which supplies, it seems to me, a remarkable confirmation of the views proposed in these pages—distinction between salvation by bare knowledge (the path of immanence and of indifferentiation with the universal Brahman—here is the natural mystical experience as we have sought to describe it), and salvation by grace (the path of love, and of access to the very Personality of the Brahman)? See the recent book of Olivier Lacombe—a contribution of capital importance to our knowledge of Vedantic Philosophy—*L'Absolu selon le Vedanta,* Paris, Geuthner, 1937, p. 372.

fatally runs the danger of identifying in some measure one absolute with the other, that absolute which is the mirror and that which is perceived in the mirror. The same word "atman" designates the human Self and the supreme Self.

❂
❂　　❂

In this attempt at analysis of the intellectual experience of the existential *esse* of the soul by means of not-knowing, as in the classification of the various sorts of knowledge by means of connaturality which I proposed at the outset, what I have attempted to winnow out have been certain pure types. In fact, as regards mystical experience, I think that the purest specimens of natural mystical experience must be sought in India (the Buddhist Nirvana doubtless corresponding to the same basic experience as the *mukti,* or Brahmanic deliverance, but understood in a deficient fashion, and more easily lending itself to impurities, by reason of the phenomenalist philosophy of Buddhism); whereas the purest cases of supernatural mystical experience should be sought in the Christian contemplatives, particularly in those of the spiritual family of Saint Theresa and of Marie de l'Incarnation (Ursuline), of Saint John of the Cross, of Tauler, of Father Lallemant. To the extent that supernatural mysticism requires human preparation, involves structures and disciplines, one should find therein structures analogically similar to those of natural mysticism— yet transposed toward a specifically different finality, and hence specifically different themselves.

It is scarcely necessary to add that the contingencies of history and of the concrete present us with every kind and every degree of mixture and juxtaposition of natural with supernatural contemplations (leaving to one side parasitic phenomena, mimetic aberrations, or simple neuropathic interferences, which are not here under discussion). So also are there mixtures of the various types of knowledge by means of connaturality which I have distinguished one from another. But I believe that one of the advantages of the distinctions which I propose here is precisely that they permit a more exact analysis of complex cases. In Plato and Plotinus is to be found, I believe, a combination of philosophic contemplation, of the poetic experience and of the natural mystical experience, the rôle of the latter being, although more or less hidden, far greater with Plotinus than with Plato. With many Soufis it could be asked if faith in the divine transcendence joined to the natural mystical experience (which of itself alone would lead rather to a monist conceptualization) does not explain certain traits of Mohammedan mysticism. While the poetic experience with its own proper affectivity adds its complications among the Persians. Among Christian contemplatives, Saint Augustine is a great example of the meeting of philosophic or theological contemplation with the supernatural mystical experience. And among Christian mystics of a Platonic cast—even in the case of a Ruysbroeck, but much more in the case of a Boehme— could there not be found a singularly exalting combination (but sometimes muddy) of the supernatural mystical experience with the poetic experience and with the natural mystical experience? In the orchestration made possible by these mixtures lies the charm—and also the danger—of all these great spirits.

I should like also to point out that in authentically contemplative souls, the poetic experience—withdrawn from its proper sphere and carried away by contemplation—can, it would seem, engage extremely complex relationships of mutual concurrence with the supernatural mystical experience, thus powerfully helping the soul to enter into the experience of union and also somewhat concealing the real extent of this union. For not only poetic *expression,* but the poetic *experience* itself can, by means of its discoveries and its intuitions, outstrip the mystical experience. And thanks thereto, precious illuminations and spiritual lessons can be given by contemplatives whose dealings with their neighbours—and this is the great criterion—still betray hardnesses of nature and ignorances of self which the grace of supernatural contemplation, achieved in the same degree, should have reduced.

A FEW CONCLUSIONS AFTER THE FASHION OF HYPOTHESES FOR RESEARCH

IT REMAINS for me only to propose a few of the consequences which seem to me to spring from the preceding analyses, and which above all I submit as hypotheses for research.

1. What relationship is it suitable to set up between the *void* of the natural mystical experience and the supernatural night of the spirit? It seems to me first of all that the distinction made by Saint John of the Cross between the night of the senses and the night of the spirit has not only a theological value but also, and first, a philosophical value. By this I mean that this distinction is based upon the nature of the human being, and upon the double disproportion on the one hand between the senses (imagination, sensible affectivity, rational discursus immersed in signs) and the spirit (in the purely metaphysical sense of the word), and on the other hand between the spirit itself and things divine (even leaving to one side the supernatural).

But there is not correspondence or parallelism between the two nights of Saint John of the Cross, nights which relate to certain painful phases of the perfecting and transfiguring of nature by grace, and the void of the natural mystical experience, which relates to the essential requirements of a movement against the grain of nature. This void, whatever suffering and terror it may carry with it, does not go so far as the night of the spirit, inasmuch as the latter dries up, disorganizes, and in some way "destroys" the spirit (not doubtless physically, but in all its operative measures and proportions and in its natural vital urge) in order that it may be made proportionate to the Godhead. For the void of the natural mystical experience does not make the soul proportionate to the supernatural, to God in His inner life; moreover, it is accomplished by means of the spirit itself, by means of the effort of the spirit, and it remains altogether intellectual, whereas the night of the spirit is brought about by means of *gratia operans* and by means of love, both of which know how to be as cruel as the grave. And this void is not, like the night of the spirit, a step on the road toward a better state (the transforming union), but the very goal to which one tends, since it is the formal means of the experience of the Self, and of the deliverance.

At the same time this void goes a great deal further than the night of the senses, inasmuch as the latter "destroys" the senses in order to make them proportionate to the spirit. The void of the natural mystical experience makes the spirit proportionate to itself. It is like an excess and a paroxysm of a night of the senses on the natural level, ordered toward passing beyond the purification of the senses, and toward a metaphysical death.

Nor is there any correspondence or parallelism between the nights which correspond in the natural order to the nights of Saint John of the Cross and the void of the natural mystical experience.

Finally, I have already indicated what a fundamental difference in my opinion separates the void—metaphysical, and by means of suppression and concentration—proper to the natural mystical experience from the void, or rather the process of stripping which is evangelic, and in the mode of a gift of oneself, of a dispossession in favour of Another, more loved—such an evangelic stripping constitutes, moreover, not the formal means, but the condition (itself attributable to co-operating or operating grace) of the supernatural mystical experience. In order to avoid all misunderstanding may I point out that this evangelic dispossession of oneself, this void, or this evangelic stripping is linked in an altogether general fashion, in accordance with differing modalities and degrees, with all the states of supernatural contemplation. Here is something different from the night of the spirit and the special void which it involves, the two latter being a very special and even violent form of dispossession—torturing and altogether passive—and produced as an effect by the implacable light of contemplation itself and of the wisdom of love.

2. The distinction between the intellectual union and the union of love must be held as fundamental.

An altogether intellectual union does not go beyond the order of nature (in the sense that Christian philosophy and theology give to this word), even when such a union goes against the grain of nature.

In the case of love, we are dealing either with experiences and modes of contemplation which are pre-mystical, or else with incidences of poetic experience, or with a supernatural mystical experience.

Wherever there really exists a mystical experience by means of union of love, this experience is supernatural (be it typical or atypical, and perhaps more or less hidden or even more or less reduced, deformed, or "crushed" by the effect of environmental conditions, and in the absence of a proportionate mental régime).

The case of bhakti, once more to take an example from India, is one of those which in this connection presents us with the greatest number of problems; for such of the Hindu contemplatives as thus place piety in the position of first importance attribute a major rôle to love. To the extent that here we have authentic experiences—particularly those which probably came with the origin of the doctrine of bhakti—the testimony is such that it must be admitted, if we are to give credence to Professor Olivier Lacombe, that these experiences involve, at least participatively, a union of love with the Supreme Being, whose grace the soul awaits. Here is something which goes beyond the experience of the Self. Since we believe that sanctifying grace is offered to all men, and that souls which do not visibly belong to the Church can effectively receive this grace and with it the organism of the virtues and the gifts which are linked to it; since, moreover, it is not believable that God should refuse Himself to souls in good faith who, even if the idea of grace is with them only a natural product of the interpretation of psychological phases of aridity and fullness, nevertheless, by means of this manufactured idea of grace, call upon grace itself, which has not been revealed to them—in view of all these things, I do not see why one should deny that the mystical experience such as is found in the school of bhakti can depend upon a sort of *composition* of the upward movement of Yoga and of the disciplines of the natural contemplation of the Self combined with supernatural touches, and with the love of charity. Explicit knowledge of the mysteries of the redemptive Incarnation and of the gifts of supernatural life creates that mental and moral régime which is proportionate to the normal development of the supernatural mystical experience. In a régime, on the other hand, where this supernatural mystical experience can gain admittance only as a stranger, and in disguise, it is possible to believe that there are many substitutions, and notably that graces by attraction from a distance come to impart to the natural mystical experience a higher value and a participation in the supernatural union of love. We are here confronted with the unexplored realm of questions concerning the state of the gifts of grace in non-Christian climates.

3. In order to survive the supernatural night of the spirit,

which is a death and a despair of *everything* (even of God)—
a lived, not a voluntarily suffered despair—at the heart of which
grace alone maintains a secret hope—in order to survive such
a night, divine power is necessary.

In the natural state there are nights of the spirit which are
also death and despair, and, in the sense defined a few lines
back, "destruction" of the spirit even unto its natural desire
and its consubstantial taste for its own proper operative ends—
a radical horror at its own life. This kind of frightful and
suicidal disjunction between the immutable ontological structure of the spirit, with which is identified its natural appetite,
and that same natural appetite, to the extent that it is grasped
and assumed by the movement of the whole conscious appetitive-
ness and of the will, in any case bears witness, along abnormal
lines, as does reflectiveness along normal lines, to the freedom
of the spirit with regard to itself and to what might be called
the fourth dimension in spiritual things. Are these nights the
result of some great abuse, causing a passage into accursed
regions? In any case they are, in their own special order, like
unto a hell.[19]

One could cite many examples of these nights of the spirit
in the natural order. May I point out that they can be found in
the realm of pure intellectual knowledge, be it metaphysical or
moral (such is the case with Faust, *drum hab' ich mich der
Magie ergeben*), in the realm of poetic experience (one naturally thinks of Rimbaud), in a mixture of these two realms
(here one thinks of Nietzsche, and those words which are so
astonishing coming from his pen: *Crux mea lux, lux mea
crux*). It should also be possible to find such nights in the
realm of the natural mystical experience (I wonder whether
tantrism has not some relationship with such a night?), it being

[19]One could here revert to the remarks made by John of Saint Thomas
concerning the state of lived contradiction wherein the spirit of the
fallen angel finds itself, and concerning the kind of radical asthenia
with which that spirit is stricken; *Curs. theol.*, t. IV, disp. 24, a.2 and 3.

understood that this night is an altogether different thing from the void which constitutes the formal means of the natural mystical experience, and of which this night would tend to induce despair.

For such nights there is no recourse. For here despair reaches, as in the supernatural night, the very ligature of the soul with the spirit. But being in the natural order and hence not including in their depths the secret power of a superhuman help, these nights of themselves end in a catastrophe of the spirit (an annihilation in the sensual; magic; insanity; moral or physical suicide). The supernatural night of the spirit is the only night from which the spirit can emerge alive.

The trials and torments of profane love are a natural analogy or an image of this supernatural night; but this love, as I have pointed out, is not a contemplative experience, and in it are not to be found natural nights *of the spirit*.

4. Is it possible to try to set forth the differential ontological characteristics of the supernatural night of the spirit? This question goes beyond the limits of the present study. Yet I shall be forgiven if I indicate that in my opinion three characteristics, when they are all present at once, and are joined to the anguish and shadows which strike at the root of the higher faculties, would seem to be characteristic of this supernatural night;

1. Mystical experience through union of love;
2. Transcendence with regard to all technique;
3. Evangelical behaviour, or detachment of perfection in perfection. I here make reference to the fact that evangelic perfection is not perfection of some spiritual athleticism wherein a man would make himself faultless, indeed impeccable, but rather the perfection of love, of love toward Another whom the soul loves more than itself, and whom it concerns the soul above all ever more to love and to join, even though the soul

in the process carries with it imperfections and weaknesses, deficiencies of the body and spirit, even sins which it detests and which it also gives Him, together with all that which He undertakes to clean away. This detachment of perfection in perfection is, it seems to me, the secret of the souls who have passed over the threshold of union; and this invisible behaviour is reflected, as in a visible mirror, in a certain typical behaviour toward one's neighbour.

APPENDIX I (CHAPTER VIII)

"There is a violation of order when capital employs workmen or the proletarian class only with a view to exploiting, at its own pleasure and for its own personal profit, industry and the entire economic régime, without in any way taking into account either the human dignity of the workman or the social character of economic activity or even social justice and the common good." . . . "It is true that there is a formal difference between pauperism and proletarianism. Nevertheless, the immense number of propertyless wage-earners on the one hand, and the superabundant riches of the fortunate few on the other, is an unanswerable argument that the earthly goods so abundantly produced in this age of industrialism are far from rightly distributed and equitably shared among the various classes of men." After pointing out that the wage contract (*salariat*) is legitimate in itself, Pius XI writes: "In the present state of human society, however, we deem it advisable that the wage contract should, when possible, be modified somewhat by a contract of partnership, as is already being tried in various ways to the no small gain both of the wage-earners and of the employers. In this way wage-earners are made sharers in some sort in the ownership, or the management, or the profits." . . . "Labour, indeed, is not a mere chattel, since the human dignity of the working-man must be recognized in it, and consequently it cannot be bought and sold like any piece of merchandise. None the less the demand and supply of labour divides men on the labour market into two classes, as into two camps, and the bargaining between these parties transforms this labour market into an arena where the two armies are engaged in combat. To this grave disorder which is leading society to ruin a remedy must evidently be applied as speedily as possible. But there cannot be question of any perfect cure, except this opposition be done away with, and well-ordered members of the social body come into being anew, vocational groups namely, binding men together not according to the position they occupy in the labour market, but according to the diverse functions which they exercise in society." . . . "Just as the unity of human society cannot be built upon class warfare, so the proper ordering of economic affairs cannot be left to free competition alone. From this source have proceeded in the past all the errors of the 'Individualistic' school. This school, ignorant or forgetful of the social and moral aspects of economic matters, teaches that the State should refrain in theory and practice from interfering therein, because these possess in free competition and open markets a principle of self-direction better able to control them than any created intellect. Free competition, however, though within certain limits just and productive of good results, cannot be the ruling principle of the economic world. This has been abundantly proved by the consequences that have followed from the free rein given to these dangerous individualistic ideals. It is therefore very necessary that economic affairs be once more subjected to and governed by a true and effective guiding principle. Still less can this function be exercised by the economic supremacy which within recent times has taken place of free competition: for this is a headstrong and vehement power, which, if it is to prove beneficial to mankind, needs to be curbed strongly and ruled with prudence. It cannot, however, be curbed and governed by itself. More lofty and noble principles must therefore be sought in order to control this supremacy sternly and uncompromisingly: to wit, social justice and social charity.

"To that end all the institutions of public and social life must be imbued with the spirit of justice, and this justice must above all be truly operative. It must build up a juridical and social order able to pervade all economic activity. Social charity should be, as it were, the soul of this order and the duty of the State will be to protect and defend it effectively."[1]

[1] *Quadragesimo anno,* May 15, 1931.

"We are here confronted with a whole mass of authentic assertions and no less authentic facts which make past doubting the proposition—already in such large part carried out—of entirely monopolizing youth from first childhood right up to adult age, for the full and exclusive advantage of a party, of a régime, on the basis of an ideology which explicitly resolves itself into a genuine and specific pagan statolatry fully as much in conflict with the natural rights of the family as with the supernatural rights of the Church." . . . "A conception which would cause to belong to the State all the younger generation, entirely and without exception from the earliest youth up to adult age, is not to be reconciled for a Catholic with Catholic doctrine; it is not even to be reconciled with the natural rights of the family. It is not for a Catholic a thing to be reconciled with the Catholic doctrine if one asserts that the Church, the Pope, should relate themselves to the exterior practice of religion, the Mass, the Sacraments; and that the rest of education belongs to the State."[2]

"For the first time in history we are witnessing a struggle, coldblooded in purpose and mapped out to the last detail, between man and 'all that is called God.'" . . . "Communism, moreover, strips man of his liberty, robs human personality of all its dignity, and removes all the moral restraints that check the eruptions of blind impulse. There is no recognition of any right of the individual in his relations to the collectivity." . . . "What would be the condition of a human society based on such materialistic tenets? It would be a collectivity with no other hierarchy than that of the economic system. It would have only one mission: the production of material things by means of collective labour." . . . "But the law of nature and its Author cannot be flouted with impunity. Communism has not been able, and will not be able, to achieve its objectives even in the merely economic sphere. It is true that in Russia it has been a contributing factor in rousing men and materials

[2]*Non abbiamo bisogno,* 1931, on the conflicts between Catholic Action and Italian fascism.

from the inertia of centuries, and in obtaining by all manner of means, often without scruple, some measure of material success. Nevertheless we know from reliable and even very recent testimony that not even there, in spite of slavery imposed on millions of men, has Communism reached its promised goal. After all, even the sphere of economics needs some morality, some moral sense of responsibility, which can find no place in a system so thoroughly materialistic as Communism. Terrorism is the only possible substitute." . . . "Communism is intrinsically wrong, and no one who would save Christian civilization may collaborate with it in any undertaking whatsoever."[3] . . . "The means of saving the world of today from the lamentable ruin into which amoral liberalism has plunged

[3]This phrase denounces the great illusion which would consist in collaborating with *Communism* in any organic or constructive undertaking whatsoever. To collaborate not with Communism, but with Communists, in putting out a fire or in succouring a wounded man is quite a different matter. The help given by England and by the United States to Soviet Russia attacked and invaded by Nazis, in the second World War, does not enter the category condemned by the Pope. It is a matter of defending England, America, the Russian people, the world's freedom, in a struggle to the death, against a formidable and threatening enemy, which is, moreover, at the same time, the most dangerous enemy of Christianity. And it is also an opportunity for helping the Russian people in the inner spiritual changes which may occur in it, by showing generosity to this people and by carrying it again into the Western commonwealth. The unquestionable difficulties and dangers occurring are less than those of a Nazi triumph or of a Communist Russia allied with Nazi Germany. Such a policy presupposes on the other hand guarding oneself at each moment against any leniency toward Communism's ideology and corrupting influence; it is not a collaboration with Communism, any more than was the policy of the Basque people during the civil war in Spain. In a pastoral letter to priests and laity of his archdiocese, the Most Reverend John T. McNicholas, Archbishop of Cincinnati, has pointed out that Pope Pius XI's denunciation of Communism "was not given as a moral direction to governments regarding aid or refusal of aid to Russia in case of a war of defense." "If we keep in mind," he added, "the clear distinction that Pope Pius made between the system of atheistic Communism, which he condemned, and the Russian people, whom he loved, we shall be able to rid ourselves of much perplexity regarding the Russian question."

us, are neither the class-struggle nor terror, nor yet the autocratic abuse of State power, but rather the infusion of social justice and the sentiment of Christian love into the social-economic order." . . . "When on the one hand we see thousands of the needy, victims of real misery for various reasons beyond their control, and on the other so many round about them who spend huge sums of money on useless things and frivolous amusement, we cannot fail to remark with sorrow not only that justice is poorly observed, but that the precept of charity also is not sufficiently appreciated, is not a vital thing in daily life." . . . "Charity will never be true charity unless it takes justice into constant account." . . . "A 'charity' which deprives the workingman of the salary to which he has a strict title in justice, is not charity at all, but only its empty name and hollow semblance. The wage-earner is not to receive as alms what is his due in justice. And let no one attempt with trifling charitable donations to exempt himself from the great duties imposed by justice. Both justice and charity often dictate obligations touching on the same subject-matter, but under different aspects; and the very dignity of the workingman makes him justly and acutely sensitive to the duties of others in his regard." . . . "Man has a spiritual and immortal soul. He is a person, marvellously endowed by his Creator with gifts of body and mind. He is a true 'microcosm,' as the ancients said, a world in miniature, with a value far surpassing that of the vast inanimate cosmos. God alone is his last end, in this life and the next. By sanctifying grace he is raised to the dignity of a son of God, and incorporated into the Kingdom of God in the Mystical Body of Christ. In consequence he has been endowed by God with many and varied prerogatives: the right to life, to bodily integrity, to the necessary means of existence; the right to tend toward his ultimate goal in the path marked out for him by God; the right of association and the right to possess and use property."[4]

"Whoever exalts race, or the people, or the State, or a par-

[4] *Divini Redemptoris,* 1937, on Atheistic Communism.

ticular form of State, or the depositories of power, or any other fundamental value of the human community—however necessary and honourable be their function in worldly things—whoever raises these notions above their standard value and divinizes them to an idolatrous level, distorts and perverts an order of the world planned and created by God: he is far from the true faith in God and from the concept of life which that faith upholds." . . . "None but superficial minds could stumble into concepts of a national God, of a national religion; or attempt to lock within the frontiers of a single people, within the narrow limits of a single race, God, the Creator of the universe, King and Legislator of all nations before whose immensity they are 'as a drop of a bucket' (Isaiah xl:15)." . . . "Human laws in flagrant contradiction with the natural law are vitiated with a taint which no force, no power can mend. In the light of this principle one must judge the axiom, that 'right is common utility,' a proposition which may be given a correct signification, if it means that what is morally indefensible, can never contribute to the good of the people. But ancient paganism acknowledged that the axiom, to be entirely true, must be reversed and be made to say: 'Nothing can be useful, if it is not at the same time morally good' (Cicero, *De Off.* 11.30). Emancipated from this moral rule, the principle would in international law carry a perpetual state of war between nations; for it ignores in national life, by confusing right and utility, the basic fact that man as a person possesses rights he holds from God, and which any collectivity must protect against denial, suppression or neglect. To overlook this truth is to forget that the real common good ultimately takes its measure from man's nature, which balances personal rights and social obligations, and from the purpose of society, established for the benefit of human nature." . . . "A Christianity which keeps a grip on itself, refuses every compromise with the world, takes the commands of God and the Church seriously, preserves its love of God and of men in all its freshness, such a Christianity can be, and will be, a model and a guide to a world which is sick to death and clamours for directions, unless it be condemned to a catastrophe that would baffle the imagination. Every true and lasting reform has ultimately sprung from sanctity."[5]

In addition to this, Pius XI condemned racist doctrines in a document dated April 13, 1938, which was addressed to all Catholic Seminaries and Universities. In November, 1938, the Patriarch of Lisbon wrote with reference to Pius XI: "Many have expressed surprise at the invincible energy of this noble old man who, with the Gospel in his hand, and fearless in his faith, condemned communism, totalitarianism, statism, racism, pagan nationalism—all those new idols of our day before which bow blinded masses of men, who lose all feeling for their dignity and their liberty from the instant when they lose Christ. Those who are scandalized at the utter condemnation by the Pope of the persecuting régimes which boast that they have saved Europe from Communism, know not (as the gospel says) of what spirit they are."

I shall conclude these extracts from the papal encyclicals by quoting some passages of the encyclical *Summi pontificatus,* published on October 20, 1939, by Pius XII, the present pope. This encyclical is exceptionally important because it was written in the first days of the second World War and because the Pope exposes in it the views he considers fundamental concerning the crisis of contemporary civilization.

"No defense of Christianity could be more effective than the present straits. From the immense vortex of error and anti-Christian movements there has come forth a crop of such poignant disasters as to constitute a condemnation surpassing in its conclusiveness any merely theoretical refutation. . . .

"Before all else, it is certain that the radical and ultimate cause of the evils which We deplore in modern society is the

[5]*Mit brennender Sorge,* 1937, on German National Socialism

denial and rejection of a universal norm of morality as well for individual and social life as for international relations. We mean the disregard, so common nowadays, and the forgetfulness of the natural law itself, which has its foundation in God, Almighty Creator and Father of all, supreme and absolute lawgiver, all wise and just Judge of human actions. . . . It is beyond question, that when the nations of Europe were still bound together by that common tie which observance of the same Christian law and tradition engenders, there were quarrels, there were revolutions, there were wars which brought havoc with them. But it is doubtful whether there has ever been an age like the present, an age in which men's spirits were so broken by despair, so busily alive to the difficulty of providing any remedy for their disorders. In earlier times, men had a clear consciousness of what was right and what was wrong, what was allowable and what was forbidden. Such a consciousness made agreement easier, curbed the fierce appetites that had been aroused, opened and paved the way for an honourable settlement. In our day, discords arise not merely from the violent impulses of an ungoverned temperament, but more commonly from a confusion and a revolt in the depths of the human conscience. . . .

"The first error, disastrously widespread in our day, is the forgetfulness of that law of human solidarity and charity which is dictated and imposed by our common origin and by the equality of rational nature in all men, to whatever people they belong, and by the redeeming sacrifice offered by Jesus Christ on the Altar of the Cross to His heavenly Father on behalf of sinful mankind. . . .

"There is a second error which, beyond all doubt, has equally baneful results for all nations, and for the general commonwealth of humanity. It is the error of those who impiously endeavour to dissociate the civil authority from any connection at all with the Divine Being; forgetting that the community quite as much as the individual depends upon Him as its first author and its supreme governor. What makes it worse is, that in doing so they seek to dispense the civil authority from observing any of those higher laws which have their origin in God. . . . The divine authority, and the influence of its laws, thus set aside, it necessarily follows that the civil power attributes to itself that absolute autonomy which belongs to the Creator alone. Thus voted into the privileges of Omnipotence, it treats the state, or the general body of the citizens, as the end to which all human actions must tend and the rule by which all legal and moral questions must be judged. It will allow of no appeal to the dictates of natural reason, or of the Christian conscience. . . .

"What happens where men deny the dependence of human rights upon divine rights, where no appeal is allowed except to the shifting phantom of earthly authority, where powers are claimed for the state which are entirely without responsibility, which are governed in their exercise by considerations not of justice but of interest? Human law itself, in its bearing on men's lives, necessarily loses all its inner hold over their consciences. When that goes, human law itself no longer receives any real recognition, is no longer in a position to call on the citizen to make sacrifices. Sometimes a civil power which in fact is based on a precarious foundation of this kind, does meet with material successes, through chance or through the special conditions of the moment. It commands the admiration of shallow minds. But there is an inevitable law which will take its vengeance in the end. The law, that is to say, that strikes down all that has been constructed upon a hidden or open disproportion between the greatness of the material and outward success, and the weakness of the inward value and of its moral foundation. . . .

"Whoever considers the State to be the end toward which all is directed, to which all must bow, is of necessity an enemy and an obstacle to all true and lasting progress among the nations. That is true, whether this unlimited dominion has been entrusted to the State by a decree of the nation or of some class within the nation, or whether the State arrogates such dominion to itself as absolute master, despotically, without any mandate whatsoever. . . .

"A special danger arises from such habits of thought and action. It is that domestic life, the primary and indispensable cell of human society, with its well-being and its growth, should come to be considered from the narrow standpoint of national power, and lest it be forgotten that man and the family are by nature anterior to the State and that a divine Creator has endowed both with their proper rights and powers, destined both for their several functions, corresponding to the fixed exigencies of nature. The education of the new generation in that case would not aim at the balanced and harmonious development of the physical powers and of all the intellectual and moral qualities, but at a one-sided formation of those civic virtues that are considered necessary for the political advantage of the country. And so, whatever furniture of the mind brings with it feelings of honour, of dutifulness, of kindness, is counted useless in comparison; its influence is only to depress and unnerve the robust vigour, we are told, of the youthful temper. . . .

"A disposition, in fact, of the divinely sanctioned natural order divides the human race into social groups, nations or states, which do not depend on one another, so far as the ordering of their internal affairs is concerned. But they are bound by mutual obligations in law and in moral right; they form a vast community of nations, which is designed to promote the general good of the race. . . . It is indispensable for the existence of harmonious and lasting contacts and of fruitful relations, that the peoples recognize and observe these principles of international natural law which regulate their normal development and activity. Such principles enjoin that each nation shall be allowed to keep its own liberties intact, shall have the right to its own life and economic development; further they enjoin that any pact which has been solemnly ratified in accordance with the rights of nations shall persist, unimpaired and inviolable. . . .

"This reservation must always be made, that in the course of time new situations may arise, which were not foreseen and perhaps could not be foreseen at the time when the pact was made. In that case, either the whole agreement or some part of it may have become, or may seem to have become, unjust to one of the contracting parties, or there may be undertakings which now would bear too hardly upon that party, or be altogether impossible of fulfillment. In such a case, the obvious expedient is to take refuge as soon as possible in a full and frank discussion of the difficulty, so that the old pact can be suitably altered, or a new pact substituted for it. It is quite a different thing to regard all signed pacts as written in water, assuming to oneself the tacit right of breaking them at one's own discretion, whenever self-interest demands it, without consulting or without having any regard for the other contracting party. Such behaviour can only deprive nations of the spirit of confidence which ought to exist between them, it is utterly subversive of the natural order, and leaves nations and peoples severed from one another by deep rivers of distrust. . . .

"It is not from outward pressure, it is not from the sword that deliverance comes to nations; the sword cannot breed peace, it can only impose terms of peace. The forces that are to renew the face of the earth, must proceed from within, from the spirit. We are hoping for a new order of things, which will govern the life of peoples and adjust their mutual relations, when these unnatural conflicts, these cruel butcheries, have died down at last. This new order must not be founded on the shifting standards of right and wrong, treacherous as quicksand, which have been arbitrarily devised to suit the selfish interest of groups and individuals. It must stand firmly based on the immovable rock of natural law and divine revelation. From these the giver of laws must derive his principle of balance, his sense of duty, his gift of prudence; if they are forgotten, the line which divides a legitimate from an unjust use of power is all too easily overstepped. It is only if he acts thus, that the awards he makes will have any intrinsic stability, noble dignity and religious sanction, and be immune to selfishness and greed.

"The troubles from which our age is suffering may be put down partly, no doubt, to the disturbing effects of economic maladjustment, partly to the competition between nations, each striving to get its fair share of the goods God has given man as a means of sustenance and progress. But the root of them lies far deeper than that. The root of them belongs to the sphere of religious belief and moral convictions which have been perverted by the progressive alienation of the people from that unity of doctrine, faith, customs and morals which once was promoted by the tireless and beneficent work of the Church. If it is to have any effect, the re-education of mankind must be, above all things, spiritual and religious. Hence, it must proceed from Christ as from its indispensable foundation; must be actuated by justice and crowned by charity."

On Christmas Eve, 1939, Pius XII announced five points which he deemed "the fundamental points of a just and honourable peace." Here follows the complete text of these five points.

"I. A fundamental postulate of any just and honourable peace is an assurance for all nations great or small, powerful or weak, of their right to life and independence. The will of one nation to live must never mean the sentence of death passed upon another. When this equality of rights has been destroyed, attacked, or threatened, order demands that reparation shall be made, and the measure and extent of that reparation is determined, not by the sword nor by the arbitrary decision of self-interest, but by the rules of justice and reciprocal equity.

"II. The order thus established, if it is to continue undisturbed and ensure true peace, requires that the nations be delivered from the slavery imposed upon them by the race for armaments, and from the danger that material force, instead of serving to protect the right, may become an overbearing and tyrannical master. Any peaceful settlement which fails to give fundamental importance to a mutually agreed, organic, and progressive disarmament, spiritual as well as material, or which neglects to ensure the effective and loyal implementing of such an agreement, will sooner or later show itself to be lacking in coherence and vitality.

"III. The maxims of human wisdom require that in any re-organization of international life all parties should learn a lesson from the failures and deficiencies of the past. Hence in creating or reconstructing international institutions which have so high a mission and such difficult and grave responsibilities, it is important to bear in mind the experience gained from the ineffectiveness or imperfections of previous institutions of that kind. Human frailty renders it difficult, not to say impossible, to foresee every contingency and guard against every danger at the moment in which treaties are signed; passion and bitter feeling are apt to be still rife. Hence in order that a peace may be honourably accepted and in order to avoid arbitrary breaches and unilateral interpretations of treaties, it is of the first importance to erect some juridical institution which shall guarantee the loyal and faithful fulfillment of the conditions agreed upon, and which shall, in case of recognized need, revise and correct them.

"IV. If a better European settlement is to be reached there is one point in particular which should receive special attention: it is the real needs and the just demands of nations and populations, and of racial minorities. It may be that, in consequence of existing treaties incompatible with them, these demands are unable to establish a strictly legal right. Even so, they deserve to be examined in a friendly spirit with a view to meeting them by peaceful methods, and even, where it appears necessary, by means of an equitable and covenanted revision of the treaties themselves. If the balance between nations is thus adjusted and the foundation of mutual confidence thus laid, many incentives to violent action will be removed.

"V. But even the best and most detailed regulations will be imperfect and foredoomed to failure unless the peoples and those who govern them submit willingly to the influence of that spirit which alone can give life, authority, and binding force to the dead letter of international agreements. They must develop that sense of deep and keen responsibility which measures and weighs human statutes according to the sacred and inviolable standards of the law of God; they must cultivate that hunger and thirst after justice which is proclaimed as a beatitude in the Sermon on the Mount and which supposes as its natural foundation the moral virtue of justice; they must be guided by that universal love which is the compendium and most general expression of the Christian ideal, and which therefore may serve as a common ground also for those who have not the blessing of sharing the same faith with us."

APPENDIX II (CHAPTER IX)

CONTAINING EXTRACTS IN LATIN FROM JOHN OF SAINT THOMAS

1. "Signum est *id quod repræsentat aliud a se potentiæ cognoscenti.*" (John of Saint Thomas, Log. II. P., q. 21, a.i.) A more precise and a more comprehensive definition than that of the lexicon of the Société de Philosophie: "An actual perception justifying in a more or less set manner an assertion relative to some other thing (and not only susceptible of evoking a representation by the play of memory or the association of ideas): A frequency of pulse—signs of fever."

John of Saint Thomas thus elaborates the scholastic definition of the sign:

"In nostra definitione ad rationem signi in communi duo concurrunt. Primum est *ratio manifestativi seu repræsentativi.* Secundum *ordo ad alterum,* scil. ad rem quæ repræsentatur, quæ debet esse diversa a signo (nihil enim est signum sui, nec significat se), et ad potentiam cui manifestat et repræsentat rem a se distinctam. Et quidem manifestativum ut sic constat non dicere relationem, tum quia potest salvari in ordine ad se et sine respectu ad alterum, ut quando lux manifestat seipsam, quando objectum repræsentat se ut videatur, etc.: tum quia potest aliquid manifestare alterum sine dependentia ab ipso, sed potius per dependentiam alterius a se, sicut principia manifestant conclusiones, lux colores, Deus visus creaturas, up peritiores Theologi docent, I. P., qu. xii et xiv. In quibus illustratio et manifestatio alterius sine relatione dependentiæ a re manifestata fit. At vero manifestativum signi invenitur, et *cum ordine ad alterum,* quia nihil seipsum significat, licet se repræsentare possit, et *cum dependentia, quia signum semper est minus significato, et ab ipso ut a mensura dependens.*" J. of S. T., Log. II. P., *loc cit.*

2. "Ratio signi formaliter loquendo non consistit in relatione secundum dici, sed secundum esse.—Dixi formaliter loquendo, quia materialiter et præsuppositive dicit rationem manifestativi seu repræsentativi alterius, quod sine dubio non importat solam relationem secundum esse. [. . .]

"Addit autem supra repræsentare, et formaliter dicit repræsentare aliud deficienter, vel dependenter ab ipsa re significata, et quasi vice illius, et substituendo. Et ita respicit significatum non ut pure manifestatum et illuminatum a se sed *ut principale cognoscibile et mensuram sui, cujus loco subrogatur, et cujus vices gerit deducendo ad potentiam.* [. . .]

"Nam D. Thomas expresse ponit quod signum est in genere relationis fundatæ in aliquo alio; sed relatio fundata in aliquo alio est *relatio secundum esse,* et de prædicamento ad aliquid si realis sit; ergo signum consistit in relatione secundum esse. [. . .]

"Ratio signi non consistit tantum in hoc quod est repræsentare seu manifestare aliud a se, sed in tali modo manifestandi, quod est repræsentare aliud tanquam inferiori modo ad illud, ut minus principale ad magis principale, ut mensuratum ad suam mensuram, ut substitutum, et vices gerens ad id pro quo substituitur, et cujus gerit vices. Sed *relatio mensurati ad mensuram et substituentis ad suum principale, est relatio prædicamentalis,* ergo relatio signi ad signatum prædicamentalis est. [. . .]

"Sic ergo signum, licet in repræsentando respiciat potentiam ut ei manifestet signatum, quia ad hunc effectum destinatur et assumitur, et in hac præcisa consideratione ad potentiam non petat consistere in relatione secundum esse, tamen in subordinatione ad signatum, quatenus respicit ipsum ut principale et ut mensuram sui, necessario debet in relatione ad ipsum consistere, sicut servus dicit relationem ad dominum, et minister, seu instrumentum ad suum principale. [. . .]

"Signum autem ratione sui fundamenti movet potentiam, non ratione suæ relationis, sicut pater non ratione relationis generat, sed ratione potentiæ generativæ; et tamen formaliter consistit in relatione. [. . .]

"Et ideo consideratur in signo et vis movens potentiam, et ordo substituentis ad id pro quo movet. Et primum est relatio transcendentalis, secundum prædicamentalis." J. de S. T., *ibid.,* a.i.

"Similiter relationes illæ, quibus signum proportionari potest ad signatum, diversæ sunt formaliter a relatione ipsa signi, v.g. relatio effectus vel causæ, similitudinis vel imaginis etc.; licet aliqui recentiores confundant relationem signi cum istis relationibus, sed immerito." J. of S. T., Log. II. P., q. 21, a.2.

3. "*Relatio signi naturalis* ad suum signatum, qua constituitur in esse signi, *realis* est, et non rationis, quantum est ex se, et ex vi sui fundamenti et supponendo existentiam termini cæterasque conditiones relationis realis. [. . .]

"Et fundamentum conclusionis deducitur ex ipsa natura et quidditate signi, quæ in eo consistit quod sit aliquid *magis notum,* quo repræsentetur et manifestetur ignotius, ut bene notat S. Thom., q. ix, *de Verit.,* art. iii, ad 4, et in IV Sent., distinct, 1, q. 1, art. i. Ad hoc autem quod aliquid sit notius altero illudque reddat cognoscible et repræsentabile, requiritur quod *cognoscibilitas istius sit habilior altera ad movendum potentiam,* et determinata seu affecta ad tale signatum, ut ad illud potius movens quam ad aliud, sive ista motio et repræsentatio fiat formaliter, sive objective. Sed *quod aliquid in seipso sit cognoscibile, non potest esse aliquid rationis;* quod vero relate ad alterum sit *cognoscibilius et reddens ipsum repræsentatum,* aliquid etiam *reale* est in signis naturalibus: ergo relatio signi naturalis realis est. Minor habet duas partes, scil. quod res in seipsa sit cognoscibilis realiter, et quod etiam relate ad alterum reddat realiter aliud repræsentatum et cognoscibile. [. . .]

"Nam quod fumus repræsentet potius ignem quam aquam, et vestigium bovis potius bovem quam hominem, et conceptus equi potius equum quam lapidem, in aliqua *reali proportione et intrinseca* istorum signorum cum illis signatis fundatur; ex reali autem proportione et connexione cum aliquo, realis relatio innascitur. [. . .]

"Ergo repræsentatio in signo naturali fundatur in propinquitate ipsius ad cognoscibile, pro quo substituit, et respectu cujus est medium; *hæc autem propinquitas in his quæ realiter proportionantur et conjunguntur, realis relatio erit,* cum reale fundamentum habeat." J. of S. T., Log II. P., q. 21, a.2.

"Ex dictis colliges in *signis ad placitum* rationem signi etiam per relationem ad signatum explicandam esse. Sed relatio ista *rationis* est, et non solum consistit signum in extrinseca denominatione, qua redditur impositum seu destinatum a Republica ad significandum." J. of S. T., *ibid.*

"Si potentia, et signatum considerentur ut termini directe attacti per relationem, necessario exigunt duplicem relationem in signo. Si vero consideretur potentia ut terminus in obliquo attactus, sic *unica relatione signi attingitur signatum et potentia,* et hæc est *propria et formalis ratio signi.* [. . .]

"Et sic signum non est mensura potentiæ, sed instrumentum signati ad illam. [. . .]

"Ad 2 confirm. resp. quod, quia signum respicit signatum præcise ut repræsentabile ad potentiam, ut vices ejus gerens, et consequenter inferius ipso, imago autem respicit suum exemplar ut imitabile, et ut principium a quo originatur et exprimitur, et sic potest illi non inæqualis esse, ideo ex parte ipsius termini quem directe respiciunt habent distinctas formalitates, seu rationes formales terminandi, licet ad unam sequatur ordo ad potentiam in obliquo, aut etiam præssupponatur, in alia non; et ita formalis ratio distinguens in utroque est ratio signati ut sic, ratio exemplaris ut sic, non ipsa potentia directe attacta." J. of S. T., Log. II. P., q. 21, a.3.

4. "Significare, seu repræsentare nullo modo est a signo effective, nec significare loquendo formaliter est efficere.—Itaque hæc propositio: *signum efficit,* nunquam est in quarto modo per se. [. . .]

"Objectum in quantum exercet causalitatem objectivam respectu potentiæ et repræsentat se, non effective id facit, sed solum se habet ut forma extrinseca, quæ ab alio efficiente applicatur et præsens redditur per species ipsi potentiæ. [. . .]

"Secundum principium est quod signum succedit, et substituitur loco objecti *in hac ipsa linea et ordine objectivæ causæ,* non autem in ratione applicantis effective, nec deducentis potentiam ad signatum modo effectivo sed objectivo, non principali sed substitutivo, ratione cujus signum dicitur instrumentale, non quidem quasi instrumentum efficientis, sed quasi substitutum objecti, non informans sicut species sed ab extrinseco repræsentans. [. . .]

"Quod si instes: Quid est ergo significare, et manifestare, si neque est excitare, neque emittere species, neque producere cognitionem effective? Respondetur quod est *vice objecti seu signati reddere objectum præsens potentiæ.* Præsentia autem objecti in actu primo vel secundo in potentia pendet a multis causis: a producente species, vel applicante objectum effective; a potentia generante notitiam, etiam effective; ab objecto se præsentante *formaliter extrinsece, seu specificative; a signo ut substituente vice illius in eodem genere causæ,* non effective." J. of S. T., Log. II. P., q. 21, a.5.

5. "Ex quo colliges quæ conditiones requirantur ad hoc ut aliquid sit signum. *Essentialiter enim consistit in ordine ad signatum, ut ad rem distinctam manifestabilem potentiæ,* et sic signatum et potentia non sunt ex conditionibus requisitis, sed ex essentiali ratione. Similiter *requiritur ratio repræsentativi, sed ex parte fundamenti,* ideoque repræsentativum ut sic non est relatio prædicamentalis, etiamsi alterius repræsentativum sit, sed transcendentalis, et in signo fundat *relationem mensurati ad signatum,* quæ prædicamentalis est. Requiruntur ergo præter ista, sed consequuntur tres conditiones jam dictæ: Prima, quod sit *notius signato, non secundum naturam, sed quoad nos.* Secunda, quod sit *inferius, seu imperfectius signato.* Tertia, quod *sit dissimile ipsi.* [. . .]

"Denique innotescit ex dictis quomodo differant *signum* et *imago.* Nam imprimis, nec omnis imago est signum, nec omne signum imago. Potest enim imago esse ejusdem naturæ cum eo cujus est imago, ut filius cum patre, etiam in Divinis, et tamen non est illius signum; multa etiam signa non sunt imagines, ut fumus ignis, gemitus doloris. Ratio ergo imaginis consistit in hoc quod procedat ab alio ut a principio, et in similitudinem ejus, ut docet sanctus Thomas, I. P., q. xxxv, et q. xcxiii, et ita sit ad imitationem illius, potestque esse ita perfecte similis suo principio ut sit ejusdem naturæ cum ipso. De ratione vero signi non est quod procedat ab alio in similitudinem, sed quod sit medium ductivum illius ad potentiam, et substituat pro illo in repræsentando, ut aliquid eo imperfectius et dissimile." J. of S. T., Log. II. P., q. 21, a.6, appendix.

6. *"Bruta proprie utuntur signis,* tam naturalibus, quam ex consuetudine.— Sumitur ex D. Thomas, q. xxiv *de Verit.,* art. ii, ad 7, ubi dicit: "Quod ex memoria præteritorum flagellorum, vel beneficiorum contingit ut bruta apprehendant aliquid quasi amicum et prosequendum,

vel quasi inimicum et fugiendum." Et videri etiam potest *Sum. theol.*
I–II, q. xl, art. iii. Et de signis naturalibus dicit q. ix *De Verit.*, art.
iv, ad 10: "Quod bruta exprimunt suos conceptus signis naturalibus."
Et de consuetudine loquitur in I *Met.* lect. i, ostendens quod aliqua
animalia sunt disciplinabilia, ut scilicet per alterius instructionem possint
assuescere ad aliquid faciendum, vel vitandum; possunt ergo bruta uti
signis ex consuetudine." J. of S. T., Log. II. P., q. 21, a.6.

7. In conditioned reflexes as in the whole field of experimentation
with animals in contact with man, and in the field of animal training,
the sign with which we are dealing is a *signum ex consuetudine* which
reduces itself to the *signum naturale.*

"Specialis difficultas est circa quædam signa, quæ non publica aliqua
institutione, i.e. ab auctoritate publica dimanante, sed ex sola voluntate
particularium frequenter illis utentium ad aliquid significandum accom-
modantur. Unde quia tota vis significandi ex ipso usu et frequentia
dependet, dubium restat an isto usu et frequentia modo naturali sig-
nificent, an vero significatione ad placitum.

"Sit ergo unica conclusio: Si consuetudo respiciat aliquod signum,
destinando illud et proponendo pro signo, tale signum fundatum in
consuetudine erit *ad placitum;* si vero consuetudo non proponat aliquid,
vel instituat pro signo, sed dicat *simplicem usum alicujus rei, et ratione
illius assumatur aliquid in signum, tale signum reducitur ad naturale.*—
Itaque consuetudo, vel potest esse causa signi, sicut si populus consuetudine sua introducat et proponat aliquam vocem ad significandum; vel
potest se habere ut *effectus qui nos manuducit ad cognoscendam suam
causam, sicut canis frequenter visus comitari aliquem manifestat quod
sit dominus ejus,* et consuetudo comedendi in mappis manifestat nobis
prandium, quando mappas videmus appositas, et in universum fere
omnis inductio fundatur in frequentia et consuetudine qua videmus
aliquid sæpe fieri." J. of S. T., Log. II. P., q. 22, a.6.

8. "Non solum sensus interni, sed etiam externi in nobis, et in brutis
percipiunt significationem et utuntur signis. [. . .]

"Q. viii *de Verit.*, art. v: 'Cognoscimus, inquit, Socratem per visum
dupliciter, et in quantum visus assimilatur Socrati, et in quantum assimilatur imagini Socratis, et utraque istarum assimilationum sufficit ad
cognoscendum Socratem.' Et infra: 'Cum visus exterior videt Herculem
in statua sua, non fit cognitio per aliquam aliam similitudinem statuæ.'
Videatur etiam in III Contra Gentil., c. xlix. Cum ergo imago et statua
repræsentent potentiæ sua significata per modum signi, si visus exterior
in statua et imagine non solum statuam attingit, sed etiam id quod
repræsentat imago, cognoscit unum minus notum per aliud notius, quod
est uti signis.

"Secundo probatur conclusio: Nam non est ulla ratio cur negetur
sensui exteriori quod *deducatur de uno ad aliud sine discursu et colla-*

tione: ad utendum autem signo et significatione non requiritur aliquid amplius, *nec necessarius est discursus;* ergo usus signi exterioribus sensibus attribui potest. [. . .]

"Cognoscit ergo signatum *ut contentum in signo,* et ad ipsum pertinens, et, ut dicit D. Thomas, Herculem cognoscit in statua. [. . .]

"Quare simpliciter respondemus quod sensus cognoscit signatum in signo, eo modo quo in signo praesens est, sed non eo solum modo quo cum signo idem est. Sicut cum videtur sensibile proprium, v.g., color, et sensibile commune, ut figura, et motus, non videtur figura ut idem cum colore, sed ut conjuncta colori, et per illum visibilis reddita, nec videtur seorsum color, et seorsum figura; sic cum videtur signum, et in eo praesens redditur signatum, ibi signatum attingitur ut conjunctum signo, et contentum in eo, non ut seorsum se habens, et ut absens. Et si instetur: *Quid est illud in signato conjunctum signo, et praesens in signo praeter ipsum signum et entitatem ejus? Respondetur esse ipsummet signatum in alio esse,* sicut res repraesentata per speciem est ipsummet objectum in esse intentionali, non reali; et sic, sicut qui videret conceptum, videret id quod in conceptu continetur, ut repraesentatum in eo, et non solum id quod se habet ut repraesentans, sic *qui videt imaginem externam, videt non solum munus, seu rationem repraesentantis, sed etiam repraesentatum prout in ea.* Sed hoc ipso quod videt repraesentatum etiam prout in imagine, videt *aliquid distinctum ab imagine,* quia imago ut imago repraesentans est, non vero repraesentatum; illud tamen videt ut *contentum et praesens* in imagine, non seorsum et ut absens, et unico verbo videt ut distinctum ab imagine, non ut separatum, et seorsum." J. of S. T., Log. II. P., q. 21, a.6.

In the concept the object of intellection is present in a mode of *intentional* existence, in the sense that there is nothing else (as a *quod* known beforehand) in the concept than the object thus present. The concept is a "formal" sign (see page 223), and the intentionality is there in act (we shall say that it is an *intentio quiescens, in actu intentionalitatis seu immaterialitatis*).

In the statue of Socrates, also, Socrates is present in a mode of *intentional* existence, but in another fashion: the statue is something itself known beforehand (according to a priority in nature, not in time), before it makes Socrates known. It is an "instrumental" sign, and the intentionality therein is merely virtual (we shall say that such a sign is an *intentio quiescens, in statu virtuali intentionalitatis seu immaterialitatis*). It is the act of vision which, immaterial as such although intrinsically subject to material conditions, awakens this intentionality in the statue—in so far as the latter is perceived or made one with the sense-power in act—and causes this intentionality to pass into act. Such is the sense in which it seems well to explain the "presence of knowability" and the *"in alio esse"* we are discussing in the text.

9. "Signum practicum dicitur illud, quod derivatur et descendit ab intellectu practico. Intellectus enim cognitionem et conceptus suos per signa a se derivata explicat; sed sicut est duplex intellectus, scilicet practicus et speculativus, sic est duplex signum ab utroque intellectu derivatum, scilicet practicum et speculativum. Et sicut intellectus ut sit practicus non debet extrahi a latitudine intellectus, sed intra limites intellectus habet rationem practici, sic ut signum sit practicum non indiget extrahi a latitudine signi, et induere rationem causæ, sed *intra genus signi habet rationem practici,* in quantum scilicet derivatur ab intellectu practico. Intellectus autem practicus et speculativus in hoc differunt, ut dicit S. Thomas VI *Ethicorum,* lect. ii, quod bonum intellectus speculativi est verum absolute; bonum autem intellectus practici non est verum absolute, sed ut concorditer et conformiter se habet ad finem rectum, seu ad opus quod intendit. Unde mensura veritatis speculativæ est res ut est in se, quia ex eo quod res est vel non est, intellectus est verus vel falsus; mensura autem veritatis practicæ non est res ut est in se, sed ut concordat cum fine intento et recto.

"Ex quo fit, quod intellectus practicus, quando respicit objectum exterius, non respiciat illud ad acquirendam cognitionem, sed ad hoc ut res ad finem aliquem intentum dirigatur, aut perducatur. Et sic respicit rem non resolvendo et abstrahendo ab ipsa cognitionem, sed potius componendo illam cum aliquo, secundum quod intendit aliquem finem, ad quem perducere intendit aliquid; et sic respectu illius finis compositivo modo procedit. Et hinc est quod intellectus practicus præsupponit actum voluntatis, quia non dicit cognitionem puram, sed directivam cum intentione finis; et supponendo intentionem finis dirigit ad illum. Quod S. Thomas explicavit loco citato dicens: 'Quod finis est homini a natura: ea autem quæ sunt ad finem, non sunt nobis determinata a natura sed per rationem.' Et sic rectitudo appetitus per respectum ad finem, est mensura veritatis in ratione practica." J. of S. T., *Curs. theol.,* t. IX, de Sacramentis, disp. 22, a.1, dubium quintum, §§ 99 and 100.

"Ab hoc ergo intellectu derivatum signum dicitur practicum, quia per illud *non intendit intellectus manifestare præcise rem, sed manifestando perficere exterius intentionem et directionem intellectus practici;* et ita in contractibus videmus, quod signa perficientia contractum habent vim ab intellectu practico perficiendi ipsum, et perducendi ac dirigendi ad finem exteriori modo id quod intendit intellectus.

"Et ideo dicuntur signa practica, quia *licet manifestent, non tamen sistunt, neque pro fine habent manifestare, sed ad intentum finem perducere et exterius dirigere;* sicut intellectus practicus, licet habeat cognoscere, non tamen cognitionem habet pro fine, sed per cognitionem dirigere et perducere ad finem. Quod ergo intellectus practicus habet intra, signum practicum habet extra, scilicet, non habere pro fine manifestare licet manifestativum sit; sed ad finem exterius perducere et dirigere, et ideo modo compositivo procedere. Quod autem ipsum signum ultra hoc sit causa rei in suo esse, et perducat ad illam sive physice, sive moraliter, est *extra rationem signi practici* et competit ei ex aliquo extrinseco; sed de ratione ejus solum est, quod eo modo quo intellectus practicus intendit finem aliquem et illum respicit interius, sic signum practicum illum respiciat exterius." J. of S. T., *ibid.,* §§ 101, 102.

"Quare ad rationem signi practici sufficit, quod significet suum significatum ut in exercitio dandum, non per causalitatem ipsius signi, sed per causalitatem alterius causæ, significatam tamen per hoc signum, quia sufficit ad rationem signi *significare* causationem, non vero requiritur quod causet significatum." J. of S. T., *ibid., dubium quartum,* § 83.

"De ratione practici est quod sit operativum, quasi efficienter et physice, nego: quasi significative moraliter, concedo.

"Unde dicitur, quod ad rationem signi practici sufficit, quod sit *operativum ex fine,* non autem ex genere causæ efficientis. Dicitur enim practicum differre a speculativo fine, seu habere pro fine opus, non autem esse causam efficientem ejus. Et sic signa hæc habent pro fine opus, scilicet, sanctificationem nostram, ut nobis dandam vel de præsenti, vel de futuro, non tamen est de ratione eorum quod effective se habeant ad hoc signatum, sed id pertinebit ad excellentissima signa practica. [. . .]

"Practicum habere pro fine opus, potest dupliciter intelligi, uno modo quasi passive, quia scilicet ordinatur et dirigitur ad opus aliquod ut ad finem, ab aliquo dirigente et ordinante sicut medium, quod assumitur passive, et ordinatur ad aliquid obtinendum; alio modo *quasi active,* quia scilicet est ordinans et dirigens ad finem, et habet pro fine ad quem dirigit aliquod opus, non vero sistit in cognitione. Primo modo habere pro fine opus, non sufficit ad rationem signi practici, sed secundo, et hujus ratio est, quia practicum invenitur in signo derivatum a practico quod est in intellectu: practicus autem intellectus non respicit finem ut directum ad illum, sed ut *dirigens et ordinans,* quia est principium operationis.

"Imagines autem sacræ, et concio et similia signa adhibentur ab intellectu ut media ad consequendum finem aliquem, et ideo solum passive habent esse ordinata, non autem habent esse signa practica, quia *prius supponuntur esse significativa et repræsentativa,* et deinde ordinantur et adhibentur pro medio ad aliquod opus. Ut autem sit aliquid signum practicum, oportet quod *ex ipsa ratione practica intellectus participet significationem,* et ordinationem ad finem, et sic *quasi active et directive habeat pro fine opus,* non quasi passive, et quid assumptum pro medio ad finem. [. . .]

"Respondetur non esse de ratione practici, quod active comparetur ad rem, quæ est opus et finis ejus, sed ad directionem in finem; et ita *debet esse active dirigens, non autem active efficiens rem ipsam.* Unde non est de ratione practici quod sit operativum rei, sed quod *pro fine habeat operationem circa rem,* tamquam dirigens ad hujusmodi finem, et non ut directum ad illum. Datur ergo activitas in practico respectu directionis operis, non tamen respectu rei, quæ est opus. Quare practicum debet esse operativum ex fine, id est, tamquam dirigens ad finem; non tamen requiritur quod sit operativum in genere causæ efficientis; et signum practicum debet esse operativum ex fine, tamquam manifestans hujusmodi directionem, et exterius dirigens, sicut intellectus interius. [. . .]

"Intellectus autem respicit finem ut movens ad illum, quia in ratione dirigentis est movens, sicut voluntas est movens quoad genus efficientis, et quoad exercitium. Quare practicus intellectus respicit finem per modum moventis, et non ut moti, seu medii assumpti ad finem; et similiter signum descendens ab intellectu practico respicit pro fine operationem non ut medium assumptum, sed ut dirigens significative et exterius, seu exterius movens et perficiens. Non autem ad hoc necesse est, quod effectio ipsius operis fiat per talem cognitionem, aut per signum derivatum a tali cognitione, quia in ratione practici sufficit, quod ex fine et directione ad eum sit operativum, non autem quod ut causa efficiens ipsum respiciat, sed id erit de perfectione practici, salvaturque vere ratio practici, si quod per aliam causam efficitur, ab ipso in finem dirigatur intentum." J. of S. T., *ibid.,* dubium quintum, §§ 108, 110, 111, 114, 115.

10. *Cf.* J. of S. T., *Curs, theol.,* IX, de Sacramentis, præamb., § 2; disp. 22, a.1, dub. primum, §§ 9 and 10: dub. secundum, §§ 25 and 31. I note here a fine quotation from the same article (dub. tertium, § 65).

"Quod vero secretum signum sit sacramentum, constat clare, quia sacramentum principaliter dicit sacrum, seu sanctum occultum; ergo sacramentum, quod est signum, debet esse occultum, et significare occulte. Unde illud proprie dicitur sacramentum, quod non debet omnibus aperiri et notum esse, nec significatio ejus esse cuilibet pervia, sed quasi clausa et abscondita. Neque est hoc contra rationem signi, de cujus ratione est quod sit manifestativum rei significatæ, et consequenter non debet celare et abscondere illam. Dicimus enim, quod de ratione signi est quod sit manifestativum, non tamen quod significatio ejus sit omnibus manifestata, sed quod cognoscentibus significationem suam sit manifestativum; sicut lingua græca nescienti significationem, potius celat significationem quam manifestat, et tamen signum est. Et ænigma signum est rei significatæ, occultum tamen, quia nescitur ejus significatio. Et hoc ideo est, quia sacramentum non solum est signum, sed signaculum; nec solum constat verbis, sed rebus; nec solum est speculativum et ordinatum ad cognitionem, sed practicum et ordinatum ad opus. Unde oportet, quod habeat significationem reconditam, et quod sit occultum, et non omnibus manifestum significatum ejus."

11. Ad secundam confirmationem respondetur, quod sacramenta legis naturæ erant determinatæ materiæ a reipublicæ institutione; quia tamen materiæ illi quam designabat respublica, conferebatur a Deo significatio

sacra, consequenter etiam fiebat ipsa materia et cæremonia, quæ a republica instituebatur, quid sacrum ac religiosum et religiose tractandum." J. of S. T., *ibid.*, dub. tertium, § 62.

See also Saint Thomas, *Sum. theol.*, III, 60, 5, ad 3; 61, 3, c. and ad 2; 70, 2, ad 1 (in this last text St. Thomas seems to give to individual initiative, in the historic state in question, a greater rôle than do his commentators: "Unusquisque pro suo libitu fidem suam profitentibus signis protestabatur"). And J. of S. T., *Curs. theol.*, t. IX, disp. 23, a.3. —John of Saint Thomas admits that in the law of nature as well as in the Ancient Law there was notably a sacrament by which little children were justified *in fide Ecclesiæ, supposita fide publica Ecclesiæ, in qua parvulus offerebatur Deo*. Not that such a sacrament worked actively (instrumentally) itself, as baptism effects the remission of original sin; but on the occasion of that sign which was itself without efficient strength,—*ad præsentiam sacramenti, non tamen ipso sacramento active concurrente,*—God, as the single active cause, forgave sins and conferred grace.

12. *Cf.* J. of S. T., *ibid.*, disp. 23, q.3, § 20.

13. *Cf. Sum. theol.*, I–II, 101, 4; 103, 2; 107, 1, ad 3: and especially 102, 5; III, 60, 2 ad 2; 60, 6, ad 3; 61, 3, ad 1; 61, 4; 62, 6, ad 2; 65, 1, ad 4. J. of S. T., *Curs. theol.*, t. IX, disp. 22, a.1, §§ 67, 68, 70, 93, 121, 124; a.2, §§ 40, 49.

14. "Esse causativum gratiæ *non est essentiale sacramento ut sacramentum est, sed ut instrumentum humanitatis Christi,* et derivatum a passione ejus. Hoc autem connectitur cum sacramento, *non ex vi et essentia sacramenti,* sicut differentiæ connectuntur cum genere, *sed ex institutione Christi Domini,* qui legem evangelicam condidit; in qua, sicut dicit S. Thomas 1–2, quæst. cvi, art. i et ii, fit justificatio non ratione scripturæ, qua traditur lex; sed ratione Spiritus et gratiæ, quæ per illam datur, juxta quod dicit Apostolus ad Rom. I: *Non erubesco evangelium: virtus enim Dei est:* unde oportuit quod sacramenta, quæ sunt fundamenta talis legis et columnæ ejus, non solum haberent signum exterius, sed Spiritum intus operantem gratiam. Hoc autem non habetur ex vi sacramenti, aut essentiæ sacramenti ut sic, sed *ex vi sacramenti Christo conjuncti, et ab ejus passione derivati.*" J. of S. T., *Curs. theol.*, t. IX, disp. 22, a.1, § 45.

15. *Sum. theol.*, III, 25, 3.

"Ad usum signi non requiritur duplicem cognitionem, nec quod ex una cognitione deveniatur in aliam, sed sufficit quod ex uno cognito ad aliud cognitum deveniatur. Aliud autem est per unum cognitum attingere alterum, aliud ex una cognitione causare alteram. Ad rationem significationis sufficit quod de uno cognito deveniatur ad aliud, sed non est necesse quod de una cognitione ad aliam. *Unde dicit Philosophus*

*in lib. de Memoria et Reminiscentia, quod idem est motus in imaginem
et in rem cujus est imago,* quod D. Thomas ibi, lect. iii, et III. P., q.
xxv, art. ii, explicat de motu in imaginem non ut res quædam est, sed
ut imago, i.e. ut exercet officium repræsentandi, ac ducendi ad aliud.
'Sic enim est unus, et idem motus in imaginem cum illo qui est in rem,'
inquit S. Thomas; quod optime Cajetanus ibi intelligit de imagine con-
siderata in exercitio imaginis, seu officio repræsentationis, non ut res
quædam est in se, quasi in actu signato. [. . .]

"Et sic non est necessarius discursus, sed simplex cognitio sufficit, ut
visa imagine seu signo res ipsa, quæ in signo continetur et significatur,
attingatur." J. of S. T., *Log.* II. P., q. 21, a.6.

16. *Cf.* above note 9, 312 (J. of S. T., *Curs. theol.,* t. IX, disp. 22,
a.1, § 111: "Imagines autem sacræ, etc.").

INDEX OF NAMES

INDEX OF NAMES